Sing My Way Home

Sing My Way Home

Voices of the New American Roots Rock

by Keith and Kent Zimmerman

Backbeat
Books
San Francisco

Published by Backbeat Books
600 Harrison Street, San Francisco, CA 94107
www.backbeatbooks.com
email: books@musicplayer.com

An imprint of CMP Information
Publishers of *Guitar Player, Bass Player, Keyboard,* and *EQ* magazines

CMP
United Business Media

Distributed to the book trade in the US and Canada by
Publishers Group West, 1700 Fourth Street, Berkeley, CA 94710

Distributed to the music trade in the US and Canada by
Hal Leonard Publishing, P.O. Box 13819, Milwaukee, WI 53213

Text design and composition by Leigh McLellan
Cover design by Richard Leeds — bigwigdesign.com
Front cover photo © Robert Altman / Retna Ltd.
Back cover photo © Tristan Fewings / Camera Press / Retna Ltd.

Library of Congress Cataloging-in-Publication Data

Zimmerman, Keith.
Sing my way home : the voices of the new American roots rock / by
Keith & Kent Zimmerman.— 1st ed.
        p. cm.
Includes index.
ISBN 0-87930-790-0 (alk. paper)
1. Rock music—United States—History and criticism. 2. Country
rock music—History and criticism. I. Zimmerman, Kent, 1953-
II. Title.

  ML3534.Z55 2004
  781.66'0973—dc22   2004012253

Printed in the United States of America

04 05 06 07 08   5 4 3 2 1

Dedication

This book is dedicated to the genius of Delaney Bramlett, whose song inspired the title, and to the memory of Jay Kahn, without whose friendship this book would not have been possible.

contents

The Death of Aquarius and the Birth (for Us) of New American Roots Rock

Everybody's musical story has a starting point. Ours is Altamont Raceway. December 5, 1969. Throngs converged for a free Rolling Stones concert, forming a tribal multitude of stoned-out humanity cradled in a dry valley between two small Northern California towns, Tracy and Livermore, about 30 miles south of Oakland.

It was an overcast day in early winter. Hundreds of thousands of revelers came to the festival site, starry-eyed with hopes of experiencing a wintry West Coast, one-day version of Woodstock, or even better, Monterey Pop. The Stones were playing *for free*. All you had to do was park your car along the desolate freeway that linked Oakland and San Francisco to Stockton and Modesto, walk another half a dozen miles along the freeway, then off into a gully a couple miles due west. There it was. Altamont. It was another major manifestation of a tribal rock 'n' roll gathering, but by the time it was over, the underground media grudgingly crowned Altamont as the Death of Aquarius.

On that gray December day, two gawky, short-haired, adolescent high school sophomores in corduroy jackets and Levis stood along the shoulder of an under-construction East Bay freeway leading to Altamont Speedway. Yeah, that's us. Now zoom in a little closer. Okay, right there. Two skinny twin brothers carrying a paper sack full of lunchmeat sandwiches and a few soft drinks. We're on our way to see the Stones. Underground FM radio and the straight press had speculated for days where the concert was being held. Our ears were glued to Jive 95 KSAN/FM and the Big 610 KFRC/AM for the announcements: first, Golden Gate Park in San Francisco; then, Sears

Point Raceway farther north near where we lived; then, finally, Altamont in the East Bay. The show was definitely on.

To get to Altamont, we tore out a map from the front page of the *San Francisco Chronicle* and headed south into Marin County, drove over the Richmond San Rafael Bridge past San Quentin Prison, into Richmond, past Berkeley, Oakland, and Hayward. We abandoned the Mustang at the First Street exit at Livermore, less than ten miles from our final destination. Traffic was already clogged, so we stuck out our thumbs, tripping clumsily along the uneven shoulder of the freeway. A few minutes later we hopped into a gaily painted VW van and sat hunched down on the floor among other young strangers, not bothering to look out the window to check which direction the long-haired, bearded driver was taking us.

All roads led to Altamont.

It's common knowledge how Altamont ended. It's been documented in books and movies. The Stones played through a nightmare. The hostile crowd was wrecked on drugs, speed, grass, and cheap wine after a daylong binge. The Hell's Angels had the thankless task of securing the stage. As it got cold, dark, windy, and scary, the Stones took forever to come out. One young man stormed the stage midway through their set waving a gun and was stabbed and killed by the Angels. Jagger, Richards, and the band watched the spirit of Woodstock West unravel.

Earlier that morning, we staked out our small square patch of earth a few yards away from an old yellow school bus. The Frisco chapter of the Hell's Angels Motorcycle Club and their hang-arounds and "old ladies" sat inside the bus and up on the roof. As they guzzled down cans of off-brand beer, the crowd hooted up at them to share. Occasionally an Angel would oblige by throwing unopened cans, full speed, into our section of the crowd. If somebody didn't get smacked on the noggin, or some fortunate person didn't make a lucky catch, then the flying cans would hit the ground hard and explode, spraying fizzy contents all around.

Young people—mostly college students, street people, hippies, and some high school kids—populated the concert. People smoked their stash openly and passed it around to the folks sitting on the blankets next to them. Others wandered aimlessly in a slurred daze, heads spinning on designer psychedelics they had saved up especially for this monumental occasion. Camera crews roamed the grounds. The documentary, *Gimme Shelter*, showed it pretty much as it was. A black man stoned out on some heavy chemicals swung a small medieval mace, calling out over and over:

"Hey 'Nardo. Where's 'Nardo? Anybody seen 'Nardo?"

By noon Santana ran through a lackluster, abbreviated set without any controversy. The sound system shorted out during the first couple tunes before it sprang to life with full decibels. When Jefferson Airplane followed, things started to get creepy. In the middle of a jam, the music abruptly petered out. Guitarist Paul Kantner deadpanned to the crowd that his lead singer had just been knocked unconscious, after vocalist Marty Balin had the guts to curse out a Hell's Angel named Animal, then jump into a fracas between some Angels and a few faces in the crowd.

The vibes near the Angels bus turned strange, so we took off on foot to check out the massive spread of humanity. Most of the backstage area was free-for-all access for anybody milling around. There were a few trailers. Security was practically nonexistent. No area was roped off or fenced in as out of bounds. The stage itself was only a couple of feet off the ground for easy access. The sound system was supported Woodstock-style by high towers of scaffolding assembled only days prior. Some stoned-out fans scrambled up and dangled on the temporary structures. Throughout the concert the stage manager would interrupt the show and plead with them to climb down.

Several yards away from the stage, we scaled a fence to the adjacent speedway surface. A pickup truck approached us slowly with passengers standing up in the cargo bed. After the engine shut off, Crosby, Stills & Nash (and Young) jumped down from the pickup, dressed in the same fur parkas they wore on the inside of the first CSN album. Following them and barking out orders was Melvin Belli, the famous San Francisco trial lawyer who helped the Stones negotiate the use of Altamont Speedway. "Where's the stage?" inquired Neil in his recognizable wavering voice. He was carrying a large Gretsch guitar case. We pointed over at the stage a hundred yards away.

"Holy shit!" We looked at each other in amazement. "Neil Young *has* joined Crosby, Stills & Nash!"

We followed the quartet of furry parkas back towards the stage locale until CSNY disappeared into a lone restricted area. Standing nearby, we gained a fairly close, behind-the-stage view and saw a band walking out and plugging in their guitars. They wore crazy painted outfits. Chris Hillman, the bass player, had a brown, frizzy 'fro doo. A lean, handsome, dark-haired guitarist, Gram Parsons, stepped up behind the microphone.

"Ladies and gentleman," Sam Cutler, the Stones' road manager emceed, "the Flying Burrito Brothers."

The whole hillside erupted into one booming cheer as the band counted off into their opening song. The Burritos launched into an energized, uptempo version of the Dave Dudley country classic, "Six Days on the Road." On top of the loping beat, a steel guitar (played by a guy nicknamed Sneaky Pete) pierced through the Chuck Berry–like chord progression and pounding drumbeat. Parsons flashed a golden grin, looked back at the band, and waved at the audience. Then as if on cue, a simultaneous flock of hundreds of Frisbees and plastic coffee tin lids went flying into the air, covering the sky in front of the stage. For one brief moment in time, albeit less than an hour, the instant Altamont City settlement was joyful, carefree, and cheery.

It was a pleasant surprise that the Burritos showed up. We had seen no mention in the papers of them playing. Throughout the year, the Flying Burrito Brothers posed like stars, gracing the pages of *Rolling Stone* magazine. And now here they were at this nutty, untamed, free concert, dressed in the same wacky Western attire as on the cover of their debut album.

We looked at each other with equal parts disbelief and relief. The playful strains of non-redneck country and good time rock 'n' roll temporarily spun a jolly mood over the atmosphere. The tense vibe around the valley appeared to loosen. The Altamont throngs seemed positively transformed. There was something about the combination of rock and country that really clicked that day. We looked up at the now bright sky with a renewed optimism and flashed on the same thought—something, as identical twins, we frequently did.

"Man, these guys are the real deal. Now maybe things will start to lighten up around here for a change." It was not to happen, and the rest is history.

When you hear the lonesome, faraway whine of a steel guitar amidst the thrashing barrage of electric guitars on Ryan Adams's "Nuclear," that same magnificent fusion of rock and country began for us back in 1969, when country-rock visionaries like Gram Parsons and Chris Hillman played Altamont.

When indie songstress Neko Case belts out a twangy, modern Dust Bowl ballad called "Deep Red Bells" from *Blacklisted*, recorded in Tucson, Arizona, we flash back (again) to 1969 when another dynamic young singer from Tucson named Linda Ronstadt blended rock, pop, and Patsy Cline into a rousing performance of the country standard "Silver Threads and Golden Needles."

When Steve Earle enraged the cable news establishment right down to their silk socks with a controversial composition entitled "John Walker's Blues" (released in September 2002), it was only because he had the audacity to step inside the head of John Walker Lindh, the reviled American Taliban fighter. Such provocation harkens back to 1969 when another twanging giant, a man dressed in black named Johnny Cash, ventured behind the stone walls of America's two most ominous prisons, Folsom and San Quentin, and dared to empathize with men locked up and doing time for a variety of criminal offenses.

In 1969, a unique and exceptional alchemy occurred between rock, folk, and country. The role of the songwriter widened in rock and deepened in folk. Then a tight group of Nashville songwriters like Kris Kristofferson, Mickey Newbury, Roger Miller, John Hartford, and Tom T. Hall added their progressive spirit to the country idiom. Bob Dylan had already ridden into Nashville and recorded *Blonde on Blonde*, but was now bringing it all back home with two more brilliant Music City works, *John Wesley Harding* and *Nashville Skyline*. The progression from *Blonde* to *Harding* to *Skyline* indicated a pronounced shift toward less dense lyrics and a warm country feel.

By 1970, the trend solidified when Kris Kristofferson scored high acclaim on his debut album, *Kristofferson*, released on the Monument label. Also by then, the Flying Burrito Brothers and the Byrds had fueled the momentum of a country-rock movement already in full swing on the California coast.

From the Byrds' 1968 *Sweetheart of the Rodeo* to Lucinda Williams's 2003 *World Without Tears*—and everything in between and beyond—this is the music that has consistently lived up to our highest expectations as fans. Since Altamont, we've called this musical synthesis "American roots rock," for want of a better, broader, media-adaptable catchphrase.

American roots rock as portrayed in this book started heating up as early as 1966, then burst into flames during the early '70s, and has been thriving ever since—well over three decades and safely into the new millennium. Today, the genre is widespread and difficult to pigeonhole. Hooray! American roots rock is a welcome rock amalgam, found wherever acoustic guitars, pedal steels, mandolins, fiddles, and dobros are free to roam. The lyrics might drill in a little deeper—they're more heartfelt—and the music feels like home.

Thirty-four years after the Altamont fiasco, time had an ironic way of catching up with those two naïve high school kids. Today, as authors of almost a dozen works of nonfiction, a biography, and a couple novels, the madness and anarchy of Altamont has proved to be a paradoxical blessing for us. While most rock historians had cast a pall over it, our phoenix had risen out of the proverbial ashes of the "Death of Aquarius." In addition to witnessing the Burrito Brothers locking into the early phases of the modern American roots rock era, another strange connection occurred that day.

When Hell's Angel visionary Ralph "Sonny" Barger came roaring into Altamont right through the crowd on his Harley chopper with his beautiful girlfriend in tow, who would have guessed that 30 years later those same two reedy kids would become co-writers of his autobiography, *Hell's Angel*? It was our first American bestseller. We, "the Zimmermen," continue to work with Sonny on his many future book projects.

Plus, not even a decade after Altamont, the two of us sat in the wings of the old Winterland Auditorium in San Francisco. On the evening of January 14, 1978, we witnessed for ourselves the onstage disintegration of the Sex Pistols. San Francisco was the infamous last show on their tarnished American tour, and again, while rock history denotes that show as a downcast event, the Pistols' demise presented a literary boon for us years down the line when we co-authored *Rotten: No Irish, No Blacks, No Dogs*, with John "Johnny Rotten" Lydon. Who'd a thunk that we'd capitalize yet again on another pothole in the rock 'n' roll highway?

Writing *Sing My Way Home* represents a personal homecoming of sorts for us. It's our first music book in a decade, and a chance to explore our own musical roots and catch up with some of the great musicians we've admired and respect today. (Between 1975 and 2001, we devoted our professional lives as journalists and editors to covering the radio and music industry beat for a San Francisco–based music trade magazine called *Gavin*.)

Fair warning: If you're an expert on roots music looking for a detailed and footnoted history and analysis, then please move on. This book is geared towards those who are curious about what newspapers, magazines, and Web sites call "Americana" or what papers like *The New York Times* describe as American roots rock. *Sing My Way Home* is an attempt to put a human face on the tastemakers we profile in each chapter. Just as we did with John Lydon and Sonny Barger, we set out to give them their say without excuses and apologies. You be the judge. Of course, the artists we highlight are not the be-all and end-all lineup of roots-rock trendsetters. In our journey they are significant milestone artisans who have helped shape the genre over the years.

Experts and critics may disagree with some of our artist selection. All we ask is that you clear your mind of any preconceptions and read what each performer has to say. Better yet, grab a couple of their CDs or download the music from the playlists that we've offered and see if the music doesn't move you after all.

The order of the artist profiles, by the way, isn't based on chronology but rather on mood, fit, and flow. Like the music, the chapters of this book draw from different genres, whether folk, country, rock 'n' roll, or blues. So in "sequencing" the book, we strove to maintain a tempo and flow that reflected the eccentricity of the music, much the same way a listener might unpredictably mix and match genres and styles of American roots rock music.

We hope you enjoy *Sing My Way Home*. It was our intention to capture the subjects' voices on the page in an informative and entertaining light. This is the music that we're truly serious about, and we hope it shows. It's our desire to 1) contribute to the movement that's been rolling along for us since that fateful day at Altamont, and 2) help American roots rock artists earn a better living (hopefully) by helping to make their joyful genre a more popular, successful, and everlasting one.

—*Keith and Kent Zimmerman*
April 15, 2004
Oakland, California

chapter 1

Cosmic American Music
and the Gilded Palace of Gram

Exploring the Gram Parsons Legacy

In September of 2003, the same week they buried Johnny Cash, we attended a music conference in Nashville staged by the Americana Music Association (AMA). It was a grand, three-day event featuring a wide agenda of meetings and various musical showcases and club performances by American roots artists including Rodney Crowell, Ricky Skaggs, Allison Moorer, the Del McCoury Band, the Derailers, Jessi Colter, and many more. Nashville was jumping that week.

At the closing gala ceremony, a few significant artists of the Americana genre were honored. Kris Kristofferson was presented with a Lifetime Achievement Award. The audience saluted Johnny and June Carter Cash with deep posthumous reverence.

The AMA also paid resolute tribute to the memory of Gram Parsons. Remarkably, it had been 30 years to the day, September 19, since his death in 1973, and it was touching to see a large Nashville music contingent honor someone who, when he was alive, was dismissed as a maverick hippie and booed by the audience at the Grand Ole Opry.

During the conference, the AMA hosted a meeting called Standing in the Shadow of the Grievous Angel. Among the panelists were author Pamela Des Barres, No Depression publisher Peter Blackstock, Rusty Young from the band Poco, and Gram's surviving daughter, Polly Parsons.

It was a curious discussion from the beginning. Des Barres reminisced about her days with the GTOs, a bizarre ensemble of Laurel Canyon-based groupies formed under the tutelage of Frank Zappa. She spoke about Parsons's glitter-and-glam appearance at a movie premiere and how she considered herself one of his biggest fans, having traveled around the country extensively just to see Gram play live.

Next, Rusty Young launched into an odd tale about meeting Gram at Disneyland. Parsons, according to Young, showed up at the amusement park with his lady and baby girl, wearing makeup and a long, flowing gown. Parsons proclaimed the dress to be the next hip attire while Disneyland authorities balked at letting him through the admission gates.

Peter Blackstock, seemingly taken aback by the accounts, volunteered that he had no such direct dealings with Parsons (by virtue of his young age) and that he had become acquainted with Parsons's music after hearing the Grievous Angel CD in 1991. He explained how Gram's legacy led to the founding of his publication.

Polly Parsons, Gram's attractive, thirty-something daughter, spoke of her father and a "Sin City" tribute she was staging that weekend at a Nashville nightclub. It all seemed a little uncanny; she was only a toddler back when Gram died. Seeing her reminded us of the day we met Jeff Buckley on a publicity tour and shared our memories of watching his famous father, Tim, live onstage. Jeff shrugged his shoulders politely and informed us that practically all of his memories of his father came from small, secondhand tidbits from people like us.

The Gram tribute panel struck a peculiar chord as we sat in the audience. Was the legacy of Gram Parsons slipping out of focus? Had he become some kind of country kitsch pop figure?

We first got acquainted with Parsons as young teenaged fans back in 1968 when the Byrds' Sweetheart of the Rodeo hit the record stores, and later when the Flying Burrito Brothers graced the pages of Rolling Stone magazine. Later, it was Gram and the Burritos who summoned a much-needed dose of good vibes when they performed their short set at the Altamont free concert. Although many choose to trace the sonic fusing of rock and country back to Elvis Presley's 1954 Sun Studio sessions (or earlier), Gram Parsons was a major lightning rod for many subsequent generations of contemporary rock fans who, from 1968 to the present, openly embraced his unique fusion of country and rock 'n' roll. It was Parsons, the Byrds, and the Burritos who steered eager young listeners like us to the music of Kris Kristofferson, Hank Williams,

*Johnny Cash's live prison records, Ray Charles, Bob Wills, and the Louvin
Brothers. It's even arguable that Parsons may have seeded the pop and country synthesis of artists such as Garth Brooks and Brooks & Dunn. And while
Parsons was not a star on the level of, say, the Eagles or Jackson Browne, his
impact was tremendous.*

*Elevating someone to historic icon status is a tricky proposition. The
question remains, how do you canonize an artist who reached only a frac-
tion of his true potential? Here's a compact history outlining the essence
and impact of Gram Parsons as seen through the eyes of one who played
with him and others who know his music well.*

The recording career of Gram Parsons was short-lived yet powerful. From his
early 1967 recordings with the International Submarine Band to his brief association with the Byrds in 1968, the formation of the Flying Burrito Brothers, the making of two essential country-rock solo recordings, and on through
his untimely death in 1973 at age 26, Gram Parsons resonates heavily within
the context of today's American roots-rock world.

Gram bottled the angst and heredity of country and western with the
luster of a rock star from that era, spawning a musical concoction sprinkled
with generous influences of gospel and R&B.

What makes Parsons so special is that he created his own brand of roots
rock 'n' roll, a poly-genre stew he termed Cosmic American Music, at a time
when country and rock were at polar cultural extremes. Not including jazz,
Gram's music was an alchemic mixture of the greatest elements of American music like rock 'n' roll, country, R&B, blues, bluegrass, and gospel. Any-
time you combine those various components into one musical tumbler, the
spiciest ingredients rise to the top. In this case it was country, which was
Gram's master plan.

What's not to like about Gram Parsons? He was lanky, dark-haired, tooth-
some, and handsome. Rich, too. He sung with a sweet, wavering, and vul-
nerable voice, tweaking the noses of the Nashville country and rock elite

alike, especially when he formed the Burrito Brothers in 1969 with ex-Byrds bassist Chris Hillman, guitarist Chris Etheridge, and steel guitarist Sneaky Pete Kleinow. They marked an indelible influence on rock 'n' roll music forever. The Burritos were American roots rockers through and through, blending country and western essentials with rock fundamentals, minus the nasal vocals and heavy twang electric guitar associated with Nashville's country output at the time.

In a gesture that was as tongue-in-cheek as it was an attempt to be outrageous and flashy, the Flying Burritos posed in exaggerated sequined cowboy suits, stitched in the style of Gene Autry and Roy Rogers. But instead of the customary cacti, horses, and embroidered lassos, Gram's suit was garnished with outrageous accoutrements of the hippie set.

"Those crazy suits were the funny part of Gram," laughed Byrd and Burrito band mate Chris Hillman. "Gram had a wonderful sense of humor. We all loved him for that. Nudie Cohen the Rodeo Tailor and Turk Nathan came from the old Gene Autry and Roy Rogers movie days, designing rhinestone suits for the film studios and the old Republic westerns. They were two competitors out of Los Angeles. Nudie created clothing designs for Hank Williams and John Wayne. Then he spread into country music and Nashville.

"We went in and ordered our own campy suits from Nudie. Each outfit became a painting of our lives. The rule was that we could put anything on our suits that we wanted. Sneaky Pete loved dinosaurs, so Nudie put pterodactyls on his. Chris Etheridge came from the Deep South, Meridian, Mississippi. He wore a long coat, a plantation owner-styled look with big red roses symbolizing the Old South. And Gram? Perfect. He chose sex and drugs. Marijuana. Embroidered pills. Naked ladies on the lapels. A cross on the back, a Mexican Pachuco thing. My suit was a potpourri with the sun on the back, Neptune, seahorses, and peacocks. Who knows where the hell I was going with that?

"But the clothes were interesting and fun. Unfortunately, every time the Burrito Brothers wore them onstage we played badly. So we only wore them two or three times. But we sparkled as we walked offstage. It was like we were wearing neon signs on our backs."

Over the past three decades Gram's influence on young songwriters like Ryan Adams and Neko Case and his own stock as a musical icon has risen steadily. Loyal readers of alternative country (aka alt.country) journals like *No Depression* or music magazines like *Mojo, Select,* and *Harp* have since anointed Parsons as the charismatic founder of country-rock, which is a dubious distinction. Over the past three decades, a number of bands have sprouted up as a result of Parsons's influence—groups like Uncle Tupelo, Son Volt, Wilco, Whiskeytown, Supersuckers, the New Pornographers, and the Jayhawks. Each and every year, younger music fans and bandleaders sign on to the list. Walter Egan, a veteran musician who wrote "Hearts on Fire," one of Gram's finest recordings, cynically describes the growing legions of Gram's hardcore followers as "Grampires."

These days, musicians like Chris Hillman who saw things firsthand seem increasingly uneasy about how the Parsons legacy has swelled and evolved.

"Sometimes it bothers me that we've put this gentleman into saintly status," said Hillman. "Gram did write a few great songs, and a bunch of good ones. He got to be in the Byrds when Roger and I hired him as a sideman. Gram had a wonderful opportunity handed to him. At that time, in 1968 and 1969, only a very few great singer-songwriters got a chance like that."

Author/musician Sid Griffin, who wrote *Gram Parsons—A Music Biography* and recently completed an extensive BBC-TV documentary on Parsons, agreed. "The Gram thing *is* a little out of control and out of proportion. And this comes from one of his biggest fans. Back in the 1980s when I played with the Long Ryders, I was a starry-eyed, rose-colored glasses devotee. Gram Parsons was good-looking, talented, charismatic, and well liked. Then he drank and drugged it all away."

In the 30-plus years since Parsons's death, there has been ample and healthy debate concerning his proper place in the American roots-rock annals. Should he be immortalized by the "Grampires" or demonized by the Nashville hardcores? Gram, who died from a deadly concoction of tequila and morphine during a desert bender outside the Mohave community of Twentynine Palms, was a musical mastermind. He was exceedingly prophetic, and decades ahead of his time. Yet Parsons also had loads of untapped potential. Few might care about his music today, some speculate, had he not OD'd and left behind a glamorous tale of death and intrigue.

Gram Parsons was born Cecil Ingram Connor on November 5, 1946—Election Day, that year—in Winter Haven, Florida. He was close to his mother, the former Avis Snively. Gram's grandfather, John Snively, struck it rich owning and operating Florida citrus groves. Gram's father, Cecil "Coon Dog" Connor, moved the family from Florida to Waycross, Georgia, where he then ran his father-in-law's orange crate factory.

Young Gram got an early taste of rock 'n' roll in Waycross in 1956 when, as a young boy, he witnessed a live auditorium performance by Elvis Presley. Immediately following the concert, Parsons ran back to Presley's dressing room. He approached the King, complimented him royally, and scored an autograph. Afterwards, Gram's ears remained glued to the radio, cruising the AM dial and enjoying a mixture of country, rockabilly, and classic R&B.

Part of the fascination that music fans have with Gram's legacy stems from his troubled personal life. His family, though well-to-do and privileged, resembled the worst aspects of gothic Southern life reminiscent of Flannery O'Connor, William Faulkner, and Tennessee Williams. There was suicide, alcohol, and familial dysfunction. Two days before Christmas in 1958, daddy Coon Dog Conner stuck a pistol to his temple and blew his brains out on the wall. Returning to Florida, Avis was soon remarried, to a man named Bob Parsons. Upon marrying Gram's mother, Bob legally adopted Gram and his sister (also named Avis), inserting his last name on their birth certificates as their legal guardian. While Bob Parsons has been portrayed as an opportunist gunning for the family fortunes, he supported young Gram's earliest musical ambitions by buying a nightclub in Winter Haven, called the Derry Down. Gram's early bands played there and were broadcast live on the local radio. In 1962 he formed a rock party band called the Legends with pop-country singer-songwriters Jim Stafford and Kent "Lobo" Lavoie.

During his formative years, Parsons's musical emphasis shifted from rockabilly to boogie-woogie to rock 'n' roll and then on to folk music. Gram tinkered with the banjo and started his own folk trio called the Shilohs, emulating his musical heroes at the time, the Kingston Trio and the New Christy Minstrels.

"Parsons was a big bluegrass fan early on," said Griffin. "He knew how to play a five-string banjo in the Pete Seeger frailing style [aka the "bum-titty, bum-titty, bum-titty" rhythm] as opposed to the picking tradition of Earl Scruggs. Before he put the banjo aside, people often said he was quite a good accompanist."

"In 1962, Parsons and I went to high school and surfed together," said Luke Lewis, co-chairman of Universal Music Nashville and founder/president of the respected Lost Highway Records label located on the famed Music Row. "We were both Ray Charles fans, especially after we heard the album *Modern Sounds of Country & Western*. A little later, Gram found the Louvin Brothers' album, *Satan Is Real*, which was a huge influence. We were folkies back then. Dylan was just starting to happen while we were listening to the New Christy Minstrels."

By 1964, Gram's Shilohs made it all the way up to Greenwich Village. He even met Bob Dylan at a party thrown by Albert Grossman, Dylan's manager. But a year later, Gram's family life unraveled further. On the day he graduated from high school, his mother died from cirrhosis and alcoholic poisoning. That fall, no academic slouch, he entered Harvard University as a divinity student. By November, his stepfather had married the babysitter of his younger sister.

With the family unit crumbling, Gram dropped out of Harvard in February 1966 but stayed in Boston where he formed the International Submarine Band, named after an episode of *Little Rascals*. The band (with guitarist John Nuese, bassist Ian Dunlop, and drummer Mickey Gauvin) recorded a few demos and singles and then drifted to Los Angeles, where (with help from drummer Jon Corneal, guitarist Bob Buchanan, and bassist Chris Etheridge) they scored a record deal with the legendary producer Lee Hazlewood on his LHI label.

By Christmas of 1967, Parsons emerged from the recording studio over budget. By the spring of 1968, the International Submarine Band released their one and only long-playing record, *Safe at Home*, which some hail as the first official synthesis of country and '60s rock and pop. However, while *Safe at Home* debuted the country-rock anthem "Luxury Liner" nine years before Emmylou Harris and her Hot Band issued the definitive version, the album's wafer-thin production blunted Parsons's impact on mixing rock, pop, and country genres.

"Personally, I don't care much for the International Submarine Band material," Hillman admitted. "To me, it's like the Partridge Family of country music, lightweight fluff that just doesn't cut it. That's not Gram Parsons at his best. I don't know why in God's name [Sony] put that stuff on the 2003 CD reissue of *Sweetheart of the Rodeo*."

The International Submarine Band was the first of many misfires that plagued Gram's abbreviated career. They were potentially "too country" for pop stations and "too pop" for country stations. *Safe at Home* slipped through the stylistic cracks and sold poorly. The album was an enigma from the day it hit the stores. *Safe at Home* sent many mixed musical signals, probably too many. Hazlewood, best known at the time for his pop collaborations with Nancy Sinatra, was listed prominently and quoted on the album sleeve. The artwork (featuring four cheery young men dressed like antebellum Confederate dandies and riverboat gamblers) proved problematic. It was neither rock 'n' roll nor psychedelic, thereby alienating the dominant younger buyers of its day. Presumably Gram saw the writing on the wall. By its spring 1968 release date, Parsons hadn't stuck around long enough to even promote or tour for the record. He had his eye on another prize. The Byrds.

Gram had already met up with Byrds bassist Chris Hillman in a bank one day, after which the group hired him as a piano sideman for a double album Roger McGuinn and his band were planning.

The Byrds had already released five bestselling albums between 1965 and 1968. However, at their first rehearsals together, McGuinn and Hillman were immediately drawn to Parsons's mission to blend country and rock. In an unparalleled move, the Byrds—considered a major rock act at the time with several radio hits *and* an underground following—boldly changed course and virtually gave Parsons unprecedented leeway to pursue his fusion of rock and country. But it wasn't the first time the Byrds had dipped their toes into country waters.

"In reality, we were recording and performing country songs way before Gram came along," said Hillman. "The first one was in 1966, a Porter Wagoner song, 'A Satisfied Mind,' off our second album, *Turn! Turn! Turn!* On *Younger than Yesterday* we adopted an early country-rock sound. Besides, to us, it wasn't so weird recording a Porter Wagoner song. It was honest music written during the golden years of country music. Prior to joining the Byrds, I was immersed in bluegrass, playing mandolin, and listening to Buck Owens."

Just before hiring Parsons, the Byrds also added pedal steel guitar fills on "Going Back" on their *Notorious Byrd Brothers* album. While "Going Back" was one of the last songs David Crosby worked on before he was sacked, it was safe to say that the Byrds weren't exactly hayseeds playing country music a couple years before Parsons joined the group. The band was already about to take the major, unmistakable plunge onto rocky Nashville terrain.

In March of 1968, with Gram onboard as a full-fledged member of the Byrds, McGuinn, Hillman, Parsons, and drummer Kevin Kelly journeyed to Nashville. After a weeklong session with a crack team of Tennessee session players, they cut a handful of songs for *Sweetheart of the Rodeo.*

"We used some fine players," remarked Hillman. "Guys like John Hartford, Junior Husky, Lloyd Green, Jaydee Maness, and Clarence White. We also had some great songs. At that particular period of time, Gram was right on the money and doing his job well. *Sweetheart* left an amazing legacy and opened the door for a lot of people to begin listening to country music."

Gram had made full impact on McGuinn and company, and not only on the Byrds, but on the whole rock 'n' roll music scene. Word spread quickly about this handsome new face that had just made a massive, controversial influence on the Byrds.

"In rock 'n' roll groups of the 1960s," agreed Griffin, "you couldn't find a better example where a newcomer to an established band with No. 1 hits was allowed to step in and help run the show like that. It's an incredibly brave thing for McGuinn and Hillman to have done."

While in Nashville, Columbia Records pulled a few strings and scored the "new" Byrds lineup a coveted slot on the live broadcast of the Grand Ole Opry at the famed Ryman Auditorium. They would perform two songs at the most sacred country venue—a stage where legends like Hank Williams, Patsy Cline, and Ernest Tubb had trod.

"When the Byrds first played the Opry, some people in Nashville were more than a little scared," said Hillman. "The powers-that-be were nervous that we were invading their closed little world. Who would break through next after us, the Temptations?"

Host Tompall Glaser was especially incensed at the group for changing one of their predetermined Opry tunes at the last minute. After performing Haggard's "Sing Me Back Home" to boos and catcalls, Parsons shifted gears on the fly as the band followed his lead and launched into another song.

"Gram decided at the last second we'd do 'Hickory Wind,'" Hillman recalled. "It was a cool song, but Tompall Glaser went nuclear, screaming at us backstage. The only person who liked us that night was [singer] Skeeter Davis."

While the incident may seem inconsequential today, Glaser's outburst typified conservative Nashville's negative attitude towards long-haired musicians invading "their" musical turf. In turn, rock musicians and fans were equally narrow-minded. They lashed out at the Nashville country compatriots as being akin to gun-toting, right-wing rednecks. That's an equally silly assumption, considering that in 1966 visionary producer Bob Johnston recorded Bob Dylan and *Blonde on Blonde*, one of the greatest rock albums ever made, smack in the center of Nashville's Music Row using many top-flight country studio players like Charlie McCoy, Kenny Buttrey, and Hargus Robbins.

Sweetheart of the Rodeo was released on August 28, 1968, to moderate reaction. The front cover art featured a drawing of a damsel in full rodeo regalia. A lone wolf (symbolizing the Byrds' lonely crusade?) howled on the back. The album puzzled rock listeners and the underground radio stations. It sold disappointingly—yet another Parsons goose egg. But *Sweetheart* soon became well respected among *musicians* and surfaced as a significant record of 1968, single-handedly launching an all-out American roots-rock revolution. The Byrds even managed to score a mid-chart Top 40 hit with the album's opener, an obscure Dylan *Basement Tapes* tune, "You Ain't Goin' Nowhere."

Sweetheart was unashamedly country and honky tonk. It featured two countrified Dylan songs (a familiar Byrds ploy), a Woody Guthrie classic, a spiffy Merle Haggard tune, one McGuinn/Hillman original (the folksy "I Am a Pilgrim"), two of the greatest Gram Parsons compositions ("Hickory Wind" and "One Hundred Years From Now"), and a magnificently cockeyed version of a gospel Louvin Brothers classic titled "The Christian Life."

"'Christian Life' was performed tongue-in-cheek," said Hillman. "After Roger sang it, he admitted to going overboard with the accent. Roger was from Chicago and here he is, doing this heavy, syrupy country twang. But now that I've heard Gram's original vocal again after they put it back on CD, I actually think that Roger's version isn't so bad. Roger sang in tune. He was a great singer and was really the best musician of all the Byrds, having spent time as an accompanist with the Chad Mitchell Trio, the Limeliters, and Bobby Darin. Roger's sense of time made him a good all-around player. Out of all of us, Roger was clearly the most disciplined musician."

The magical collaboration of McGuinn, Hillman, and Parsons on *Sweetheart* was stung by Lee Hazlewood's contractual claim that Parsons had prematurely abandoned his International Submarine Band obligations to LHI in favor of joining up with the Byrds. That limited Gram to two lead vocals on the original *Sweetheart of the Rodeo* pressings.

Gram Parsons's tenure with the Byrds would be nearly as brief as his time spent with the International Submarine Band. Weeks after *Sweetheart*'s release, after a charity show at the Royal Albert Hall in London, Parsons followed his conscience. He jumped ship and left the group behind in England, refusing to join in on the Byrds' plan to play a few dates in apartheid South Africa. Other reasons may have interceded. Some say Parsons was irked that the band didn't have a pedal steel player onstage, and that his fear of flying also had to do with his leaving. Either way, Gram chose to stick around London with a new acquaintance, Rolling Stones guitarist Keith Richards.

When the Byrds returned stateside without Parsons, Hillman left the group and soon joined Gram to form the Flying Burrito Brothers with Chris Etheridge and Sneaky Pete Kleinow. They quickly inked a deal with A&M Records in late 1968. Their timing proved opportune for Gram's next serious stab at realizing his vision of Cosmic American Music.

On the eve of the Burrito's musical unveiling in 1969, *Rolling Stone* magazine and its Los Angeles correspondent Jerry Hopkins had already championed the entire burgeoning country-rock scene emerging out of Southern California. Even before that, in San Francisco, the young *Rolling Stone* publisher/founder Jann Wenner had liberally applauded country acts like Flatt & Scruggs, Johnny Cash, and Merle Haggard inside the pages of his biweekly newsprint music publication.

Many influential rock opinion leaders were now looking to Los Angeles for some fresh musical inspiration. Ex-Buffalo Springfield guitarist Richie Furay and Jim Messina had formed Pogo (later renamed Poco to avoid legal problems with the popular comic strip's author) with a young steel guitarist named Rusty Young and drummer George Grantham. Taj Mahal, though primarily a blues singer, fronted a mixed band of players who incorporated subtle strains of country, while Native American guitarist Jesse Ed Davis combined blues and country-and-western licks. Songwriter Jackson Browne was perfecting his craft with the Nitty Gritty Dirt Band.

Roger McGuinn retrenched his ever-changing Byrds lineup with *Sweetheart* session guitarist Clarence White and included "Drug Store Truck Drivin' Man" on their next record, a countrified tune poking more fun at Southern rednecks.

Gene Clark, another ex-Byrd, and arguably the band's best songwriter, teamed up with bluegrass banjo picker Doug Dillard and signed with the Burrito Brothers' label, A&M Records, as Dillard & Clark. Back in Tennessee, the Everly Brothers released a country crossover LP in 1968 on Warner Bros. titled *Roots*, which featured two famous Haggard tunes, "Sing Me Back Home" and "Mama Tried."

Ex-Monkee Michael Nesmith began recording with the First National Band, which included pedal steel prodigy Red Rhodes and other legendary Nashville sidemen. Nesmith scored a modest Top 40 hit with "Joanne," a song with country and western tendencies. Linda Ronstadt, who, with the Stone Poneys, had a folk-rock hit with a Nesmith composition titled "Different Drum," launched her solo career singing country music not unlike a modern day Patsy Cline. She recorded two fabulous solo records on Capitol called *Hand Sown, Home Grown* and *Silk Purse*.

The country-rock train had left the station. It was an important birthright for the American roots-rock movement, which was now penetrating the mainstream airwaves and local record stores. Few would dispute that Parsons was a prime architect, except for the sad fact that, officially, he had

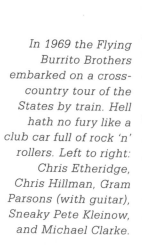

In 1969 the Flying Burrito Brothers embarked on a cross-country tour of the States by train. Hell hath no fury like a club car full of rock 'n' rollers. Left to right: Chris Etheridge, Chris Hillman, Gram Parsons (with guitar), Sneaky Pete Kleinow, and Michael Clarke.

yet to drink from the cup of success with his own hit single. Rather than merely aping country music licks and verbatim vocals, Gram was taking a much more difficult and innovative route.

"Gram is not really the founder of country-rock music. Rather, Gram attempted two major feats that the others hadn't," Griffin explained. "First, he wanted to bring the country and the rock audiences together. Oddly, that was something the others hadn't thought of. That's how far apart both cultures were. Gram stated in interviews that he wanted the country crew cuts and the rock 'n' roll longhairs of the late '60s and early '70s to come together as one, as a single audience at concerts, realizing that there was something to each other's music. You *never* heard guys like Gene Clark, John Sebastian, or Mike Nesmith say anything close to that back in the day. Give Gram credit for that.

"The second thing is that Gram understood the philosophy of young, hip, and long-haired guys—probably no strangers to smoking marijuana—and the value of playing country and western music with rock 'n' roll attitude. He looked at the Beatles (who had covered Buck Owens), the Stones, and the Byrds and *knew* you could play country music with the same rock 'n' roll look. Plus, it would be a whole new thing and not a bunch of straight-looking musicians alienating young music buyers with corny country album covers."

In celebration of the Burrito Brothers' debut record, *Gilded Palace of Sin*, A&M Records excitedly sent out press invitations with pieces of straw enclosed. Parsons enjoyed the critical limelight tremendously, although the album fell far short of gold by initially selling only about 40,000 copies.

"I really enjoyed that period," Hillman recalled. "I wrote some of my best stuff with Gram. I wrote half of 'Sin City' while he was asleep in the morning. I shouted, 'Gram, wake up. I've got something really interesting, a verse and a chorus.' He thought it was great, downed a cup of coffee, and we finished the song in ten minutes. It was a song that wrote itself."

"For my money," said Griffin, "*Gilded Palace of Sin* is the best Gram you can buy. Psychedelic Cosmic American Music that can't be beat. Gram incorporated all of America's roots music at once, not just on one song, but across all 12 songs on the album. *Sweetheart* was his first real start at it. *Gilded Palace* was the second and final, and most successful, stab, since *Burrito Deluxe* and the two solo albums that followed mainly combined country and rock.

"According to Ed Tickner, who managed Gram, the Byrds, and the Burritos, Cosmic American Music mixed rhythm & blues, straight blues, country music, bluegrass with mandolin and fiddle, and gospel all in one package. That's what Gram meant by his concept of Cosmic American Music."

Throughout his career, Parsons didn't have to play the part of the starving musician. As an heir to his grandfather's citrus fortunes, Gram was a trust fund kid, spending his annual stipend on limos and drugs.

"He emulated stardom and dressed the part on one hand," said Ben Fong-Torres, journalist and author of the Parsons biography *Hickory Wind*, which has been optioned by Rolling Stone Keith Richard as a possible movie. "He acted the part and spent the money that normally came with fame, except the money didn't come from musical success."

"Gram had a crutch in that he was a trust fund kid," Hillman explained. "He didn't experience that literal hunger most musicians felt. Gram had that fifty or sixty grand a year coming in. But he had a terrible family history of alcohol and drug abuse. Genetically it probably all led to his demise."

Gram was haunted by the shadows of death, suicide, alcoholism, and addiction within his dysfunctional family. At one point, Gram's stepfather confessed to him that he had smuggled booze to Gram's mother on her deathbed, which apparently accelerated her death. Parsons was emotionally shaken by his stepfather's admission and delved heavily into alcohol, psychedelics, cocaine, pills, mescaline, magic mushrooms, heroin, and morphine.

In the limited time (roughly two years) that Gram played with the Burritos, one of their most bittersweet accomplishments was being placed on the bill at the free Rolling Stones concert in December 1969.

"Gram got us that gig at Altamont by hovering around the Stones," said Hillman. "He was like a lapdog with those guys. But when we jumped on that stage and played 'Six Days on the Road,' a Dave Dudley song, we quieted down the crowd. Taj Mahal did that song, so we started doing it live.

"I knew that day it was a bad omen when we drove up and got into a minor car accident. Sneaky Pete was driving and we got knocked off the road. I had to walk through that crowd with my Fender bass over my head. It was like weaving through New Delhi during monsoon season. I had gotten up to the stage where our equipment guys had backed up the van. The Burritos mastered the Altamont stage for about 30 minutes. For a brief moment everybody stopped hurting each other.

"I was backstage when a couple of Hell's Angels were sitting there calmly. Then they'd see somebody jump onstage and go from Dr. Jekyll to Mr. Hyde and start beating them up.

"We actually took that big fat naked guy [who you see in all the famous pictures] and put him in our van. He was stoned on something. We told him, 'Get inside and stay in there. You're gonna get hurt.' Then he climbed out and the Angels jumped on him again. It was barbaric and brutal."

Parsons's short attention span for playing in bands continued during his time with the Burritos. He lasted through two Burrito albums, *Gilded Palace of Sin* and the more rock-centric *Burrito Deluxe*. During the *Deluxe* sessions, Parsons got sidetracked, hanging out with the Stones in Laurel Canyon while they remixed the tapes for *Let It Bleed*. It's been speculated that by then he had become addicted to heroin, using the drug along with Keith Richards.

As his relationship with the Burritos deteriorated, Gram and the band entered the studio anyway with producer Jim Dickinson and recorded a collection of strange cover tunes, including Ray Price's "Crazy Arms," "Sing Me Back Home," "The Green, Green Grass of Home," and a wistful remake of the Bee Gees' "To Love Somebody."

"Gram's concept of taking rhythm & blues songs and doing them in a country style was amazing," Hillman reflected. "'Dark End of the Street' and 'Do Right Woman' on the first Burrito album are right out of left field. To pick those kind of soulful, rhythm & blues songs and put them inside a country setting was quite ingenious."

By June 1970, the Burritos' relationship with Gram had collapsed. Parsons's fear of flying limited their tours and his attitude worsened. Hillman sacked Parsons from the group. "It was only a matter of time, actually, before we fired him. He wasn't showing up on time for gigs. We had a job playing for $350 in El Monte in Southern California. We all drove out there together while Gram hired himself a limo. It was two sets for a mostly Latino high school dance.

"We played another club in the San Fernando Valley where Gram showed up late. We started into one song while he played another. We were doing a country shuffle; he was singing a ballad in a whole other key. That's pretty hard to do. I said, 'That's it. We're done. He's over.'"

After leaving the Burritos, Parsons spent the next several months in the French Riviera hanging out with the Rolling Stones while they wrote and recorded *Exile on Main Street*. As Gram palled around with Richards during the *Exile* sessions, the two became poster boys for heroin chic. Gram was banned from the actual sessions, but his influences on Richards seeped into songs like "Sweet Virginia" and "Torn and Frayed."

"The Rolling Stones loved country and western," noted Griffin, "but up to then, they couldn't record it because it ended up sounding like a joke. Gram was the first guy to show Keith and Mick how to do it, how to play country, how it felt to play it, and how it felt getting it right. That was Gram's gift to the music world, through the Rolling Stones. He showed them authenticity. Being a Southerner, hearing country on the radio daily, he knew what it should sound like and how the lyrics ought to feel."

By 1972, Parsons returned to the United States after recording with producer Terry Melcher and nearly signing a solo record deal with Rolling Stones Records. Ever the musical tactician, he was searching for a female singer to launch his new band featuring a vocal duo in the tradition of George Jones and Tammy Wynette.

Through a chance meeting in Baltimore with ex-band mates Hillman and Rick Roberts (Gram's replacement in the Burrito Brothers), Gram was urged to contact a young female folksinger in Washington, D.C.

"When Gram came back from England," said Hillman, "I told him about a young lady in Washington, D.C. 'You need to call her up, I envision you two singing together.' That was Emmylou Harris. I had to literally beg him to call her. He finally made the call and went to D.C. to meet her. After that, *she* would have to put up with his behavior.

"But once again, the concept was right; he led Emmylou into a career starting in country music. She wasn't a country singer at that time, doing more folk music then, though she had a knack for country and even sang a couple of country songs during her sets when she worked in Georgetown."

Flying back to Los Angeles, Gram prepared for the next phase of his career, negotiating a solo deal with Reprise Records. Merle Haggard even met with him, but turned down the opportunity to produce his solo debut. At the time, Gram's addictions had shifted from the needle to the bottle. Bloated from extended bouts with alcoholism, Parsons changed course and flew to Las Vegas to enlist Elvis Presley's red-hot TCB band, notably hiring guitarist James Burton, pianist Glen D. Hardin, and drummer Ronnie Tutt to join him in the studio to record *G.P.*, his debut solo record.

Harris was flown in from Washington, D.C. and Gram sobered up so he wouldn't look ridiculous in the studio in front of Elvis's guys. *G.P.* was yet another astounding, genre-bending effort. But this time Parsons the solo artist devoted himself to an amalgamation of rock and country (though he loathed the term "country-rock"), as opposed to his more idealistically eclectic (and up until then, elusive) strain of Cosmic American Music.

Unable to finagle tour support from Warner/Reprise to put Elvis's TCB band on the road, Parsons instead assembled the Fallen Angels in 1973. With Emmylou at his side, he hit the concert trail. The loose-knit group grew tighter and tighter as they crisscrossed the United States. Soon they played to enthusiastic full houses at the Armadillo World Headquarters in Austin and at Max's Kansas City in New York. Parsons and Harris's duets, both live and on record, proved to be legendary stuff. Fresh off the road, Parsons entered the studio again and recorded what was to be his final album, *Grievous Angel*. Paying tribute to such writers as Tom T. Hall ("I Can't Dance"), the Louvin Brothers ("Cash on the Barrelhead"), and Roy Orbison (featuring a haunting duet with Emmylou of "Love Hurts"), and penning two moving, original ballads ("$1,000 Wedding Dress" and "In My Hour of Darkness"), Gram unfortunately would not live to see the release of his *Grievous Angel*.

A more pure country approach, *Grievous Angel* paled in comparison to the Burritos' eclectic *Gilded Palace of Sin*.

"While I have a soft spot for the last solo album," admitted Griffin, "a lot of country singers could have sung *Grievous Angel*. But nobody, not the Byrds, not the Beatles, not anyone, could have made an album like *Gilded Palace of Sin*."

Between completing *Grievous Angel* and preparing another tour, Parsons and three friends visited the Mohave Desert for some much-needed time off. He and a lady friend binged heavily on drugs and alcohol. In their Twentynine Palms motel room outside Joshua Tree National Park, Gram slipped into unconsciousness and turned blue. After being resuscitated and walked around, he laid back down on his motel bed and slipped into yet a deeper altered state, after which his organs shut down. His system went into shock. By 12:30 a.m. on September 19, 1973, Gram Parsons was pronounced dead in a Yucca Valley emergency ward. The final determination of his death was an overdose—a combination of morphine, cocaine, and barbiturates—and a blood alcohol level of 0.21%.

Contemporary musical folklore ignited on September 20, when Gram's body was stolen from the cargo section of the Los Angeles airport as it was being readied for loading onto a plane bound for Louisiana. Gram's former road manager Phil Kaufman and personal assistant Michael Martin had engineered the theft of the body. According to Kaufman, Parsons had requested that his body be cremated in the desert rather than undergo traditional funeral and burial services.

Less than 48 hours after his death, Gram's body was burned on Cap Rock at Joshua Tree National Park. After the police discovered the charred remains, Kaufman was arrested. Gram's ashes were then sent off to New Orleans to his stepfather, where they remain to this day just off the airport highway, next to a plaque proclaiming: "God's Own Singer: Gram Parsons." A plaque is also present near Cap Rock with the inscription "Safe at Home."

"What I remember about Gram are the good things," said Hillman. "I recall a very young kid who was motivated and full of dreams. He really worked hard for a brief period—from the Byrds' *Sweetheart of the Rodeo* through the first Burrito Brothers album. After that—bang! He was gone.

"Gram wrote some amazing stuff. We wrote some great songs together. 'Hickory Wind' and 'A Hundred Years from Now' from the *Sweetheart* album are priceless. Those were his greatest songs, while 'Hot Burrito #1' and 'Hot Burrito #2' were probably the best vocals he'd done on record.

"Up until the first Burrito album, Gram was focused. He had discipline. He was hungry. Then we lost him. What else can I say about the guy? He had talent and he wasted it. He died at 26 after a drug overdose. So, are we making this guy a role model here, or what?"

"Gram at his worst," Griffin added, "was a guy singing all these country covers [released on A&M] that have since come out posthumously, disastrous readings of songs like 'Tonight the Bottle Let Me Down,' 'Honky Tonk Women,' and 'Close Up the Honky Tonks.' He sounds sad, tired, and drugged out. The outtakes are equally heartbreaking. The man shouldn't have been in the studio. He should have been home in bed or in detox."

The joy of making music ended prematurely for Gram Parsons in the mysterious way timeless myths are launched. Had Gram survived and battled his addictions successfully, would he have maintained his current status as a legend? Or for that matter, would his output have matched that of Emmylou Harris? Even with less than a decade's worth of recordings, Parsons's contributions, measured by today's standards, are remarkable. There are dozens of anthology and tribute discs out there.

"Gram had a purity of vision, and a devotion to the sound he heard in his own head," said Fong-Torres. "He didn't care much about the conventions of the music industry."

"Gram was really good, but was he great?" Griffin asked, posing the final, most troubling question. "Probably not, because he didn't apply himself. We've seen other performers with drink and drug problems, like for instance, Steve Earle, bounce back. But Gram didn't have the work ethic. That's the heartbreaking side of it; he really pissed it all away.

"Because Gram died young, he's always going to be 26, handsome, and sexy, his remains burning on a flaming pyre in the desert. I guess that's a dramatic, page-one-headline-grabbing way to go out, which is a lot sexier than just dying quietly like Tim Hardin. He'll never be overweight and bald, and for a legend, that's a good thing."

Download This!

No Nasal, No Twang: Cosmic American Music Leaves Its Mark

Here are eleven of Gram's most prolific recordings and a few of his antecedents.

1. "Hot Burrito #1"—Flying Burrito Brothers (A&M).
   Gram's masterpiece from *Gilded Palace of Sin* was co-written with Chris Etheridge and represents Cosmic American Music fully realized. A pleading, soulful vocal performance that Otis Redding could have felt at home adapting.

2. "California Cotton Fields"—Gram Parsons and the Fallen Angels (Rhino).
   The best tune pulled from Gram's *Live 1973* release, taken from a live radio concert in Long Island. It's got a loping beat with loose-knit guitar fills quite reminiscent of prime live Grateful Dead from the same period.

3. "Dancing with the Women at the Bar"—Whiskeytown (Outpost).
   Ryan Adams is all of 22 on this 1997 track from *Strangers Almanac*. It's a windshield-wiper-slapping, haunting road song with mysterious whining pedal steel and vocal backing from Alejandro Escovedo.

4. "Hickory Wind"—The Byrds (Columbia/Legacy).
   The signature Gram tune from *Sweetheart of the Rodeo,* the same song the Byrds broke into unannounced on the Grand Ole Opry stage.

5. "Truck Drivin' Man"—International Submarine Band (LHI).
This obscure 1966 B-side single is available on the 2003 *Sweetheart* reissue.
A Buck Owens cover, it's a much funkier style of performance than what
appeared a year later on the original International Submarine Band album.
The ISB material appeared against the wishes of both Roger McGuinn and
Chris Hillman.

6. "The Christian Life (Master Take GP Vocal)"—The Byrds (Columbia/Legacy).
This alternate take is available on the 2003 *Sweetheart* deluxe reissue.
Parsons's lead vocal did not appear on the original release for contractual
reasons. This signifies Gram's love for the Louvin Brothers with nice subtle
background vocals by Roger McGuinn.

7. "Far, Far Away"—Wilco (Reprise).
Some say Wilco singer Jeff Tweedy currently plays down his alt.country influ-
ences even though that's what brought him to the dance. What's up with that?
From the 1996 *Being There* release.

8. "Wild Horses"—Flying Burrito Brothers (A&M).
The Burritos' second record, *Burrito Deluxe,* was more rockin' country and less
experimental. But Gram's rendition of this song preceded and eclipses the
Stones' own on *Sticky Fingers* by a country mile.

9. "Sweet Virginia"—Rolling Stones (Rolling Stones/Virgin).
The Stones tackled country on *Exile on Main Street,* but Jagger's lyrics and
harmonica work sounds like a parody. Nice acoustic blend of mandolin, slide
dobro, and mellow-roasted Gibson guitars. Gram claimed he sang in the
background, but it could not be substantiated.

10. "Streets of Bakersfield"—Buck Owens (Capitol).
Buck Owens had a string of country hits on Capitol in the 1960s, but he was
a Nashville outsider, much to the delight of young hipsters like Gram and later
Dwight Yoakam.

11. "(Sweet) Mental Revenge"—the Long Ryders (PVC).
From their 1983 debut EP called *10-5-60,* Sid Griffin's Long Ryders were
the first alt.country band to pay major homage to the Burritos. This is a
punky version of a song written by Mel Tillis, which also appeared on Linda
Ronstadt's extraordinary *Silk Purse* album recorded in Nashville by producer
Elliot Mazer.

chapter 2

Sing My Way Home

The Delaney & Bonnie Connection

Credit Gram Parsons for 1) pushing Chris Hillman and Roger McGuinn to create Sweetheart of the Rodeo; 2) championing the fusion of red-neck country with long-haired rock 'n' roll; 3) turning the Rolling Stones on to real country music; 4) co-founding the Flying Burrito Brothers; and 5) introducing Emmylou Harris into the American roots-rock continuum. One can argue whether or not Parsons is the father of progressive country, but one thing is certain: by today's vernacular, Gram Parsons had amazing networking skills in mixing people and music styles.

While all of the above is remarkable, Parsons's most far-reaching achievement was helping to bring Delaney and Bonnie Bramlett to influential prominence. The duo would intertwine rock 'n' roll music with Southern gospel, blues, and soul. The domino effect Delaney & Bonnie and Friends had on American roots-rock music during the genre's preeminent surge from 1969 to 1972 helped to significantly raise the level of musicianship leaps and bounds among even the top players like Eric Clapton, Joe Cocker, George Harrison, Dave Mason, Leon Russell, and many others.

In 1965, Mississippi-born Delaney Bramlett played bass and guitar with the Shindogs, the original house band for the go-go ABC-TV "live" music show, Shindig! The Shindogs boasted a hot lineup—Elvis TCB band guitarist James Burton and pianist Glenn D. Hardin, drummer Chuck Blackwell, and guitarist Joey Cooper. At the time, Delaney had yet to find his true musical calling in Los Angeles, that is, until 1967 when he met up with an attractive blonde blues singer named Bonnie Lynn O'Farrell.

Bonnie was a newcomer to the Los Angeles music scene, fresh from the St. Louis blues and jazz circuit. When Delaney met Bonnie, it was love at first sight. They made sweet music immediately and were married within a week. Between 1969 and 1972, the duo recorded six essential roots-rock recordings.

The enormous impact Delaney & Bonnie made on the evolution of American roots rock has been overlooked in favor of the Byrds and the Burritos. Much like Gram Parsons, Delaney and Bonnie Bramlett were extremely influential, attracting a posse of high profile musicians who were in musical and spiritual transition. Delaney & Bonnie's "open-door policy" gave their band a feeling of family and unity. Under Delaney's watch, the band was also tight and disciplined.

This is the story of a couple who hit the worldwide rock circuit and taught a few bored, super-rich, genteel, white British musicians how to roll up their sleeves and make their music down and dirty, more soulful and honest. Four decades later, their impact remains.

Contrary to popular belief, Bonnie Bramlett isn't from the South. But today, she still speaks with the same wavering, bluesy, Midwestern drawl you hear when she sings. Headquartered in Nashville, however, and still musically active, Southern hospitality flows from her friendly demeanor.

"I first came out to California in 1967 with a dude out of Detroit named Sam the Soul. Sam the Soul sounded black, played sax like Junior Walker, but looked like Bobby Hatfield. We came to Los Angeles as a rhythm & blues show, Sam the Soul and Bonnie Lynn. We truly sounded black, and we were *really* good."

Prior to rolling into Los Angeles, Bonnie sang the blues in her hometown of St. Louis, Missouri. "Albert King, Little Milton, Ike and Tina Turner, and Chuck Berry were all local musicians where I grew up," said Bonnie. "I sat in with some of the greatest artists before I left St. Louis."

After Bonnie Lynn O'Farrell dropped out of school at14, she started hanging out at jazz clubs in the Gaslight Square club district of St. Louis. Her band opened for Count Basie and she sang with several renowned jazz players including Dexter Gordon, Cannonball Adderley, Maynard Ferguson, and Wes Montgomery. But she also worked the rock circuit, making famous friends early.

"I was just a young kid playing in Gaslight Square," Bonnie recalled. "I remember when Duane and Gregg Allman, Johnny Sandlin, and Paul Hornsby had a band called Hourglass, which was before the Allman Joys. They played Pepe's A Go-Go. I was across the street at The Living Room. The bands from both clubs took breaks at different times. When the Hourglass was on break, Duane would bring his guitar over while my band was in full swing. When we took our break, my horn section would go over and play parts with Hourglass because they didn't have horns."

The concept of a soul revue would reap a strong influence that would follow Bonnie for the rest of her career.

While an underage teenager, Bonnie became the first white Ikette in the Ike and Tina Turner Revue. By rubbing skin-darkening lotion on her body, she toured convincingly with the all-black R&B show. Onstage and off, Ike ran a tight ship, tolerating little or no hanky-panky.

"I was 15 years old when I played with Ike and Tina. I had written permission from my mother so Ike could take me across state lines, and there was an adult guardian with me. Ike and Tina's band, the Kings of Rhythm, all rode in the bus while us girls—Tina and the Ikettes—rode in the Cadillac with Ike and his nephew, Jimmy. Ike *never* let the band and the girls mess together."

Bonnie later relocated to Memphis where she sang backup vocals in the studio with many of her idols, including Fontella Bass and Albert King, after which she decided to take a once-in-a-lifetime shot and move west to Los Angeles.

Delaney Bramlett was raised in the Deep South in Mississippi, migrating to Los Angeles during the late '50s. He played guitar on the legendary instrumental hit "Tequila" by the Champs. As a young singer, Delaney sang lead vocals on demos for Elvis Presley. As a Shindog, he'd landed the plum gig, playing guitar and bass on a network TV show. When Delaney met Bonnie Lynn at a Shindogs nightclub gig, the two made an instant love connection and formed a quick musical bond.

It was 1967. Bonnie was 23 years old; Delaney wasn't much older, a worldly five years her senior. The two had other differences. Bonnie belted out a blues and soul scream that legitimized her art of singing flat. Delaney sang in perfect key with a sweet Southern gospel tinge. Bonnie loved to sing live onstage; Delaney preferred the controlled atmosphere of the recording studio.

"We fell instantly in love," Bonnie said, "and got married in a bowling alley bar that had topless dancers. Our first song together was absolute magic because our styles contrasted one another. It was magic and that juxtaposition of separate styles is how we came up with our sound."

With the duo concept intact, Delaney used his connections to assemble all the best players for a recording session with his new bride. A collection of Los Angeles' best on-call musicians was contacted. Included in Delaney's black book was Leon Russell, rock's top session player who had appeared on various Phil Spector productions and Herb Alpert's hit instrumental "A Taste of Honey."

"Delaney had a special pool of musicians. We didn't know who would show up," Bonnie explained. "When we had a gig, we never knew who the drummer might be. It could be Jim Keltner, Jimmy Karstein, or Jim Gordon. All we knew was there'd be a drummer named Jim. We let them suss it out amongst themselves. We were sure pianist Bobby Whitlock would be there, because he lived with us. We knew either John Galley or Leon Russell would play piano. That's why the band was called Delaney & Bonnie and Friends, because they all wanted to play with us and everybody in town knew our charts."

Delaney pulled out all the stops calling numbers from his black book. Many of Delaney & Bonnie's "friends" went on to become world-class artists and major session players, including musicians like Rita Coolidge, Jim Keltner, J.J. Cale, Merry Clayton, Jim Horn, Bobby Whitlock, Carl Radle, Bobby Keys, Leon Russell, Jerry McGee, and Jim Price.

"Delaney brought in *all* the musicians," said Bonnie. "I didn't know any musicians in L.A. I was so in love with Delaney and met everybody through him."

Because Bonnie came from a blues, soul, and jazz background, not to mention working under a strong male leader like Ike Turner, entering the pop and rock world proved to be a learning experience for her.

"Delaney knew all the white musicians. Me, I didn't know one Beatle from another. I didn't know Jeff Beck from Eric Clapton. But I sure knew B.B. King, Albert King, and Chuck Berry. I was a snobby blues purist, very narrow-minded at the time. I thought most rock 'n' roll was a poor excuse for white kids trying to sound black. I thought I knew everything.

"Being from St. Louis, I had incredible black and religious influences. That's what I brought to this L.A. crowd. Religious expression, blues, and gospel."

While fraternizing among the Los Angeles rock elite in 1968, Bonnie met another extremely influential character at a gig outside of Los Angeles. That meeting would propel Delaney & Bonnie's career ambitions.

"Gram Parsons was a friend who helped break [introduce] us by helping us secure management," Bonnie noted. "Gram was also a catalyst amongst fellow musicians. He spread the word. He was our buddy, and he was famous then. Delaney was semi-famous. I wasn't famous at all.

"When I first met Gram I'd heard about the Byrds, but I wasn't much interested in them. I didn't like their music. I saw the Flying Burrito Brothers, and wondered, 'What the hell are these guys doing?' I watched the Rolling Stones and thought, 'Oh my god, would you guys tune up? Is this what the white kids are buying?'

"Gram was a glamour hippie. We were both born in November. 'What sign are you?' he'd ask me. 'Scorpio? Oooh. So am I.' That's how we met. Then we started singing together, Delaney, Gram, and I. Gram and I started hanging out. He wasn't really that macho. Gram was more like one of the girls. Delaney was rugged and macho, like Toby Keith is today.

"Later on, we spent a lot of time with Gram when he was with Emmylou. They were singing partners. Delaney and I were singing partners. That was the attraction. We were all best friends when we met and stayed that way until the day Gram died."

While it may be difficult to comprehend today, when Delaney & Bonnie presented white rock fans with a blend of rock, blues, soul, and gospel, the debate lingered as to whether young, long-haired white rockers had the right or the ability to convincingly sing and play blues, gospel, or soul with the same heart and conviction as black musicians.

Bonnie views the situation as a paradox.

"Lightnin' Hopkins and B.B. King are this country's Beethoven and Mozart. Kids like me embraced the black sound while many black activists rejected the blues as sounding Uncle Tom. So the blues got lost in the shuffle between civil rights and the black power movement."

Racial barriers were being crossed when Delaney & Bonnie scratched for their first record deal in 1968. The duo ironically found themselves in the same trick bag as many black performers, except their experience was reversed.

"We broke the color line at Stax. At the time, you never saw a picture of Booker T. & the MGs on an album cover for a reason. People didn't know Steve Cropper and Duck Dunn were white. We were the first all-white act signed to Stax. When the label signed Delaney & Bonnie, they must have thought they were signing two black kids.

"They had no idea we were white, never mind that I was eight months pregnant. I was bursting when we showed up in Memphis in 1968. Isaac Hayes opened the studio door. 'Hi, we're Delaney & Bonnie.' He looked shocked. 'Uh, oh.' After we cut the record, black radio stations said they wouldn't play it because we were white. Still, we'd broken a color line, and that was an important thing."

Delaney & Bonnie's first record, entitled *Home*, was recorded that same year, in 1968. Just like in Los Angeles, the Stax house band was all-star caliber. Delaney & Bonnie were accustomed to playing with the tightest, most grooving "friends." *Home*'s backup band was Booker T. & the MG's, with Delaney & Bonnie's keyboard player Bobby Whitlock, and no less than Eddie Floyd, Isaac Hayes, and William Bell adding vocals.

Stax Records, unsure of what to do with their new white act, sat on the master tapes and delayed release of the album. Later, back in Los Angeles, Leon Russell had also produced three tracks of Delaney & Bonnie singing together, but Russell followed a more pop "Sonny & Cher-like" approach. The logjam broke when Delaney & Bonnie scored a *second* recording contract with Jac Holtzman's Elektra Records.

"When we went into the studio to cut *Accept No Substitute*, the Doors had taken a 30-day vacation from the album they had been working on for months. Until I met Delaney, I didn't appreciate what a producer did. We

Much like the Flying Burrito Brothers, in a relatively short burst of time Delaney and Bonnie Bramlett invigorated rock 'n' roll with their ingrained mix of blues, gospel, R&B, soul, and roots-rock influences.

rushed in and quickly cut our record. We played live and we wrote live. We set the band up, cut 12 songs, mixed it, and were done in 15 days. We made the whole album for ten grand."

By mid-1969, Delaney & Bonnie and their new band of Friends had a hit album playing on underground FM radio. They also developed a reputation around Southern California for being the premiere roots-rock big band.

Enter Gram Parsons again, sprinkling more fairy dust on Delaney & Bonnie's future.

Parsons introduced the Bramletts to yet another musician in transition, ex-Traffic guitarist Dave Mason. Delaney & Bonnie and Friends scored a coup by adding the British guitarist as a band member. Mason's slide playing soon became an attraction at live shows. Gram Parsons's evangelizing of Delaney & Bonnie's music continued, this time for Beatle George Harrison, who secretly taped one of their sets from his table at an American nightclub. Harrison in turn passed the tape on to guitarist Eric Clapton, who reportedly went ballistic. His enthusiasm led to his offering Delaney & Bonnie a coveted slot on the 1969 American tour of Blind Faith, Clapton's post-Cream supergroup that included Steve Winwood, Ginger Baker, and Ric Grech.

Blind Faith fizzled after one tour. Clapton was disgusted with the pressures of being branded a "guitar god." He was weary of leading high-maintenance bands like Cream and Blind Faith. After working with John Lennon and Yoko Ono on their Plastic Ono Band projects, Clapton was eager to explore purer American roots on the level of *Music from Big Pink* by the Band, the group and album responsible for Clapton dismantling Cream in the first place.

As an ardent lover of the blues and eager to simplify his own approach to rock 'n' roll, Clapton began a low-key association with Delaney & Bonnie in the fall of 1969. Delaney became Eric's mentor, of sorts. In return, Clapton arranged for Delaney & Bonnie to bring their band over to Europe for a tour. At the insistence of promoters and record labels, Clapton's name was co-headlined on the tour. His tenure with Delaney proved to be a fortuitous time, allowing him to creatively refuel, build his confidence as a singer, and retool his bluesy fundamentals in order to record a solo album and pursue looser, less ego-based band projects.

"Clapton grew leaps and bounds after he left Cream and Blind Faith," said Bonnie. "He took a whole other turn. The stuff he played with the Yardbirds was raw. Then I think he got sidetracked with his own importance for a minute. All of a sudden, everything got so clean, deep, and intellectual. With us, he came back to being raw and real."

It was an incredibly fertile time for Clapton to step away from the limelight as a guitarist in a close-knit band. Also joining Delaney, Bonnie, and Clapton for the onstage party was Dave Mason, drummer Jim Gordon, horn players Bobby Keys and Jim Price, organist Bobby Whitlock, singer Rita Coolidge, percussionist Tex Johnson, and Carl Radle on bass.

The early shows in Germany drew mediocre response, but throughout the British dates, which ran through December of 1969, Delaney stayed the course. He ran the band in the tradition of James Brown and Ike Turner, as a Southern soul revue. Delaney emphasized precision, threw dirty looks at lackluster playing or missed notes, and kept an iron grip on quality and tightness. Audiences in the UK were thrilled to see Dave Mason and Eric Clapton ripping hot leads as relaxed sidemen. Delaney & Bonnie's blazing, all-American sound had provided British rockers with a fresh outlook on roots-rock inspiration.

"We were a monster band," Bonnie admitted. "We had instant communication. James Brown had it; Ike Turner had it, too. There's a prevalent saying in rhythm & blues: too many chiefs and not enough Indians don't make it. There was only one boss onstage and that boss was Delaney. All eyes were on him.

"Delaney followed the black way of running a band, except he didn't fine anybody. Delaney had 'the glare.' If he turned around and you got the glare, you'd better snap out of it. That included Eric.

"Delaney was a hard man to work for, but you learned every second. He was the chief, period. The band moved in absolute unison at all times. Delaney could change at any time. He might want to go into a whole different groove or song, and if you're looking away for a second, you might miss it. We could all end up flat on our faces. But that didn't happen often. It was a magnificent band. It was Delaney's ear. He could hear harmonies I couldn't hear if my life depended on it."

While Bonnie was comfortable being a frontline blues singer, playing live was a nervous experience for Delaney, who, according to Bonnie, vomited before every live show. Then his Southern macho took over, drawing in the more reserved, moneyed, and cultured British rock gentry.

"They came to learn from us, and you know, I gotta credit myself, I was a good singer when I walked out there, but Clapton didn't come to sing with me. He came to play with Delaney. They wanted to learn from him."

Another guitarist who was curious to "learn" and play a few hot licks was George Harrison. When Delaney & Bonnie hooked up with him, he was in a restless, anxious state, just like Clapton. Bonnie, the typical loud, brazen American, invited the quiet Beatle to join them on the road, not as a superstar, but as a guitarist, which thrilled Harrison to no end.

"I asked George, 'You wanna go play with us?'

"'It would please me, yes.'

"'Well c'mon then.'

"Delaney said, 'Yeah, just get on the bus. Let's go.'

"'Yes, but Patti [Harrison's wife] won't let me go.'

"We knew English people were too polite to say no to our faces," Bonnie remembered, "so we just drove up to George's place in the bus and like rude Americans, grabbed George. 'Come with us.' What's she gonna say, no?

"So we did. George got on the bus and toured with us. We stopped at the airport so he could pick up a paper to see what the hell John and the guys were up to. We were already set to meet up with John and Yoko at the Lyceum two weeks later to do the Plastic Ono Band thing. It was a crazy show. Eric played guitar using a cigarette pack for a pick. Keith Moon played bass. John Lennon and I played drums. People loved it, even though we all played horribly."

Touring Britain in December 1969 wasn't the first time Delaney & Bonnie met George Harrison. They'd met prior to the Beatles' *Abbey Road* sessions.

"George wrote this song," said Bonnie, "and at the time, the Beatles hadn't played together for a while. I remember George telling Delaney and me about the tune.

"'I've got this song, Delaney. I keep giving it to Paul and John. They're putting it on the back burner.'

"George played 'Something' for us in a hotel room. Delaney looked at him, and playing the pushy American said, 'George, you're a rich man. Go cut it. You want me to help you? You can do it, and you don't have to wait for Paul or John. Go cut the freaking song.'

"George did, and it became Harrison's first big hit with the Beatles."

Blazing the UK motorways, Delaney, Bonnie, Eric Clapton, and Friends were tearing up the British concert halls. At the same time, a former plumber's apprentice from Sheffield, England named Joe Cocker had released two hot albums. Like Delaney & Bonnie, Cocker worshipped blues and soul musicians like Ray Charles and sang with a raucous technique that delighted British and American rock fans. By 1970, Leon Russell recruited Delaney & Bonnie's entire band to join Joe Cocker on the successful but ill-fated, two-month Mad Dogs & Englishmen tour.

"We were boot camp for dang near everybody. I look at it this way. If God hadn't put Delaney and I together, then none of this would have happened. But like I said, we brought the blues to this crowd like serious business and because *we* could do it, we made them believe *they* could do it, too."

By 1970, Delaney & Bonnie entered the next phase of their careers. Just before the band's mass exodus to the Cocker and Russell camp, the entire crew joined Eric Clapton in the studio with Delaney Bramlett as arranger and producer. They would record Eric's long-awaited solo debut. Clapton's self-titled LP stunned many fans on first listen. The music was unmistakably rootsy and American-sounding. Instead of a pinched, self-conscious singing style, Eric's vocals were now wholesome, fuller, more relaxed and confident. They closely resembled Delaney Bramlett's own Delta dulcet tones.

"Delaney walked Eric through that record, line by line. He'd sing the line, punch it out, Eric would sing the same line, punch it in. Line by line, that entire album. Delaney did that for Eric.

"Delaney was not the easiest person to be around, but you knew that after you left him, you would leave a better musician than when you showed up. Was he a perfectionist? Yes. Did he get everything done? Yes. Did he sense that you had more talent than you realized? Yes. Did he demand that you use it? Yes."

In June of 1970, Delaney & Bonnie and Friends' late-1969 European tour was documented with the release of a bestselling live album appropriately titled *On Tour with Eric Clapton*. Rarely had a large rock group sounded so agile and tight. Bonnie's charisma shone through the record's eight songs. But by the time the disc was released to the public, Delaney & Bonnie's all-star revue had already splintered and moved on.

A parade of records with the Delaney & Bonnie stamp would follow throughout 1970. In July, Clapton debuted his solo record, which mined multiple hits on Top 40 radio. In August, Joe Cocker released a double-set, live *Mad Dogs & Englishmen* LP and movie. Also that summer, prior to Clapton, Dave Mason re-emerged with his very first solo album, *Alone Together*, which included Delaney & Bonnie and Friends as key session players. Delaney & Bonnie's musical mark would saturate the radio airwaves worldwide. But the best by-products were yet to come.

By November of that year, a more confident Clapton stepped back into the spotlight with Derek and the Dominos, a band made up of Delaney & Bonnie alumni. Clapton's blues chops had evolved tremendously, and the masterpiece *Layla and Other Assorted Love Songs* showed Clapton singing and playing with more passion and fury than ever before. A few days later, an even more musically liberated George Harrison released his tour de force, *All Things Must Pass*, featuring songs with Derek and the Dominos playing prominent backup roles.

Bonnie looks back on those days as a time for fun and games. And in the final analysis, touring with Delaney & Bonnie was the rock equivalent to joining a good ole Southern R&B/gospel/soul road show, right down to the group prayer sessions.

"Delaney and I both came from deeply religious Christian homes, so we always prayed on the road," she reminisced. "Leon was raised that way in Oklahoma. Praying was the big difference between what we did and what other bands didn't. Eric got on his knees and prayed with Delaney and I. Gram prayed with us. So did Joe Cocker.

"We prayed before every show, after the show, and in our hotel rooms. We prayed before we got on the bus. We joined hands and stood in a big circle. Leon got to the point where he almost became the preacher."

Not many bands at the time formed prayer circles.

"We weren't being hypocritical. It was us saying, 'Be with us, Lord. We're scared and we don't know what we're doing.' And everybody got into it. It shook Eric down to his boots. And George Harrison, too. But that's why people came with us. We didn't put on any delusions of grandeur. This was who we were. You want what we got? This is what we do. We'd pray before every show. We thanked God for our blessings; we asked God to keep us safe."

After the 1970 recordings deluge, Delaney & Bonnie's most powerful musical offering was yet to come.

When the couple returned to Los Angeles, they arranged for a low-key recording session to try and summarize what they felt were the most inspirational aspects of being traveling musicians. In 1971, Delaney & Bonnie released the roots-rock masterwork, *Motel Shot*.

"*Motel Shot* wasn't cut as a hit record," Bonnie explained. "It went absolutely against the grain. It was a *real* record. The whole concept of *Motel Shot* was inspired by the fact that after each gig, we'd go back to the motel and sing. Eric, Delaney, Duane Allman, or me, or whomever, would sit around singing and picking and strumming guitars all night long. We thought we should try to recapture that spontaneity of those motel rooms, because that's where the real genius comes from."

Motel Shot highlights all the important genres of Gram Parsons's Cosmic American Music concept—the blending of rock, gospel, hillbilly, country, blues, and soul. There are no electric instruments or drum kits. Handclaps and tambourines were the loudest percussion. Even Gram Parsons was on hand to bestow his blessing.

"*Motel Shot* wasn't made in a studio. It was recorded in [producer/engineer] Bruce Botnick's big front room in Los Angeles. We really wanted to be 'in the house,' in the living room, not in some studio with baffles, none of that stuff. We wanted everything to be as live as if we were sitting around jamming. Everything was recorded from the time we opened the door to the last note, in one day."

Like the old days, Delaney & Bonnie put the word out. If you wanted to be a part of *Motel Shot,* show up at Botnick's house by 6:45 p.m., no later than 7:00 p.m. After that, the door would be closed and locked. It would be a one-day shot, a *Motel Shot.*

The official lineup became Delaney & Bonnie, Bobby Whitlock, Jim Keltner, Gram Parsons, Dave Mason, Duane Allman, Iva Bramlett (Delaney's mother), Eddie James, Buddy Miles, Carl Radle, Leon Russell, Joe Cocker, Jay York, Sandy Konikoff, John Hartford, Kenny Gradney, and Ben Benay.

"There were no drums, just a briefcase. Buddy Miles, by the way, played great briefcase even though he wasn't credited on the record. The big bass drum you hear? That was Joe Cocker banging on the side of the piano. All that percussion on 'Going Down the Road Feeling Bad' was me, Gram Parsons, and Duane Allman smacking our laps. As a matter of fact, Duane played briefcase, too. Briefcase, lap, and slide guitar. Jim Keltner played briefcase, too. John Hartford was there as a friend and singer. John and I grew up together in East St. Louis near the Mississippi River."

There were no multiple takes on *Motel Shot.* The tape machine was turned on as the musicians played for about four hours. The session lasted a single night. Twelve songs were elected as keepers.

"We did many more songs, it was that spontaneous. We had a general idea of what songs we were going to do. Leon sat down at the piano and sang 'Rock of Ages.' 'That's a good key. Okay, 1-2-3-go.' That's Mamaw [sic], Delaney's mother, singing 'Rock of ages, cleft for me' with Leon and I.

"The record opens with 'Where the Soul Never Dies,' an old, really white mountain gospel song. 'Talkin' about Jesus' and 'Going Down the Road Feelin' Bad' were black gospel expressions, which shows you there's not a whole lot of difference between black and white mountain gospel. It's a hoot hearing Joe

Cocker screaming 'talkin' 'bout Jesus' over and over. We wanted to go from white-on-white hillbilly church music to black gospel, and I believe we succeeded. If you think about or listen to the wheels of a traveling tour bus, listen to the rolling rhythm of 'Lonesome and a Long Way from Home.' It's self-explanatory, isn't it?"

Delaney & Bonnie's homey, heartrending version of "Faded Love" signifies Delaney's Southern lineage in Pontotoc County in Southern Mississippi, where he was raised.

"'Faded Love' is a song that Mamaw and Papaw Preston Bramlett and Papaw J.R. Bramlett—that's Delaney's grandpa and great-grandfather—sang whenever they got the family together. The patriarchs and the matriarchs of the Bramlett clan, from the time Delaney first sang as a pre-teenager, would say, 'Now Lane, c'mon in here now and sing 'Faded Love' for your Aunt Merle.' That's why we included that song."

As down-home and organic as *Motel Shot* sounds, Delaney & Bonnie surprisingly scored their biggest radio hit from that simple session.

"Delaney had partially written 'Never Ending Song of Love' in Nashville, even before he came to California. After we got together, Delaney told me I needed to start writing songs.

"'You need to know how to do this,' he would tell me, 'you're a songwriter now.' I said okay and commenced to writing. It was a rainy day and I was going through Delaney's catalog of half-written songs. I asked him about 'Never Ending Song of Love.'

"'Yeah, I started that one in Nashville. It's kinda corny.'

"'How's it go? It looks cute.'

"Delaney sang me the song.

"'Man, this song is so sweet, our kids can jump rope to it. Let's finish it.'

"'Oh Bonnie, it's so corny.'

"Then Duane Allman came over. 'Look Duane,' I said.

"'Bonnie, don't play that song for him,' Delaney pleaded.

"'Listen to this cute song Delaney wrote.' Then we finished it.

"Duane gasped, 'Oh my god,' so we cut it during the *Motel Shot* session. If Delaney had anything to do with it, other than writing the dang thing, it would not have been recorded. Duane and I rediscovered it and it became a huge hit record."

Perhaps the most astounding tune on *Motel Shot* is a composition buried toward the end of side two. "Sing My Way Home" weaves lyrics and a sweet melody gently wrapped around strumming acoustic guitars. The vocals are entwined with Duane Allman's recognizable, masterful slide dobro. The words, the singing, the accompaniment, and the serene eloquence of the song are indigenous to American roots-rock music at its best.

"Isn't it a wonderful song? Delaney co-wrote 'Sing My Way Home' with Steve Cropper. What an amazing lyric. 'I'd like to tell the birds and trees and all the leaves that fall before my feet that I'm in love.' Remember, Steve Cropper wrote '(Sittin' on) the Dock of the Bay,' but I think they both wrote the lyrics for this song. I don't know who wrote what line, but Delaney is also very good at lyrics. 'It's not so hard to understand the satisfaction of a man who's had the only thing this world has had to offer him.' I hear that as being Delaney's line, but I can't guarantee it. The first line sounds much more like Steve Cropper to me. Either way, it's just a monster song written by two incredible songwriters, so who can tell?

"After we cut *Motel Shot*, Delaney and Bruce Botnick went through the tapes in the studio. I went home to cook and take care of the kids and my mother-in-law. Months later, for another record, Delaney wrote a song called 'Country Life' that longs for simple times. 'Oh to be back in Tennessee, baby you and me, just once again. Down near the end of the road you can see where I live, with my wife and three lovely daughters.' Delaney was charismatic that way."

The good times couldn't last. Delaney & Bonnie's musical partnership burst onto the musical landscape like a supernova, and it ended as suddenly as it began. In 1972, the couple left Atlantic Records after label executive Jerry Wexler sensed trouble in their marriage and sold their contract to Clive Davis at Columbia Records. Their first Columbia release, *Delaney & Bonnie Together*, featured strong material from their Atlantic days along with new music, including an energized studio rendition of "Only You Know and I Know." Eric Clapton and Dave Mason reunited with a frenzied, double lead-guitared version of "Comin' Home." Rounding out the album, Delaney & Bonnie performed more soul duets in the tradition of their early Atco and Stax recordings, punctuated by punchy, Memphis-styled horn charts. All-star cameos decorated *Delaney & Bonnie Together*, with return appearances by Clapton, Mason, and Russell, as well as Tina Turner, Billy Preston, King Curtis, and Steve Cropper. Bonnie's original 1969 version of "Superstar," the huge 1971 Carpenters hit she and Russell penned, also appears on *Delaney & Bonnie Together*, suggesting a tying-up-of-loose-ends approach to the record.

A year after *Delaney & Bonnie Together* was released, the couple's relationship collapsed and they abruptly divorced, ending an illustrious and condensed career as a rock and soul duo. Delaney recorded two subsequent solo efforts for Columbia. Bonnie did one. Bonnie looks back at their breakup as a result of the fast times of the era, where booze, drugs, and loose sex was encouraged and almost expected of the rock 'n' roll elite. An overindulgence of cocaine ravaged its way through the inner circles of rock 'n' roll during the early '70s. Bonnie saw the devastating aftereffect of rampant drug use as gradual.

"I didn't notice the drug or alcohol problems. It's what we did in those days, and we were encouraged by the powers that be. You could tell who had the best record deals by the quality of coke they snorted. That's no joke.

"When cocaine came along, I was innocent about drugs," recalled Bonnie. "Early on, we'd have a drink or took a bennie. When that other stuff came into our lives, with all the fame, Delaney and I were pitted against each other. Man, it was bad. When one of us would get too caught up, the other one would see the ditch down the road.

"Being a Christian girl, I didn't do well with all that behavior. This wasn't about a band and a girl and guy singer. That was my husband and the father of my children, and we were behaving horribly. And it was not what I had in mind for the big time. It was not Christian behavior. It was not what we were praying for.

"What can I say? When I needed to get sober, I went to a nuthouse. There were no recovery centers yet. It seemed like everybody was dying. I didn't want to die and I knew we were doing wrong. He knew we were doing wrong. Delaney just didn't know how to get out of it.

"Gregg Allman and I became the pioneers of sobriety in rock 'n' roll during that time. That was over 30 years ago. We were the first ones to hit the program. It was an intense time because, like I said, there were no recovery centers and so many people were using."

Bonnie Bramlett prefers to remember the productive and the influential times as a bygone musical era that cannot be forgotten nor duplicated.

"We had a ball, and nobody wants to write about how funny things were. It was a funny time. There were no rules, and I wasn't just a girl singer, I was part of the band. We'd tell our war stories. The guys could tell one and we'd all laugh. Leon would tell one, and we'd all laugh. Then I'd tell one, and Delaney would get so mad. 'Why do you have to tell a story every time somebody else tells a story?' We had freedom galore and I just wouldn't shut up. Sometimes Delaney wanted to tape my mouth. I was quite the outspoken one.

"I remember one time when Eric, Delaney, myself, Eric's girlfriend, and Jerry Wexler were all riding in this limo to go see Little Esther Phillips. Little Esther wanted to make a record and she fancied Delaney might want to produce it. Delaney hadn't done Eric's record yet, and at the time I didn't know all that much about Clapton's music.

"All of a sudden, this song comes on the radio. 'I'm so glad, I'm so glad, I'm glad, I'm glad, I'm glad.' It repeats two or three more times and goes on and on, the long version. Now I'm a blues person, and it didn't sound anything like the original by Skip James.

"'Holy hell,' I yelled out, 'I know that sucker's glad, but Jeez, would somebody please turn that radio off?'

"'Bonnie,' Eric spoke in a low tone. He looked like he was going to cry. 'That's me.'

"I guess I did that a lot. That was my arrogance, but you know, I think that's why Eric liked us. We didn't treat him like anything other than a great guitar player."

Download This!

The Delaney & Bonnie Traveling Medicine Show

Just as Gram and those darned Burritos messed with country and rock, Delaney and Bonnie Bramlett dosed rock and pop with a much-needed shot of blues, gospel, and soul. Here's a short list of essentials by Delaney & Bonnie and related artists. *continued on the next page*

The Delaney & Bonnie Traveling Medicine Show *continued*

1. "Sing My Way Home"—Delaney & Bonnie and Friends (Atco).
   A roots-pure, acoustic strum-along from the legendary *Motel Shot* record,
   co-written by Delaney Bramlett and Steve Cropper, with Duane Allman playing
   slide. So poignant we named the book after the tune.

2. "Talkin' about Jesus"—Delaney & Bonnie and Friends (Atco).
   Six-minute jam with Joe Cocker testifying "talkin' 'bout Jesus" over and over
   again with Leon Russell pounding out ham-fisted gospel piano rhythms.

3. "Never Ending Song of Love"—Delaney & Bonnie and Friends (Atco).
   The last thing Delaney & Bonnie were fishing for on *Motel Shot* was a Top 40
   hit. But it happened. Contact www.rhinohandmade.com and suggest they
   re-release an expanded edition of *Motel Shot.*

4. "Soul Shake"—Delaney & Bonnie and Friends (Atco).
   A mid-chart Top 40 hit from May 1970. As the title suggests, it's a fine little
   soul-shakin' duet.

5. "When This Battle Is Over"—Delaney & Bonnie and Friends (Elektra).
   The quintessential Delaney & Bonnie anthem? Notice the tasty fade-up on the
   percussion jam that begins the song. Delaney & Bonnie trade vocal lines while
   Leon Russell's punch-drunk piano lines stagger around the verses. The song
   appeared during the closing credits of an episode of the HBO series *The
   Sopranos.*

6. "Look at You, Look at Me"—Dave Mason (MCA).
   Tommy LiPuma has produced many fine jazz talents including Diana Krall,
   but he'll always be the man who produced Dave Mason's masterpiece, *Alone
   Together*, on Blue Thumb Records in 1970.

7. "Only You Know and I Know"—Delaney & Bonnie and Friends/Dave Mason
   (Columbia/Legacy).
   Both the Delaney & Bonnie and the Mason versions measure up nicely.
   Delaney was the master at beefing up guitar hooks to songs. While Mason
   wrote the tune, the opening guitar riff that kick-starts the song sounds like it
   may have come from Delaney.

8. "The Art of Dying"—George Harrison (Apple/Capitol).
Derek and the Dominos backing up the late Beatle in a Phil Spector fog from
All Things Must Pass, Harrison's masterwork recording.

9. "Speak Your Mind"—Marc Benno (A&M).
From Marc Benno's second album, *Minnows,* here's an extremely rare jewel.
Benno was originally Leon Russell's partner in a short-lived duo, Asylum Choir.
Guitarists include Clarence White, Jesse Davis, Bobby Womack, and Jerry
McGee.

10. "Delta Lady"—Leon Russell (Shelter).
Leon Russell's debut solo record had all the great songs, including "Delta
Lady," "Hummingbird," and "Your Song." It was one of the first records on
Denny Cordell's Shelter Records, which was the early inspiration for today's
Lost Highway label, home of Lucinda Williams and Ryan Adams.

11. "Comin' Home"—Delaney & Bonnie and Friends (Columbia/Legacy).
Originally released as a single in 1969. A trio of frenzied guitars by Eric
Clapton, Dave Mason, and Delaney lead the charge. Available on the Sony
reissue *Delaney & Bonnie Together,* Clapton's rave-up clearly crosses the
finish line first.

12. "Cry Me a River"—Joe Cocker (A&M).
From the *Mad Dogs & Englishmen* package, the Leon Russell-led band sounds
a bit unwieldy and ego-driven compared to Delaney & Bonnie's tight Friends
ensemble. The vocals are fresh and earthy. One of Joe Cocker's better
performances.

13. "Why Does Love Have to Be So Sad?"—Derek and the Dominos (PolyGram).
What would have happened if Derek and the Dominos had had the stamina to
stick around for a few more albums? One shudders to think of the possibilities.
This tune from *Layla* recalls Delaney & Bonnie's influences. By this time,
Clapton had a new sound and direction nailed.

14. "I Don't Want to Discuss It"—Delaney & Bonnie and Friends (Atco).
The high-water mark from the *On Tour with Eric Clapton* CD. Someone needs
to mine the original tapes, and expand and re-master the CD.

continued on the next page

The Delaney & Bonnie Traveling Medicine Show *continued*

15. "After Midnight" (alternate version)—Eric Clapton (PolyGram).
A hit version of J.J. Cale's classic, furiously sped up. This is a slightly different version culled from Clapton's *Crossroads* box set with a hotter horn mix and grittier guitar solos. Delaney works the knobs on these sessions, which became Clapton's first official solo album.

16. "Me and a Friend of Mine"—Marc Benno (A&M).
Another scarce tune from Marc Benno's third solo record gem, *Lost in Austin*. Sessions were produced by Glyn Johns, and featured Benno, Clapton, and Albert Lee on guitar. The late bassist Carl Radle, nicknamed Mr. Peepers by Bonnie, also appears. Again, no Delaney & Bonnie, but what a fine shuffle groove former "Friend" Jim Keltner plays.

17. "It's Been a Long Time Coming"—Delaney & Bonnie and Friends (Stax).
This is the opening track from *Home,* their first and only record on Stax. The backup band is Booker T. & the MGs, Bobby Whitlock, and "background singers" like Eddie Floyd and Isaac Hayes.

18. "Just Plain Beautiful"—Delaney & Bonnie and Friends (Stax).
Back in the day, the *Home* album on Stax was less important in the grand scheme of other Delaney & Bonnie releases. But today, the richness of Stax's signature horn charts and arrangements makes this well worth seeking out.

19. "Piece of My Heart"—Delaney & Bonnie and Friends (Stax).
When Delaney & Bonnie cut "Piece of My Heart" in Memphis, Janis Joplin owned the song hands down, but this version demonstrates the duo's tremendous absorption of black musical influences.

chapter 3

Joe Ely

*Freight Hopper, Hitchhiker,
and West Texas Whirlwind*

Every widespread musical influence that emanates from Texas—be it rock, country, Norteno, Cajun, Mariachi, punk, folk, blues, honky tonk, rockabilly, or western swing—seems to stick to Joe Ely like glue.

"Texas is bombarded on all sides by a variety of musical influences," explained Ely. "West Texas has honky tonk and rockabilly. South Texas has that Mexican border feel, everything from Norteno to the Tex-Mex stuff. East Texas is pretty much the blues and the traditional Louisiana Hayride country, and between all of those, everything sooner or later converges in Austin. That's why Austin is so important. It's the center of the wagon wheel."

Ely spent his formative years in West Texas—Lubbock, to be exact, the home of rock legend Buddy Holly. As a youngster he watched as Mexican migrants pined for their homeland playing their music. As a teenager he dropped out of school to pursue a career in rock 'n' roll. As a young man he forged his own sound from the rudiments of barrelhouse, rockabilly, honky tonk, blues, and country.

Later on, Ely nurtured a valuable friendship with two boyhood acquaintances, Jimmie Dale Gilmore and Butch Hancock. Ely, Gilmore, and Hancock went on to become a highly respected Texas songwriting triumvirate in the American roots-rock genre, called the Flatlanders. (Their tale is told in chapter 14.)

Ely breaks the mold of the rowdy Texas rocker. He writes poetry, has just completed a novel, and has amassed several journals jammed with prose, pencil sketches, and amateur photography.

"My family came from the trains," said singer/guitarist Joe Ely, relaxing with a latte on the patio of a downtown San Francisco motel located in the heart of the city's red-light district. "They followed the railroads from Arkansas to Texas in the post-Dust Bowl days. We were fortunate to have jobs with the railroads when nobody else had jobs.

"My early childhood was fun. My family took the trains out to California. We moved around a lot. We lived for a little while in Amarillo, San Antonio, and Fort Worth, never far from the tracks. Then we came to Lubbock when I was 12."

Ely and his family happily rolled into Lubbock from Amarillo in 1959, the same year rock 'n' roll legend Buddy Holly perished in a plane crash over Clear Lake, Iowa, with the Big Bopper and Richie Valens. Holly had already made a lasting impression on the Lubbock townsfolk.

"I didn't even know Buddy Holly was from Lubbock when we first moved there," recalled Ely, whose relationship with music began as a child. "I'd been seriously playing the violin in school in Amarillo since I was seven. When I came to Lubbock, there was no school orchestra, but there *was* a guy down the street who owned an electric Fender guitar. Because of Buddy Holly, everybody in town had Fender electric guitars. After Buddy died, garage bands sprouted everywhere.

"Music was Lubbock's main form of entertainment. There was no theater, very few movies, a pretty desolate place. Not quite as desolate as *The Last Picture Show* movie, but almost. The main thing that saved Lubbock from becoming a totally bleak town was that it had a big university nearby."

A stable of jukebox stars came from West Texas, more than enough to whet Joe's appetite to become a professional musician himself.

"Besides Buddy Holly, Waylon Jennings originally came from Lubbock. Roy Orbison started out 80 miles south, and Bob Wills lived 60 miles northwest. They all came through and played in Lubbock all the time.

"It was amazing. I've always wondered how local guys like Holly and Orbison came up with those classic, drop-dead, beautiful melodies like 'Only the Lonely' and 'True Love Ways.' I think Mexican music was a real melodic influence. Buddy's guitar playing reflected that Mexican two-string harmony style."

Ely and his parents lived modestly in Lubbock. After working for the railroad, Joe's father settled down and ran a thrift store in the center of town. Back in the day, cotton was the cash crop in West Texas and the region drew masses of pickers and field hands from South of the border.

"My father operated a used clothing store on Broadway, the Disabled American Veterans Thrift Store," said Joe. "The townspeople donated their old stuff, and my daddy sold things for as cheap as he could. The Mexican pickers visited my daddy's store because he sold ten-cent shoes."

It was a bygone era, before the sprawling corporate farms and automated machinery. In the summertime, tens of thousands of migrant workers were trucked in to pick the sea of cotton that stretched hundreds of miles in every direction. Lubbock was the place the migrant workers flocked to on the weekends to do their shopping. During the summer, Ely remembers the vibrant Tex-Mex atmosphere that charged downtown Lubbock.

"On Fridays, Saturdays, and Sundays, downtown Lubbock went from being a deserted ghost town to a thriving, Spanish-speaking metropolis. It was as if you were in Mexico City, surrounded by amazing Mexican music. Our store was at the center where the Mexican shops were. There were bars across the street where mariachi bands played, and I would listen to accordion and bajo sexto players as conjunto bands roamed the streets."

Almost as quickly as Ely settled into Lubbock and its colorful surroundings, tragedy struck his family.

"My daddy died real quick of leukemia when I was 13," said Ely. "He got sick and was gone in six months. Times got tough at our house. We had to shut the store down and I had to go to work to bring in money. I was in junior high working after school washing dishes at the neighborhood chicken place. Most of the guys that hung around there were gamblers, poker players, and bootleggers."

Having given up violin for a Fender guitar and classical music for rockabilly, throughout Joe's early teens music became his emotional life raft among the Texas ramblers and gamblers he met washing dishes. He soon started up his own bands.

"I had this music thing going, but pretty soon it took over my life. I started playing in honky tonks and speakeasies at 15. Lubbock was dry so you couldn't have a bar that sold alcohol. So they had these weird little private clubs where everybody stored their alcohol inside lockers. It's a little like that today. While they have bars now, you still can't buy a six-pack in the stores. Lubbock is probably the longest-running dry city in America."

As a young fatherless musician scratching out a livelihood on honky tonk stages, playing music professionally collided with Joe's education.

"Because I worked and played in the clubs, that made it harder and harder for me to go to school. I'd be up until two in the morning, so it was impossible to get up early and go to high school. I got a job at a nightclub in Fort Worth called the Cellar Club. That led to the opening of another Cellar Club in Houston, where I alternated sets with ZZ Top. My band would play an hour and they'd play an hour from six in the evening until six in the morning."

Back in Lubbock, Joe's boyhood friend Jimmie Dale Gilmore sang around town in the folk bars for the university students. Butch Hancock, another friend of Joe's and Jimmie Dale's, attended Monterey High School at the same time. A capable athlete, Hancock played varsity basketball and later studied architecture at Texas Tech University. He soon took up songwriting and became a folksinger like his pal Jimmie Dale.

Having known each other in high school, Jimmie, Butch, and Joe became close friends, playing the same music venues in and around Lubbock. Still in their late teens, they bounced back and forth between California and Lubbock, separately and together, sampling the budding counterculture. Ely experienced the West Coast psychedelic movement firsthand.

"After I dropped out of school," he recalled, "I followed the music west. That brought me to Venice Beach in California in 1966. I lived in Venice for a couple of months, and then in 1967 I drifted up to Telegraph Avenue in Berkeley during the height of the Summer of Love."

In the tradition of Jack Kerouac, Woody Guthrie, and Jimmie Rodgers the Singing Brakeman, a young and footloose Ely continued to explore the dusty trail.

"I literally rambled for a few years," said Ely. "A pencil and a guitar was my tape recorder. A sketchbook was my camera. I traveled light, a backpack, a sleeping bag, and a guitar. I learned how to get from Texas to California by rail-hopping a freight train to Clovis straight on to San Bernardino. It beat hitchhiking because you didn't have to deal with the nuts that would pick you up on the highway."

Joe laughs out loud at the naïveté of the times.

"I felt because it was the '60s you could do anything you wanted. There were no rules, and as I look back on it now, it's a wonder I wasn't killed. I remember when my train car got disconnected in the middle of the desert. I was stuck out there for hours with no water.

"We were all big fans of Woody Guthrie and Jack Kerouac, the writers of the day, so we'd sorta blow with the wind. If Woody sang about the California fruit fields, I would go out and see them for myself. If I heard a song about San Francisco, I'd go there to check it out. I needed to see where the songs came from. And in doing so, I connected with the images. But it was not exactly like the songs. You created your own experiences; you brought back something different. That's where my songs came from. They might have little to do with the original ones I chased down. It was all part of one big journey. I kept a little notebook in my back pocket and scribbled down phrases. I'd do sketches and drawings, too. I didn't have a camera, so I'd draw wherever I was."

While visiting Los Angeles and San Francisco together, Joe, Butch, and Jimmie Dale witnessed different musical forms colliding. Musicians like Gram Parsons and bands like the Byrds and the Burrito Brothers were experimenting with conflicting styles, just like "the new Texas three" back in West Texas.

"I loved the Burrito Brothers," Ely smiled. "And I could relate to them. It was the same thing Jimmie Gilmore and I were doing back in Lubbock. We were blending stuff out of love for old folk songs, country tunes, and whatever new was going on in rock 'n' roll.

"When country met rock, it opened up a whole new thing in music. It happened first back in the early '50s with rockabilly. Hillbilly music and the blues collided. That was one form. Then there was this different form, the Gram Parsons thing, where sophisticated rock met country. Everything was exciting; whole worlds were being turned upside down."

At the time, though, Ely wasn't quite sure whether Parsons's synthesis signaled a lasting trend.

"We didn't know if it was media hype or what. There was something weird about it all. It didn't have that raw feeling like when Jerry Lee Lewis or Carl Perkins started singing country music. It had more of a hippie polish to it, but everything was changing so much in the mid- to late '60s that it was exciting no matter what it was." The formation of the Flatlanders during the summer of 1971 with Jimmie Dale and Butch represented a two-year stopgap between Ely's hitchhiking and jumping freights to and from California. Joe returned to Lubbock for two years, while he, Gilmore, and Hancock shared a house for eight months, working out a new batch of tunes. Butch contributed "Boxcars," which recalled Ely's youthful days next to the railroad tracks in Amarillo. Jimmie Dale wrote "Treat Me Like a Saturday Night" and "Dallas," which had a lonesome Lubbock and Texas aura. While the Flatlanders' harmonies were tight and disciplined, the band also covered a variety of styles from Little Richard to Bob Wills.

After assembling a decent set of road-tested songs, Jimmie Dale signed a record deal in February 1972 so that the Flatlanders could journey to Nashville to record a single and an album for Shelby Singleton, label executive and producer of artists like Jerry Lee Lewis, Merle Haggard, and Burt Bacharach. Conceptually, their record was several years ahead of its time. With its blend of acoustic and electric guitars, dobro, fiddle, harmonica, string bass, and even a whining musical saw, the album was not officially released on Singleton's Plantation label. While the original version of "Dallas" came out as a country single under the banner of "Jimmie Dale and the Flatlanders," within months the group amicably split up and returned to Texas.

Back in the Lone Star state, times were volatile for bohemian, anti-war longhairs like Ely, Gilmore, and Hancock. Being a hippie in a large, redneck state like Texas had its bizarre moments, including a spell for Ely in the Lubbock jail.

"I had brought back some pot from San Francisco. Plus they had caught me with LSD and dried psilocybin mushrooms on the very first day that stuff was made illegal in the state of Texas.

"Every morning I'd hear Merle Haggard singing train-riding songs and 'Mama Tried' on the radio in the jailhouse. 'I turned 21 in prison, doing life without parole.' To me, Merle Haggard was authentic, right up until the time he recorded 'Okie from Muskogee.' We were trying to get out of the draft, totally against the war in Vietnam. I had a two-year battle going with selective service, so when 'Okie from Muskogee' came out, I thought, 'Wait a minute, he's on the other side.'"

In 1974, after the stint in the Lubbock jailhouse, it was time for Ely to leave Texas again, resuming his role of rambling troubadour. This time, instead of heading out to the West Coast, Joe changed course, passed through Nashville, and hitchhiked north. Growing up as a rock 'n' roller, fortified with country and folk credentials, Ely took off for the skyscrapers of Manhattan.

"After the Flatlanders thing, I decided to go up to New York City and stick around there for six months. I wanted to put some gigs together and get something going. I went to Folk City and the Bitter End to stand in line for auditions. But after six months I didn't get hired anywhere, except for one single

Road warrior Joe Ely is a perennial attraction on the roots-rock festival circuit.

gig. Kenny's Castaways put me on the third back slot for one night. This was before the days of the Lone Star Cafe."

By mid-1975, Ely formed one of the first American roots rock bands, combining honky tonk, barrelhouse, rock 'n' roll, rockabilly, waltzes, Cajun rhythms, and Texas swing—a hodgepodge unheard of back in its day. In 1977, Ely scored a contract with MCA Records and soon released his self-titled debut. The artwork featured a pencil sketch of a haggard Ely, cowboy hat tilted on the crown of his head. For the album, Ely combined showstoppers like "I Had My Hopes Up High" and "Mardi Gras Waltz" alongside Gilmore and Hancock Flatlander pieces like "Treat Me Like a Saturday Night" and "She Never Spoke Spanish to Me."

Labeled as "progressive country" and "country-rock," Ely's MCA debut arrived at the height of the outlaw country movement.

"I guess the radio guys had to call us something so they lumped us in with the outlaws," Ely explained. "Willie was doing *Red Headed Stranger*. Waylon had already cut *Honky Tonk Heroes* and the Billy Joe Shaver songs. We had a whole separate thing going on. Later on, we did play some shows with Waylon and we hit it off good, mostly because we were both Lubbock guys. But I still felt they were Nashville while we were real Texas guys.

"Yeah, we got thrown into the outlaw country genre all right, but we didn't feel much a part of it. That was Waylon, Willie, Tompall Glaser, Jerry Jeff Walker, and all those guys. By calling it outlaw music, we felt it was all a Nashville invention. Back in Lubbock, I didn't feel a part of *any* movement. The music we played was a whole different deal."

Bolstered by a strong sophomore effort on MCA, *Honky Tonk Masquerade*, Joe toured the United States heavily. Jimmie Gilmore's "Tonight I Think I'm Gonna Go Downtown" augmented "I Let My Fingernails Grow So They Click When I Play the Piano" on the road. Hancock, arguably Joe's best songwriter, contributed "Boxcars," yet another lonesome railroad anthem, to his sets. With hard-earned artistic credibility, Ely and his band found a larger fan base oceans away from the dusty cotton fields of Lubbock. In Great Britain, the punk movement led by the Sex Pistols had exploded. Another wily London quartet, the Clash, had become ardent Joe Ely fans.

"The Clash had a sincere appreciation for the kind of music that came from West Texas. They were huge fans of rockabilly and Marty Robbins's ballads like 'El Paso,' 'Big Iron,' and 'The Streets of Laredo.' Texas was completely romantic to them. To listen to their music, you wouldn't think they would be a romantic band of any sort, but they really loved the stuff that came from that dusty old part of the country where I grew up.

"I met them in England in 1978 when they came to one of our shows. Our first couple of records sold better in England than they did in the USA, so we found ourselves working across the ocean. We toured America, but radio wouldn't play our stuff because it had screaming steel guitars. But in London, we found a huge audience.

"We couldn't figure out the British connection. The Clash liked us. Pete Townshend from the Who was in the audience. It seemed weird that anybody would like our stuff in the UK because we sang so much about West Texas, hardly an international topic."

Like the Sex Pistols, the Clash had a hankering to visit the Southern regions of the United States. So the band asked Joe Ely if they could muster up a joint tour of Texas and the Southwest. The Clash didn't care about playing Dallas and Houston. They longed to play towns like Lubbock, El Paso, and Laredo, all cities immortalized in song. Ely arranged for he and the Clash to hook up and crisscross the Texas nightclub circuit together. The Clash returned the favor in England.

"In 1980 the Clash invited us back over to England to do the London Calling tour with them. There was an amazing scene going on there with reggae, garage rock, and rockabilly. Guys like Dave Edmunds and Nick Lowe were doing cool rockabilly stuff. Elvis Costello was writing incredible songs. It was basic rock 'n' roll, sorta Lubbock–style.

"Lloyd Maines manned the steel, Jesse Taylor played guitar, and Ponty Bone was on accordion. Nobody could believe how well we played. Musicians showed up to our gigs to check out everything we did. They scrutinized us so hard, we thought we had spaghetti on our shirts. They couldn't believe we had a steel player *and* an accordion player in the same band. But to us, it was just a group of friends, whoever happened to join the band, onstage. We were good musicians because in Lubbock there wasn't much else to do but learn your craft."

Ely then teamed with country music legend Merle Haggard, exporting even more American roots music overseas.

"I toured with Merle in Europe in 1980. We hadn't met when this English promoter set up the tour. We played 20 dates together in England, Ireland, and Norway. Our band was a bunch of wild West Texas crazies. Meeting Merle's guys became a big competition of who could out-drink, out-party whom. Haggard's band won hands down. We just gave up. They'd be drinking Vodka at six in the morning, getting on the tour bus, mooning all the people as we drove by."

Invigorated by his success overseas and an association with the UK and the Clash, Ely returned to the US to step up his touring schedule. Road weariness and exhaustion soon started to set in. In 1981 *Musta Notta Gotta Lotta* received a load of positive attention from fans and critics on both sides of the Atlantic. Ely appeared on the front cover, hair greased and combed back like both an English Teddy Boy and an American fifties greaser. The album included a revised version of Jimmie's "Dallas" alongside Hancock's yearning "Wishin' for You," the two highlights of the record.

"*Musta Notta Gotta Lotta* has a lot of spark," admitted Ely. "Playing harder and faster influenced that record, but I listen to it now and everything sounds *too* damn fast. We were out with the Clash at the time, performing every night to wild audiences."

By 1982, the constant touring on the road had worn Ely out.

"From the middle of 1981 to New Year's Eve 1982, I didn't go home. I didn't have a family at the time. I wasn't married. I was totally loose. I lived in a suitcase. We jumped from the Clash tour to a Kinks tour to the Rolling Stones to Tom Petty and the Heartbreakers and so on, until the next band called. At the end, I just collapsed. The road ground me down. Muddy Waters said it best. I once picked him up at the airport in Lubbock in my 1957 pink Cadillac Coup DeVille. I asked him about hitting the road so hard and how was he doing? What he said made complete sense to me. It was exactly how I felt. 'Joe, being on the road is 22 hours of misery and two hours of ecstasy.'

"Muddy was right. The road can be miserable. Either you're in a hurry or you're waiting. You can't find anything good to eat after hours. It's a quagmire. Sheer chaos."

Playing larger arenas, concert halls, and nightclubs, Ely watched his studio output take a backseat to all the live shows and touring.

"I actually like my records from 1990 to the present better than the earlier ones," said Ely. "A lot of it has to do with the fact that I didn't really care much about making records in the early days. I cared more about being on the road. I liked putting a hot road band together. We'd stop in the studio every once in a while just to make a record. While the first two albums captured the early energy and arrangements of the band, they have this sound that's squashed and compressed, which is how we made records up until the 1990s."

Today Joe Ely lives comfortably in Austin, and is highly respected among the scores of musical peers who also reside in the artistic hub of Texas. In the early days, Austin was primarily known for being home to Kenneth Threadgill ("the grandfather of Austin country music"), Janis Joplin, and Johnny and Edgar Winter. But since the seventies, an army of singers, songwriters, and guitar pickers have at one time or another converged on Austin, including performers like Guy Clark, Ray Wylie Hubbard, the Fabulous Thunderbirds, Shawn Colvin, Ian Moore, Lucinda Williams, the Derailers, Willie Nelson, the late Stevie Ray Vaughan and Townes Van Zandt, Lou Ann Barton, Kelly Willis, Marcia Ball, Jerry Jeff Walker, Tish Hinojosa, Chris Duarte, Angela Strehli, Asleep at the Wheel, Alejandro Escovedo, Stephen Bruton, Eliza Gilkyson, Jimmy LaFave, and Darden Smith.

"When I first got there, Austin was paradise. It was a little old college town where you could live for practically nothing. Today, everybody, including the politicians and the lawyers, support the music. Unlike other cities, Austin and music go hand-in-hand. You can see former governors like Ann Richards in the audience at shows. People in government sit alongside the old hippies, farmers, and pot dealers. It's a supportive place where musicians can eek out a living."

Ely has added a home studio to his remote Austin spread, and writing and recording songs isn't the rushed process it used to be. Nowadays he takes his time developing and finishing projects. *Streets of Sin*, a recent album, portrays real-life, plot-driven songs about everyday people battling common adversity. Characters include carnival drifters, hard-luck horse race gamblers, farmers who have auctioned off their land, and rural townsfolk surviving devastating floods. Butch Hancock contributed two songs while Ely wrote the remaining ten.

"After I wore myself out, I put together a little studio in the house that, over the years, I've added to. That's where I bring my ideas. There are a lot of sketches of songs I build from the ground up. I've got several recordings on file."

After recording and re-recording *Streets of Sin* three times, Ely reunited with Gilmore and Hancock to re-form the Flatlanders. They recorded a disc aptly titled *Now Again*. Following a successful tour, the trio was so struck by the smooth reunion process that they cut an encore release titled *Wheels of Fortune* on the New West label. *Wheels of Fortune,* one of 2004's finest roots rock releases, is a satisfying, rocking, front-porch-friendly, laid-back collaboration. From its inception, the Flatlanders band was founded on the friendship of three talented Texans, and from the opening number of *Wheels of Fortune,* it's clear the Texas trio hasn't lost their sense of unity.

These days Joe Ely lets his artistic side shine beyond the music. He's been collecting and recompiling the lost journals he kept during his rambling days spent hitchhiking and jumping freights. He's also dabbled in fiction.

"I finished a novel which takes place when I was rambling on the road, playing, trying to keep a family together," he noted. "It's called *Super Reverb.* It's not a biography, but I follow some West Texas characters and combine their personalities. I started it in July of 1999 and finished in July of 2001."

Like many other songwriters who have crossed over to novels and short stories, Ely found it was not an easy undertaking.

"Writing a novel is much harder than songwriting. There's continuity and character development. You have to outline and follow the story. I even wrote a long poem and included that. I got snagged on it several times. I even quit writing for a couple of months. But once I got 30 or 40 pages deep, I decided I'd finish even if it killed me."

Download This!

From Lubbock to Austin

Joe Ely's musical journey began in Lubbock, then moved to Austin. Here is a track-by-track highlight of his screaming pedal steel and ripping blues guitar licks.

1. "She Never Spoke Spanish to Me"—Joe Ely (MCA).
   A classic Butch Hancock composition from Joe's self-titled debut cut in 1977.

It employs a standard style of Nashville production with subdued pedal steel and novelty Mariachi horns.

2. "Boxcars"—Joe Ely (MCA).
Another Butch Hancock anthem cut by Joe on his second album, *Honky Tonk Masquerade*. The song is closer to Joe's trademark style, using accordion and double lead guitars. The song alludes to the lonesome feeling of Lubbock and Joe's fascination with jumping freights.

3. "Down the Line"—Buddy Holly (MCA).
Here's a fine, vintage 1950s rock song made during Buddy Holly's early days with Bob Montgomery. Holly was Lubbock's favorite son and Ely's local idol.

4. "Tonight I Think I'm Gonna Go Downtown"—Joe Ely (MCA).
Jimmie Dale Gilmore's contribution to *Honky Tonk Masquerade*. The song has a prime blend of accordion, acoustic guitars, and pedal steel. British punk bands were in awe of Joe's ability to mix such instruments.

5. "Coma Girl, Long Shadow, X-Ray Style"—Joe Strummer & the Mescaleros (Epitaph).
Strummer's last band (before he died in December 2002) made no bones about their love for West Texas influences. In these three songs, there are shreds of rockabilly, El Paso border sounds, and Marty Robbins cowboy balladry—the same styles passed on to the Clash by Ely himself.

6. "Pancho & Lefty"—Townes Van Zandt (Tomato).
Ely first encountered the hard-drinking, wandering troubadour when Townes hitchhiked through West Texas with a guitar and a backpack full of hand-pressed LPs of his work. Van Zandt slipped him a copy, and the material affected Joe deeply.

7. "Dallas"—Joe Ely (MCA).
Joe Ely makes another Jimmie Dale song his own. Jimmie sings it and it sounds lovelorn; Joe cuts it and it sounds as raunchy and boozy as the beer-soaked walls of a honky tonk. From Joe's 1981 *Musta Notta Gotta Lotta* release.

continued on the next page

From Lubbock to Austin *continued*

8. "My Way Down"—Chris Duarte (Silvertone).

The perfect medicine for those who dig steamy Austin guitar blues but are a little burned out on Stevie Ray Vaughan. From Chris's acclaimed 1994 *Sugar Texas/Strat Magik* release. Duarte is less polished and grittier than Stevie Ray.

9. "Letter to Laredo"—Joe Ely (MCA).

This Ely-penned song shows that Joe can compete with Hancock and Gilmore as a writer. The 1995 re-cut version features smoldering flamenco guitar, but the vibe tilts decidedly more toward Texas border town (with its added slide dobro) than the Spanish gypsy Andalusian style.

10. "The Right Place"—Derailers (Sire).

Lots of Buck Owens, Bakersfield, and roadhouse twang by another tight Austin band, the four-piece Derailers. Two-fisted, rockabilly, country, and dang proud of it, this tune comes from the 1999 release *Full Western Dress*.

11. "Shelter from the Storm," "You're a Big Girl Now," "Walk Away Renee"—Jimmy LaFave (Bohemia Beat).

Although the gravelly voiced singer Jimmy LaFave is headquartered in Austin, he's originally from Oklahoma. LaFave gets our vote as the prime interpreter of Bob Dylan compositions. His reading of the Left Banke's "Walk Away Renee" is jaw dropping. All three songs are extracted from a live package called *Austin Skyline* on the Bohemia Beat label.

12. "Fingernails"—Joe Ely (MCA).

This has been one of Joe's big onstage numbers, saluting that rockin' Louisiana-Hayride-East-Texas element of his music.

13. "Levelland"—Robert Earl Keen (Arista Austin).

Gotta sneak in some props to Robert Earl Keen, who lives and writes near San Antonio, just down the road from Kinky Friedman's ranch. While Keen is a gifted writer in the style of Gilmore, Ely, and Hancock, this particular tune was written by another talented Texan, James McMurtry, son of the famous Lone Star novelist/screenwriter Larry McMurtry, author of *The Last Picture Show*. Got all that?

Don McLean Harpoons the Great White Whale of Fame

Few hit songs have broadsided modern culture as powerfully as Don McLean's "American Pie." Released on the album of the same name in October 1971, a few months later in 1972 it became a massive radio hit of mythic proportions. An eight-verse masterwork, "American Pie" deals symbolically with the death of Buddy Holly and the rippling effect such a musical event had on the popular culture at large.

It was a time when America was losing its idealism, headed for deeply cynical times. McLean's imagery was meant to signal the loss of innocence using clever rock 'n' roll metaphors. But when the song sprang onto the Top 40 airwaves with its upbeat piano and sing-along chorus, the general public became engrossed with deciphering line-by-line McLean's lyrical imagery of "the day the music died." The song encapsulates a lot. Amazingly, each verse makes direct or indirect references to personalities, music, and slices of pop culture, including Elvis Presley, Buddy Holly, the Byrds, Bob Dylan, James Dean, Mick Jagger and the Rolling Stones, John Lennon and the Beatles, Janis Joplin, the Fillmore West, Woodstock Nation, Altamont, the Weavers, the Hell's Angels, Hank Williams, Pete Seeger, Woody Guthrie, Connie Francis, John and Bobby Kennedy, the Lovin' Spoonful, the Monotones, Richie Valens, the Big Bopper, Little Richard, Marty Robbins, and a small record store in New Rochelle, New York.

This chapter is not meant as a tribute to the historic significance of "American Pie." There's already been plenty written about that. Rather, it's an analysis of how the song's overwhelming success deeply affected an artist who *wrote and sang one of America's most famous declarations. It's about the psychological drama that occurred after an artist relentlessly pursued fame and fortune, attained it against insurmountable odds, and then watched it all unravel.*

Why Don McLean as American roots rocker? Why not? On the surface, McLean is known primarily for his pop hits, yet his music is forged from traditional folk (circa New York state, Greenwich Village, and the Hudson River area) and rock 'n' roll legends like Holly and Orbison. Once Don had his fill of the pop music machinery, roots-folk became his sanctuary and he created albums like Playin' Favorites *and* Homeless Brother. *In his earliest days, McLean toured the Hudson River onboard a sloop with Pete Seeger and a troupe of hootenanny-crazed folkies. And he continued an association with leftist folk-blues legend Josh White, for whom he had a deep professional admiration.*

When American Pie *the album was released in October 1971, it was colorful and vibrant, and, for the most part, upbeat. "American Pie" and "Vincent" became huge and beloved worldwide hits. By November 1972, the self-titled follow-up, in contrast, was dark, gray, and bitter. No Top Ten hits, just stark, gloomy presentations from a self-absorbed artist imprisoned by the demands that fame had brought his way. Today, it is customary for celebrities to rely heavily on tabloid attention to remain in the limelight. They routinely hire legions of PR staffers to leak personal tidbits of their lives to keep their names in front of the public lexicon. But sometimes, as was the case with Don McLean, a musician's sensibility is violated by such intrusion, so he uses the only weapon in his arsenal to fight it off: songwriting.*

This is what happened when a musician caught up in the friendly crossfire of public adoration had to choose between grinding out what sells and declaring his independence as an artist and human being.

It was extraordinary watching "American Pie" rocket to the top of the charts. At the time, America, knowingly or not, was drifting into a jaded era. Like the song's main character, who senses an abrupt end to the innocence of the psychedelic age, within a matter of months many Americans were experiencing the same wistful feelings as the song's narrator.

The playful idealism of the hippie movement had already faded. War headlines plagued the newspapers, magazines, and evening news. Nixon's Watergate scandal was only a few months away, lurking just beyond the political horizon, bringing with it deep, widespread feelings of suspicion and resentment towards the ruling hierarchy and its leaders.

Don McLean saw the storm coming as he sat in his small Northeastern writing room, composing "American Pie."

"I was fascinated with the implication that America was going bye-bye," McLean commented, "and that by 1971 we were a horribly divided country with tremendous anger directed at the government over the Vietnam War.

"It's an anomaly hearing these angry lyrics in a clear, sweet voice, an odd combination. If you sing sweet, you should be singing sweet songs. But 'American Pie' is sweet and sour together. There was an ironic mismatch intended in the performance. The song was created as a rock dream. A visual world. The imagery was meant to draw you in."

While *American Pie* was No. 1—four weeks on the American singles chart and six weeks on the album chart—in every city and town Don McLean toured he saw himself on the television and in the newspapers. Constantly. The media burn became a distraction to him.

"Joni Mitchell once described her fame like this: 'People have put me on a pedestal and I was wobbling.' I hadn't heard it put quite that way," said McLean. "But that was what I experienced. I was wobbling.

"In the months after the *American Pie* album and single hit, everywhere I went, I was news. If I performed in a city, I was on the evening news. I was like Springsteen. In fact, I did meet Bruce Springsteen back when he was just getting started. I guess I was about as big as you could possibly get."

Don McLean started out as a hardworking folksinger singing his way up and down the Hudson River. He was a picker and player deeply influenced by artists like Josh White, the Weavers, and Pete Seeger. He was born and raised in bucolic New Rochelle, home of American heroes like Willie Mays, Buffalo Bob Smith, and the fictional Rob and Laura Petrie of the *Dick Van Dyke Show*. McLean's father, also named Donald, was a meek gentleman who worked for Consolidated Edison.

"My father died the death of a salesman," McLean recalled. "He burned himself out. He was a sweet little man who gave everything to everybody. He wore a suit to the dinner table every night. Then one day he turned white as a sheet and died of a heart attack. He was 56 years old when he left behind a wife and a little boy. It all came tumbling down one terrible January of 1961."

Fatherless at age 15, sullen, and wound up tight with rage and bitterness, McLean made a vow never to conform to a nine-to-five existence. A career in music was his way out.

"I made up my mind after my father's death that even though I lived in New Rochelle—the American capitol of conformity—I would never, ever work for anyone as long as I lived."

McLean pursued his show business dreams vigorously. His work ethic was relentless. While boys and girls his age were carefree high school students, McLean was already venturing to New York City's Greenwich Village to play backup guitar for die-hard folkies in dingy nightclubs and smoky coffeehouses.

McLean's promise to himself meant a lot of struggling during the early '60s. He played dank folk clubs on Manhattan's Lower East Side to support himself and his mother. He was determined and single-minded about achieving a reputation as a writer and performer.

"I didn't think about commercial success in terms of acquiring wealth," said McLean. "I was thinking about art, the music, and trying to get better on stage—improving myself without worrying about reaching for the brass ring. I had this constant desire to grow in order to reach that dream."

In 1970, after literally 30 labels passed on signing him, Don McLean scored a one-record deal with a small imprint called Media Arts. *Tapestry,* his first album, contained two of his finest compositions, "And I Love You So" and "Castles in the Air." It sold respectably, affording McLean the chance to tour heavily, tighten up his act, and make a modest living on the road. *Tapestry* (released before Carole King's mega-hit album of the same name) also scored him a subsequent major label contract with United Artists Records.

The first United Artists sessions included just enough folksy ballads to fill one album, including an eight-and-a-half-minute piece of musicology that, at the last moment, was sped up in the studio by a session pianist named Paul Harris. That song became "American Pie," which would catapult McLean into the American consciousness. McLean, a sweet-voiced journeyman folkie, soon became a world-famous pop star.

"I was living in a rented gatehouse up in Cold Spring, New York, when 'American Pie' hit. I remember getting a check for $400,000. Six months later, I got another check for $600,000. I was earning thousands of dollars a night, selling out concert halls everywhere. I was now internationally famous."

McLean faced the demands of skyrocketing fame. Nonstop interviews. Special appearances. Travel. All his hard work had paid off; he was now a star. But McLean soon found the "star-making machinery" unexpectedly intrusive and incredibly intense. As Don McLean and "American Pie" became household names, cracks in his psyche had already started to appear.

"It was more than I had dreamed of, way beyond anything I had expected," McLean reflected. "I suddenly found myself in a strange position. Instead of running *toward* the dream, I was soon running *away* from the dream." McLean shudders at the memory. "Then suddenly the dream was chasing *me*; the dream was hounding me. I had awakened this entire media. Psychologically, it was like pursuing the great white whale. When you harpoon it, all of a sudden it's dragging you across the ocean."

Suddenly, McLean's life was no longer his own.

Prior to his runaway pop success, Don McLean's music leaned heavily in the folk genre, à la the Weavers, Pete Seeger, and Sonny Terry & Brownie McGhee.

"When you're poor and you've achieved fame, you realize the many opportunities you didn't have. Prior to success, everything you did was based on your own choices. Now you had to be in five places at once, with handlers ordering you around. 'You're booked here and you're booked there. Go to this radio station. Do this TV show. Sit with this magazine interviewer.'"

McLean was already accustomed to a heavy concert schedule. He loved performing live, but the intense heat of the media spotlight made music much more demanding. He was now being tugged at from every angle. His schedule and obligations expanded exponentially. Still, it wasn't a predicament that prompted much sympathy.

"I can understand that. But there's one thing people don't realize. When this happens to an artist," said McLean, "for the next five years you are absolutely exhausted *all* the time. You're constantly going from one place to the next. Physically, it ties you in a knot. It breaks people down. I became clinically depressed because of the physical exhaustion. It's what a lot of young pop acts get swept up into. John Lennon broke down. Britney Spears broke down. Mariah Carey lost it. And that's what happened to me."

At the time, McLean was in a bad place emotionally. His marriage was on the skids. As he felt little or no sustenance from his family, his thoughts drifted as he began feeling more and more alone in his life.

"Of course, I didn't have the time or energy or emotional wherewithal to establish supportive relationships. I couldn't deal with the subtleties that went into serious relationships. But sadly, you need relationships more desperately than ever because you're feeling very isolated."

Once overexposure sets in, the same critics and pundits who marvel at an artist's ascendance will write them off. Don McLean watched himself being set up for such a fall. The pressure became enormous. Would there be another "American Pie"? More important, did he even *have* the desire to write another "American Pie"?

"The press set me up. They said I would never follow up. I was marked for failure. I felt trapped, as if the whole country was watching me, and for a while, I went through a period of feeling very unworthy of all the attention. I don't have that super-sized ego that felt that everything that was happening to me was what I deserved. While I did have a sense of self-worth and humility of my own relative importance, this situation was way over the top."

After a hectic career burn that lasted a couple of years, McLean suffered a breakdown. As a result, he went into temporary seclusion.

"I never thought about suicide because I loved life, but I knew I was in the grip of something terrible," Don said. "I had a breakdown in 1974. I went back to work a year later. But 1975 and 1976 were the worst years."

The ultimate absurdity set in. Today, McLean looks back with disdain at the very decade that launched his career and rewarded him with enormous material riches and fame.

"The '70s were terrible for me," deadpanned McLean. "I hated the '70s. It's ironic. They were the worst years of my life.

"I was in such a dark place and I was so depressed, I couldn't see out. But I would go onstage, sing, and do my shows, and for a few hours I would feel nice again."

In his paranoia and exhaustion, McLean foresaw death emerging from fame. His fear was rooted in reality. That's when he decided to slow down.

"Something frightened me. I was afraid that if I moved too fast I might be killed. And shortly after that, in 1973, Jim Croce was killed flying around in some lousy little airplane, trying to get to three places in one night. A lot of people in show business have died moving too fast. Harry Chapin was killed racing into New York to meet with somebody to get his career started up again."

McLean thought back to his hero, Buddy Holly, the very man who inspired "American Pie." Like Croce, Holly, in his haste, died in a plane crash trying to scrape together a few extra hours to sleep and get his laundry done. Suddenly Don's moneymaking anthem cast an ominous shadow.

"I realized that what had happened to Buddy Holly could happen to me. So I made the decision that I wanted to live to be an old man."

McLean had a plan. He plotted his next move for a crucial follow-up album to *American Pie*. He would make the hard choice of staying true to his art and create an album of songs that would document the struggles he faced against the "American Pie-driven" machinations of fame. But he encountered another problem—a lack of fresh, new material.

For McLean's first album, new music had flowed at a brisk pace. "I wrote 20 or 30 songs for *Tapestry* in a year and a half. I was really into it, taking songs off and adding new ones. During *American Pie*, I was tapped out. Luckily I came up with 'American Pie' [the song] and it saved my ass. For the third record, there wasn't a single song left. The cupboard was bare."

From the depths of writer's block and melancholy came ten new tunes, his most introspective yet, linked as if written as a total-concept album. While McLean's self-titled third album is hardly recognized as being on par with *American Pie, Don McLean* is an astounding outpouring by an artist howling his inner pain while addressing the cursed cult of celebrity and media overexposure. It's an unabashed journey into one man's self-absorption.

There comes a time for all of us to define or reinvent ourselves at the next critical phase of our life's work. Songwriter Leonard Cohen, for example, addressed this theme of personal reinvention. In his song "A Thousand Kisses Deep" he refers to being "summoned now to deal with your invincible defeat," meaning, in every person's creative cycle, there is a time to replenish or start over.

Released in November 1972, *Don McLean* signaled a new era in McLean's life. Looking back, it was ingenious to self-title the record since it epitomized such a personal inner journey.

"The 'old me' ended with *American Pie*," McLean confessed, "the 'new me' started with the *Don McLean* record, documenting the experiences and the changes that occurred.

"I decided to be completely true to myself. I wanted to slow things down by writing an album about what was happening to me. I came up with the songs very quickly and I hoped I could come out of my depression and carry on with a reasonably normal career where I could make records and play live without this hyperkinetic energy around me all the time, which I couldn't handle."

You only need to compare the artwork of *American Pie* and *Don McLean* to gauge each work's temperament. *Pie* features a self-assured, literal "thumbs-up" by McLean, with his thumb painted in American-stars-and-stripes colors. Yet *Don McLean* pictures a dour artist looking downcast and dejected.

"My usual rollicking happiness was gone," said McLean, "and I was in a very dark place. That place didn't have the oranges, reds, whites, and blues, and the happiness of *American Pie*. That was by design. A guy named John

Olsen took the picture for an article in *Life Magazine*. I chose a black-and-white photograph for the cover to replicate what was in my heart and soul. I was gray and dark, so the album got a gray and dark response from the public and the press."

Don McLean begins with a vigorous, accelerated/decelerated piece titled "Dreidel." On it, McLean examines the frenzy of whirling through life like a spinning top. The lyrics begin with the central theme of the album, the need to slow life down. McLean confesses to all the poisonous feelings that loomed in his psyche during the previous months of fame—the feelings of self-doubt, personal fraud, dizziness, and confusion. McLean's own soaring vocal range dramatizes a scathing tale of tremendous pessimism. While the lyrics are bleak, the arrangements roar with blaring horns and a rousing electric piano. Oddly, the song ends with a hint of reaffirmation.

On the next tune, "Bronco Bill's Lament," McLean uses oblique symbolism reminiscent of "American Pie." This time, Bronco Bill is a washed-up cowboy actor who "worked his youth away" and is ripped-off and cast aside by the changing movie studio system. As it turns out, Bronco Bill's venomous rants against "the voyeurs and the lawyers" bare a thin disguise to McLean's own feelings of professional disillusionment. Close in the background, Don's father Donald also seems to lurk.

"If We Try," one of only two romantic songs on the album, is more about looking *at* affection from a distance than attaining love from the inside.

"There was love in 'If We Try,' although I wasn't in love at the time. I saw a lot of women I liked being with, but I stopped short. It was a longing thing."

One of *Don McLean's* most vivid musical parables is "The More You Pay." In it an aging mare is paraded around at the end of a horse auction to the laughter and derision of the crowd. A young boy steps up and bids two bits for the tired broken animal, as the auctioneer cruelly winks and remarks, "That what they don't sell, they shoot or give away."

"Both the horse and the little boy are symbolic of me as an artist," Don explained. "The horse is my dream. The more you pay, the more it's worth. Yet the horse has one foot in the glue factory. What they don't sell, they shoot or give away. That's show biz."

Don McLean ends on a solemn note, with a gloomy indictment called "The Pride Parade." The song's main character is a masquerade of a human lost in the emptiness of his own public image. The despicable character is painted as the epitome of evil and deception. Who is this character that McLean lashes out at so viciously?

"That's me, angry with myself. It's weird, the self-hatred, isn't it? At the time, I thought of myself as a fraud. People from my past would turn up and visit me after the shows. They would see me sign autographs. 'My friends are together where the people are all gathered.' I'm this one-man parade, and as I'm passing them by, it presents a lonely image.

"*Don McLean* was the bluest record I ever made. It's very sad in many ways, like a Billie Holiday record.

"But it's very important to understand," stressed McLean, "that, as an artist, if you're feeling a certain way, no amount of production can take out that indescribably blue sentiment you have in your voice. It's what makes you an artist; it's what's in your soul that comes out through your singing that affects people. No amount of echo or production could hide the pain."

When the album was released, it received the chilly reaction it probably deserved. The big press party was over. The reporters had all packed up their gear and gone home. No glimmering sequel to "American Pie." Although the record sold well initially, it merely pierced the top 30 of the album sales charts. Yet three decades later, *Don McLean* can be construed as an artistic victory on a whole new level. An artist stands up and bares his soul—and not for the money, the sequels, or the follow-ups.

"Looking back, I am proud of it," McLean proclaimed. "I didn't do it for the money. I did it for what was inside of me. You know, I sincerely believe a real artist doesn't go into the music business with the singular idea of becoming rich. We do it more for the applause, love, and approval, and to make people aware."

Don McLean was able to exorcise his inner ghosts and find professional contentment alongside his art. In 1983, he cleaned professional house and took over his own business affairs. He renewed his career path with a hit rendition of Roy Orbison's "Crying." And today, he's happily married and the proud father of two. McLean tours and plays to audiences around the world. During his time off, he spends time settled in a rural section of Maine.

Not many fans prefer the darker intensity of "that album after *American Pie*." It marks the tale of a man who crawled out from under the bell jar of depression, shook his fist, and maintained artistic independence. Looking back, McLean doesn't regret opening the emotional floodgates with such a dark, introspective effort.

"When the *Don McLean* album came out, yes, I was confused and self-indulgent. I realize that. But you don't want to stay in a place like that any longer than you have to. Luckily I came out of it—and without therapy, I might add, although I did need it, especially at such a low point in my life."

Download This!

A Few Slices Beyond "American Pie"

Here are the ten tunes that appear on the 1972 *Don McLean* release, plus a few extra tidbits.

1. "Dreidel"—Don McLean (BGO-UK).
   The declarative "slow it down" song written by McLean. "I never thought this would happen to me," he sings.

2. "Bronco Bill's Lament"—Don McLean (BGO-UK).
   The song uses traces of steel guitar and Gene Autry and Roy Rogers–styled western arrangements.

3. "Oh My What a Shame"—Don McLean (BGO-UK).
   Another heartrending song of lost opportunities with symphonic overtones and lush piano by former Steps Ahead jazz pianist Warren Bernhardt.

4. "If We Try"—Don McLean (BGO-UK).
   During this period, McLean was involved with an elusive Israeli woman. He spent time wooing her in the Middle East and after living there a while learned how lucky Americans like himself really were.

5. "The More You Pay"—Don McLean (BGO-UK).
   One of McLean's main songwriting strengths is his expert use of symbolism and allegory.

6. "Narcisissima"—Don McLean (BGO-UK).
   McLean lofts another personal attack on himself, this time a play-on-words tune that probes his own narcissism.

7. "Falling Through Time"—Don McLean (BGO-UK).
   One of the many symptoms of depression is the feeling that one is falling into a void of darkness. The lyrics here contain such images.

continued on the next page

A Few Slices Beyond "American Pie" *continued*

8. "On the Amazon"—Don McLean (BGO-UK).
This novelty piece is the only song from the album not written by Don. Presumably from a 1930s musical, it's the one comic relief portion of the album.

9. "Birthday Song"—Don McLean (BGO-UK).
On the surface, it's a charming song, but digging deeper, McLean broods over his inability to open up to others.

10. "The Pride Parade"—Don McLean (BGO-UK).
Cruel, cutting, and autobiographical.

11. "Crying"—Don McLean (Hip-O).
A chilling rendition of the Roy Orbison hit, from Don's 1978 *Chain Lightning* album. "'Crying' is a holdover from the nervous breakdown I had from the *Don McLean* album experience," Don said. "I understood the pain and I was able to sing the song in the same way Orbison did it. I wasn't faking it; I lived that song."

12. "Killing Me Softly"—Roberta Flack (Atlantic).
Charles Fox and Norman Gimbel wrote this hit after a singer friend, Lori Lieberman, told them about seeing Don McLean live at the Troubadour. When a friend of McLean's told him about the song, his initial response was, "Does it suck?"

13. "Vincent"—Don McLean (Capitol).
Stevie Wonder called "Vincent" one of his favorite songs. It also was the song Tupac Shakur's girlfriend played for him over and over in his hospital room as he lay dying from bullet wounds after a drive-by shooting.

14. "And I Love You So"—Don McLean (Capitol).
"The last song on the last album Elvis did, *Elvis in Concert*, was 'And I Love You So,'" Don recalled. "The album was done in 1977, but released two months after his death. Every time I look at that LP, I get the chills."

15. "True Love Ways"—Buddy Holly (MCA).
Buddy inspired "American Pie." McLean once compared listening to Holly's music as being just like "tasting corn flakes for the very first time."

16. "Mountains O' Mourne"—Don McLean (BGO-UK).
A charming classic Irish ballad, McLean sings the story of a villager visiting Londontown for the first time. Note the line about watching his friend stopping traffic "with the wave of his hand." He's the traffic cop.

chapter 5

The Nashville Rat Pack

Newbury, Hartford, Hall, and Miller
Writin' "Them Heartbreakin', Achin',
Eggs and Bacon Country Songs"

Hank Williams is the king of all country music songwriters. He is the great communicator. Stylistically, Hank broke the mold. His impact and over-lying spirit is massive and indelible, spanning the days of Jimmie Rodgers, Ernest Tubb, and the Grand Ole Opry, right up to Lucinda Williams, Robert Earl Keen, and Rodney Crowell.

Harlan Howard is another Nashville songwriting kingpin. Howard, the writer of several country smash hits including Patsy Cline's "I Fall to Pieces" and Jim Reeves's "He'll Have to Go," rose to prominence with a multitude of hits represented in each and every decade from 1950 up until his death in May 2002.

But in terms of who paved the golden road of American roots-rock song-writing by way of Nashville's Music Row, four tremendous writers, all born between 1936 and 1940, made a momentous impact on the art of melody and verse. They are Mickey Newbury, John Hartford, Tom T. Hall, and Roger Miller. (Note: Kris Kristofferson is also part of our "Nashville Rat Pack," but he'll be revisited more fully in the next chapter.)

All four individuals are worthy of being categorized as cult figures to the generations of younger roots-rock fans now just discovering classic country and acoustic music. Beginning songwriters would be wise to study these four men line-by-line, verse-by-verse, and analyze their compassionate con-tributions to American roots rock.

Each of these four artists arrived in Nashville with a head full of dreams and a few dollars in his pocket. All four went on to sign publishing deals with major song-peddlers like Acuff-Rose and Tree Music Publishing. Mickey Newbury lived and wrote in the back seat of his car during his first days in Tennessee. John Hartford was spinning records on the air at WSIX-Nashville before he was discovered. Tom T. Hall came to Tennessee on New Year's Day in 1964 from a radio DJ gig in Virginia with forty-six dollars and a guitar. Roger Miller putted around town on a moped and went from working as a hotel bellhop to playing fiddle for Minnie Pearl and pounding drums for Faron Young. After scoring hits for others, all four strolled the hallways of the record companies and auditioned with their guitars for recording deals of their own in front of label patricians like RCA's Chet Atkins and Mercury's Jerry Kennedy.

Of the four, only Tom T. Hall is still with us. All have been hailed as "writer's writers." Their talents and musical bodies of work have crossed beyond the realm of country. They wrote huge hits for famous singers like Elvis Presley and Glenn Campbell to pay the bills. Afterward, their own solo careers flourished throughout the 1960s, '70s, and '80s. It was during a time when, as up-and-coming solo artists, these Nashville rebels butted heads in the studio with "old school" record executives and producers. On their earliest solo LPs—particularly in the case of Hartford and Newbury, who first recorded for RCA Records, and less so for Miller and Hall, who were Mercury artists—they fended off clock-watching staff producers from spoiling their unique songs with goopy layers of MOR (middle of the road) string orchestras and canned instrumental arrangements. With country often resorting to pop-oriented, string-section-heavy, "countrypolitan" sounds, 1963 until 1968 was a tricky time to be a new artist. Artists were beholden to staff arrangers and producers who couldn't differentiate between what was "hip" and what sounded "square."

With the exception of Miller—who chose to project an affable, apolitical, goofy image on nationwide television—Hall, Newbury, and Hartford were ideologically out of step with Nashville's conservative, right-wing majority. They leaned politically left of center. Hall even championed liberal causes in his songs. Hartford fancied himself an aloof nonconformist, comfortably pictured alongside longhairs like Gram Parsons and the Byrds inside the pages of a young Rolling Stone magazine. From his early folk days, Newbury was receptive to the anti-war movement and the civil rights struggle. His biggest hit, "American Trilogy," wasn't so much pro-Confederate,

*stars-and-bars flag waving. Rather, it respectfully signified a modern South-
ern optimism for a post-civil rights America.*

*The most significant attribute these four writers have given to the genre
of American roots rock is the depth and dimension they added to the science of songwriting. Their songs dabbled with literary imagery and probed
into deeper, more adult emotions like estrangement, loneliness, and sensuality. They debated social issues and critiqued American society. Newbury,
Hartford, Hall, and Miller, as well as Kristofferson, elevated popular country music to a higher plateau of expression through their unique styles of
verse, chorus, and rhyme. Their music ran against the grain. Today, they set
the standard for the subject matter people have come to expect from modern songwriters.*

Mickey Newbury didn't tour with a full band when he played live. He performed alone in smaller nightclubs with just an acoustic guitar. Newbury was
a moving target, his music tough to categorize. He wasn't exclusively rock,
country, or folk, but his live gigs reflected a comfortable folksinger side.

Milton J. Newbury, Jr., was born and raised in Houston, Texas. From the
beginning of his life he felt uncomfortable in his redneck Texas surroundings. As a teenager, he wrote poetry before he learned to play guitar. He re-
cited his poems in Houston coffeehouses during the Beat 1950s. Frustrated
with living in Texas, Newbury joined the air force and was stationed in England. When he was discharged, in the tradition of Jack Kerouac, Newbury
rambled through Texas and worked for a spell as a fisherman on a shrimp
boat. Buoyed by his love of poetry, Mickey had little difficulty combining it
with melody and making the leap to songwriter. He moved back to England
and began an early association with Kris Kristofferson while Kris attended
Oxford University. He also knew fellow Texan Townes Van Zandt, and such
associations moved Newbury closer towards becoming a folksinger, performing at hootenannies and writing songs.

Newbury migrated to Nashville in 1963 through an introduction from a
friend to come and work at the Acuff-Rose publishing house. Through Acuff-
Rose, singers like Eddy Arnold and Andy Williams began recording Newbury's
tunes. Newbury scored his first Top Ten record in 1966 with "Funny Familiar

Forgotten Feelings" by Don Gibson. With the counterculture in his creative rear view mirror, Mickey experimented with psychedelia when Kenny Rogers and the First Edition recorded his mind-bending "Just Dropped In to See What Condition My Condition Was In." Soon Newbury signed with RCA for two records. Newbury's first album, *Harlequin Melodies,* came out in 1968, and pictured him fresh-faced on the cover with close-cropped wavy hair, a charming half grin, and a campy Nehru shirt with embroidery on the collars and cuffs. Newbury's sweet tenor voice blended rudiments of country and folk, accented with the slightest traces of blues and R&B from his Texas days.

His songs were far more introspective and personal than traditional Nashville fáre. Predictably, a lack of sophisticated production and arrangements buried the sheer sentimentality, angst, and dejectedness that were such important components of Newbury's later sounds. But in 1969, Mercury Records came damned close to the mark when they released *It Looks Like Rain.* The opening "Write a Song a Song/Angeline" stretched out past seven minutes with the melancholy flavor that made Newbury's music so distinctive. Mickey liked to blend compositions together, a technique that would later be another one of his songwriting trademarks. One tune, deceptively titled "She Even Woke Me Up to Say Goodbye," was anything but a two-fisted, honky tonk send-up. Much like Kristofferson's "Sunday Mornin' Comin' Down," the song was doused in sorrow and emptiness.

Producer Jerry Kennedy gave *It Looks Like Rain* the toned-down restraint the songs deserved. Aural ingredients included a lone whistler, delicate notes on glockenspiel, a lonely church organ mixed far in the background, the pitter-patter of rain, subdued background choirs, and simple chord picking on Newbury's lone guitar. Kristofferson penned the liner notes and appropriately quoted William Blake.

The record label didn't really promote *It Looks Like Rain* with much enthusiasm, so Newbury left Mercury in 1970 to begin a remarkable five-record association with Elektra Records. Still, *It Looks Like Rain* captured the spellbinding hypnotism of Newbury's forlorn abilities. It marked the first (of many) appearances of his signature song, "San Francisco Mabel Joy" (misspelled on the album sleeve as "Mable Joy"), an aching ballad about a starving wanderer from Waycross, Georgia (Gram Parsons's home town), who falls for a Los Angeles street girl on the Sunset Strip. She loves him and casts him aside. Soon after, he turns 21 in a federal prison. Then, at the end of the song, beneath her doorway bathed in red light with a bullet in his side, the farm boy is told that Mabel Joy left four years ago in search of him. Classic Newbury.

There were plenty of doubters in Nashville's skeptical songwriting circles of a melodrama's chances for success. But soon Kenny Rogers, John Denver, Waylon Jennings, and Joan Baez all picked on up the song.

"I consider 'San Francisco Mabel Joy' to be the most successful song I have written for several reasons," Newbury once said. "First, it was a five-minute song written in a two-minute world. I was told it would never be cut by any artist. Second, I was told you could not use the term 'redneck' in a song and get it recorded. It has sold in excess of 55 million records. It broke the rules and it broke the walls down. It became the foundation for a new form of expression in country music. It was chosen in the millennial year as one of the top 100 folk songs of the past century."

It was a typical scenario. Characters in Newbury's songs were often the victims of gross misfortune and were left abandoned under clouds of depression and shame. Passionate lovers who "broke down walls for doors" soon saw

Just Mickey Newbury and his guitar: It was his favorite way to perform.

their relationships crumble into an eery silence and estrangement. They would wander the streets late at night, tip a flask of whiskey, and suck it dry.

Newbury, himself a recluse and a bohemian, lived alone on a Tennessee houseboat or sometimes 100 miles away from Nashville in a cabin. But after moving to Los Angeles, he married a former singer with the New Christy Minstrels, started a family, and signed his dream deal with Elektra Records, a progressive label that encouraged him to explore his country roots, and expand his dramatic songwriting capabilities.

The opening song on his Elektra debut LP, 'Frisco Mabel Joy, rendered a fascinating, unique glimpse of traditional Americana. With an expertise not unlike an exquisite filmmaker, he seamlessly fused three traditional Southern anthems together into one swelling ballad. "An American Trilogy" was another trademark Newbury medley that blended the familiar strains of "Battle Hymn of the Republic," "Dixie," and "All My Trials" into one grand suite. It was so triumphant and stirring that the king himself, Elvis Presley, used the song for no less than a climactic finale to his live performances.

In the meantime, Newbury toured modestly as a solo acoustic act, distrustful that accompanying musicians might dilute the majesty and anguish of his songs. A live FM broadcast in 1973 captured a typical live set (not to mention his talkative between-song banter) and before it reached bootleg status, Elektra rush-released it as *Live at Montezuma Hall*. In another shrewd marketing move, the label packaged the live disc with a reissue of *It Looks Like Rain*. It was a golden year. A few months earlier, Newbury had released his finest collection of songs on *Heaven Help the Child*, and scored his biggest Top 40 hit with "Sunshine," another inspired ballad of loneliness.

On *Heaven Help the Child*, practically every song blended into another without pause. The title track ends with a brief rendition of "Auld Lang Syne." A typical Newbury motif is the presence of a rainstorm and faraway trains sprinkled throughout the record. Newbury, an audiophile in the studio, claimed it was there to cover up nagging vinyl surface noise, but it also contributed to the starkness and desolation of his compositions. In 1975, the back cover of *Lovers*, another exceptional Newbury confessional, pictured a pocket-sized whiskey bottle turned empty on its side with the last few drops spilled on a table.

After an astounding, groundbreaking run between 1969 and 1975, Newbury's recording career seemed to run out of steam. It was as if the advent of punk and power pop drowned out his delicate musings. In 1976 Newbury terminated his contract with Elektra, bought up all his masters, and returned to the Nashville label scene, signing a deal with Hickory for three records and a final one in 1981 for Mercury. But none of those recordings quite captured the magic of his previous efforts. Newbury spent the next 20 years in failing health and semi-retirement in Oregon with his wife and family. He released a handful of homegrown and live recordings available by mail order on his Web site. The master tapes of his records on Elektra, Mercury, and Hickory were tragically misplaced and lost, but a box set of all ten albums was made available on CD by means of digitally re-recording virgin vinyl copies of each release.

The heartrending spell of what came to be known as "Newbury's train songs," particularly the acoustic Elektra sides, holds up remarkably well on the box set transfers. Newbury loved to re-record versions of his best tunes like "San Francisco Mabel Joy," "How Many Times Must the Piper Be Paid for His Song?," "Sunshine," and "An American Trilogy." He also peppered his recordings with overt, traditional country cryin' songs like "If You Ever Get to Houston, Look Me Down" or a rare upbeat tune titled "How I Love Them Old Songs."

On September 28, 2002 (the very day we began working on the concept to write this book), Newbury died at home in Vida, Oregon, of respiratory complications.

John Hartford was another American roots player who performed at his best playing solo. He would drop a large square slab of plywood on the center of the stage and place a microphone at floor level. Dressed in a white shirt, black vest, jeans, work boots, and a bowler hat (resembling a riverboat bartender), Hartford would sing, play the fiddle, and soft-shoe-shuffle-clippity-clop his tune's rhythm in grand hillbilly fashion.

One night between songs in a crowded music hall, as he tuned up his fiddle, a request came down from the balcony.

"Play 'Tall Buildings.'"

Without hesitation, Hartford put down his fiddle and reached for a small vintage Martin guitar. "This is a very sad song," he told the audience, and launched into a half-humorous, dead-serious account of a person who was leaving the countryside and his pretty damsel to move to the city and work in a skyscraper.

"I'm going to work in tall buildings," sang Hartford in a deep baritone croon. Nobody in the audience quite knew whether to laugh or cry. Such was the ambivalent, cheeky style of Hartford's music.

To make his name more palatable to country DJs, John Harford added the "t" to his name at the suggestion of Chet Atkins when he signed his first label deal for RCA Records in 1966. Hartford was born in New York City, but was raised near the banks of the Mississippi River in St. Louis. Like Samuel Clemens, he had dreams of working on a riverboat and did just that at the tender age of ten. At night he listened to the Grand Ole Opry and became a skillful fiddle and banjo player by age 13. In high school Hartford played in bluegrass bands and pursued a career in graphic arts in Illinois. He added guitar and mandolin to his instrumental arsenal.

Hartford's baritone pipes also made his voice suitable for the radio as a DJ. By 1965, he moved to Nashville and took on an air shift on WSIX. Hartford made his acquaintance with Newbury, Kristofferson, and other young writers in Music City. A year later, after signing Hartford to RCA, Chet Atkins entered the studio with the young singer-songwriter/instrumentalist. The cover art of Hartford's debut album, *Looks at Life*, pictures John on a back porch with a pipe in his mouth and a banjo on his lap. Johnny Cash wrote the liner notes. The overall feel is equal parts bluegrass, folk, and country ballads. Hartford's lyrics are clever, witty, cerebral, zany, and kooky. The instrumentation is mostly rolling banjo picking, fluid guitar lines, and breezy orchestral string charts. Hartford's music comes across as folksy and lofty. Wordy yet snappy, traditional yet experimental, academic yet street-smart, supercilious titles include "I Shoulda Wore My Birthday Suit," "Untangle Your Mind," or "Eve of My Multification." Sometimes he would chuckle between the lines of a song. Because his music was often obtuse, Hartford cultivated an image as one of the early Nashville stoners. Like the Beatles did during the *Sgt. Pepper* dates, during recording sessions Hartford must have, on more than one occasion, retired to the back alley or the rooftop for a puff or two of Mary Jane.

Signed by RCA label exec Chet Atkins, John Hartford often used his banjo to compose his most fluid, stream-of-consciousness melodies and verses without choruses.

If Hall, Newbury, and Kristofferson were the early architects of an alternative movement among Nashville songwriters, then Hartford represented the most idiosyncratic part of that spectrum. In 1967 Hartford's career exploded when he entered the studio with another cache of far-out tunes. The result was an album called *Earthwords and Music*. Buried midway through the album is the title track, "Earthwords," a minute-long, artsy-fartsy, spoken-word poem set to random banjo finger picking. But the song that follows changed the face of country-pop forever.

"Gentle on My Mind" was written exclusively on banjo, like practically all of Hartford's tunes at the time. The song contained no chorus or bridges; it was a straight shot of four verses stitched together aurally from end to end. Like Hartford's previous song contraptions, "Gentle on My Mind" had the same amiable rolling motion, but it didn't indulge in imagery overload.

"Gentle"'s juggernaut of tumbling metaphors of impermanence captured the imagination of an entire generation: the feeling of rambling cross-country like a hobo; warming next to a fire in a windy train yard; assorted sea-to-shining-sea landscapes of wheat fields, coal mines, and railroad tracks; a nomad leaving his sleeping bag rolled up and stashed behind some girl's couch. The song's freewheeling, no-rings-no-strings treatment of love and commitment clicked in synch with the then-modern ruminations of free love. It also dredged up images of Woody Guthrie's best dusty road anthems. When Glen Campbell recorded the mass appeal version a few months later, it became an automatic, across-the-board radio smash.

Its effect rippled worldwide. Legend has it that as a result of "Gentle on My Mind" being one of the most-played songs on the radio, Hartford was assured an annual six-figure royalty check for the rest of his life. In the late '60s, Hartford reportedly earned $170,000 per year, quite a bounty at the time. His financial independence afforded him the luxury to not compromise his music—not that he would have in the first place. As a result of the fame he gained from composing "Gentle on My Mind," Hartford moved to Los Angeles and became involved with network television through his appearances on CBS's controversial *Smother Brothers Comedy Hour* and the *Glen Campbell Goodtime Hour.*

Prior to departing Nashville for Los Angeles, Hartford was booked as a session player for another important record that would skew his musical attitudes even farther. In the spring of 1968, Hartford joined Roger McGuinn and the Byrds in Columbia Studios on Music Row in their quest to fuse rock and country with the renowned *Sweetheart of the Rodeo.*

Subsequent solo recordings in 1968, *The Love Album* and *Housing Project*, were considered unconventional and highbrow for their day. "I Would Not Be Here" is another wacky, stream of consciousness play on words. The verses are decked out with multicolored images that bleed together into a single run-on, two-minute sentence. Beneath the vocal track is a spacey, typical late '60s psychedelic sound bed. Although lyrically verbose and dense, "Natural to Be Gone" (from *The Love Album*) and "A Simple Thing as Love" (from *Housing Project*) are also free-spirited melodically and lyrically in the tradition of "Gentle on My Mind," although neither caught on with anywhere near the magnitude.

With the advantage of hindsight, the five albums Hartford recorded for RCA—*Looks at Life, Earthwords and Music, The Love Album, Housing Proj-*

ect, and *Iron Mountain Depot*—do sound a bit dated and a tad pompous. Like his musical contemporary, composer/guitarist Mason "Classical Gas" Williams, Hartford's RCA work emits a passé "canyons of your mind" approach. But, at the time, it was truly one of the first Nashville psychedelic experiments to come from a major label.

After the RCA sessions, subsequent recordings Hartford made in the late '70s for the Flying Fish label, including the Grammy award-winning *Mark Twang,* are far better and more timeless representations from which to measure his art. After striking his fortune, Hartford returned to Missouri and earned his riverboat captain's license. In 1971 he appeared uncredited on Delaney & Bonnie and Friends' *Motel Shot,* another important recording in the American roots rock vein. From 1971 until his death in 2001 from non-Hodgkin's lymphoma, Hartford remained exclusively devoted to traditional and acoustic country and bluegrass. His last great recordings appeared on the Rounder label, culminating with his participation in the mammoth, multi-platinum *O Brother, Where Art Thou?* soundtrack of 2000.

A senior editor at a New York publishing house once advised us that if somebody reads a book, finds four or five great stories, and then shares them with their friends, that book will become a success. Tom T. Hall's discography is loaded with hundreds and hundreds of great stories, which explains why he's had such wide appeal as a writer and singer over the past three decades.

Hall's avuncular songwriting technique relies on the same tools that accomplished authors use for short stories and novels (i.e., developing vital elements like setting, characterization, plot, and theme). Rather than proselytize in song, Hall chooses a nonbiased, almost journalistic observation angle in his songs. And he rarely breaks the cardinal rule of creative writing: show, don't tell! He lets his characters live and breathe and interrelate on a believable level.

Tom T. Hall's song protagonists are every man and every woman with an unusual spin: The guy who didn't marry his high school sweetheart and is relieved; the poor working stiff who moves into a subdivision when havoc breaks loose; two naïve GIs involved in a donnybrook in a German beer garden; a man turns 40 and reflects on his life; a truck-stop child grows into a starry-eyed, pretty waitress with a Daddy complex; a man sits in a shopping mall and describes the many slice-of-life scenarios he sees; a young man gets sage advice from a wise, old hillbilly; a fella has two left feet on the dance floor and loves beer. Like many of Hank Williams's classics, these tales are told in a succinct pace with a precious moral to ponder after the last note.

Tex Ritter first nicknamed Hall "the Storyteller" during an onstage introduction and the name stuck. Born in a log cabin in 1936 outside of Oak Hill, Kentucky, Hall was dealt some tough breaks as a kid. His mother died when he was 11, and four years later, his father, a bricklaying minister, was shot and wounded in a hunting accident. Hall dropped out of school at age 15 to provide for the family.

Tom wrote his first song at age nine when he heard two neighbors arguing. He recreated the spectacle into song as a detached observer, and that became his signature style. Realizing he was given the gift of verse, he continued to compose tunes for family picnics and played in bluegrass bands as a teenager. After a series of factory jobs, Hall broke into radio in Morehead, Kentucky, and even wrote a jingle for one of the station's main sponsors, a flour company.

In 1957 Tom Hall joined the army and was stationed in Germany. He performed in bands on armed forces radio, and even met Elvis a few times when Presley was stationed in Germany. When Tom returned to the States, he went back into radio in Salem, Virginia. He'd accumulated a stockpile of wisecracking songs he wrote from the army bandstand, including "36 Months of Loneliness and 30,000 Gallons of Beer." His friends at the station encouraged him to make the pilgrimage to Music City.

When Hall went to Nashville in 1964, the country clique totaled only a few hundred tight-knit folk—musicians, songwriters, producers, session players, arrangers, and publishers. Pretty soon Hall was tipping beers at Tootsie's Orchid Lounge with his new songwriting buddies, who included Mickey Newbury, Kris Kristofferson, and Roger Miller.

"Kris Kristofferson was a bartender; Roger Miller was riding a Honda; Mel Tillis hadn't learned to stutter; and Dolly Parton was a 32-B," Hall once quipped. "Songwriting was more a calling than a profession. When I got to Nashville, it was a folk art. Now it's an industry."

Lauded by country's old-five-and-dimers, honky tonkers, and No Depression devotees alike, Tom T. Hall is America's quintessential storyteller.

Tom Hall dutifully wrote songs from nine to five for a publishing outfit called New Keys Music. Every Friday afternoon he turned in a full reel of finished tunes and typed up lyrics for fifty dollars a week. Adding the middle initial "T." to make his name catchier, Tom penned a few radio hits, but really struck the publishing mother lode in 1967 when he wrote a huge crossover country hit by Jeannie C. Riley called "Harper Valley PTA." It was an accusatory story of a mini-skirted, widowed, single mother accused by the townspeople of dressing like a tramp. She shows up at the PTA meeting and exposes the parents as drunken, lecherous, and hypocritical fools.

The song rattled America's social psyche. Seemingly every suburban woman in America ran out and bought the single until "Harper Valley PTA" racked up six million units in sales. It became a cottage industry, spawning a movie and a television series. Hall's fortunes were set. Starting in 1970 he began a fruitful recording career on Mercury Records guided by producer Jerry Kennedy. Tunes like "Ravishing Ruby," "I Like Beer," "Faster Horses," "Old

Dogs, Children, and Watermelon Wine," "The Year That Clayton Delaney Died," and "A Week in a County Jail" were hit staples on country radio. Hall logged in a slew of country hits for the Mercury label (and a few for RCA) throughout the 1970s and through the mid-'80s. He was his own man, musically and politically. Like few writers in Nashville, Hall shunned the politics of Nixon and Republicanism. He recorded a satire of the Watergate scandal and another about a monkey in the White House. He often spoke out, unashamedly, in favor of liberal causes and in support of the Democratic Party.

Hall's clever narrative songwriting style has been an inspiration to several American roots rock artists. Besides Boudleaux Bryant's "Love Hurts" and the Louvin Brothers' "Cash on the Barrelhead," Gram Parsons's only other cover song on his *Grievous Angel* record was a rocking version of Tom T. Hall's "I Can't Dance." In 1974 guitar virtuoso Leo Kottke iced the definitive version of "Pamela Brown."

A who's who of roots rockers recorded a tribute CD honoring Hall in 1998. *Real: The Tom T. Hall Project* features a notable line of talent. Johnny Cash sang one of Hall's more serious songs, "I Washed My Face in the Morning Dew," a tune about purification and personal redemption. Whiskeytown revisited Tom's darker side with "I Hope It Rains at My Funeral," a witty but dark account of one man's cradle-to-grave struggles. Kelly Willis interpreted a pure country/honky tonk ballad called "That's How I Got to Memphis." Joe Henry offered a bittersweet, boy-who-makes-good-visits-home song called "Homecoming," and Syd Straw ripped a version of "Harper Valley PTA."

What draws such a fashionable cross-section of admiring musicians and fans to Tom T. Hall is his total lack of pretension. Or it's his ability to read people like a trained psychologist. But ultimately, it's his calling as an old-fashioned storyteller, because, after all, *everybody* loves a good story.

Roger Miller was a goofball genius, a way-out square hipster who failed over and over before achieving fame. Who else would record a tune called "My Uncle Used to Love Me but She Died," perhaps the most ridiculous song ever written?

"My songs come from the soul, and I guess God just gave me a funny soul," Roger Miller surmised.

When Miller was on his hot streak (ten consecutive country and pop hits in just two years, from 1964–1966), he was known around Nashville songwriting circles for being the king of the one-liners. Fellow songsters carried notepads and followed him around town to pick up spare quips and quotes. Any remark that flew out of Roger's mouth could make for a potential song:

"My family was so poor, I was made in Japan.

"L.A. cop: 'Can I see your driver's license?'

"Roger: 'Can I shoot your gun?'"

Roger Dean Miller was born in Fort Worth, Texas, in 1936. His aunt and uncle raised him in Oklahoma after his father died and his mother was too ill to take care of him. Music came naturally to the young boy. By age 11 he learned to play guitar and fiddle. After he left school in the eighth grade to work on ranches and in the rodeo, he mastered the drums, banjo, and piano.

Serving out a hitch in the army, he moved to Nashville and arranged for a personal audition with Chet Atkins at RCA. Miller was so nervous seeing Atkins behind the desk, he began singing and playing his guitar in two different keys.

With his music aspirations consequently on hold, Miller toiled as a bellhop at the Andrew Jackson Hotel. He wrote a few tunes for Mercury Records through an introduction by honky tonk crooner George Jones, whom he had met as a hang-around at WSM radio. But again, Miller came up empty. All of his songs stiffed, so he joined Minnie Pearl's revue as a fiddle player, and toured as a drummer for singer Faron Young. Later off the road, he gave up music for a few months and moved to Amarillo, Texas, to become a fireman.

Only Roger Miller could get himself fired from a firehouse.

Luckily, Miller picked up a gig with Ray Price and his Cherokee Cowboys when Price rolled into Amarillo on a tour. Roger played guitar and sang harmony in the band, but his unique vocal timbre and crazy phrasing drove Price, the consummate country Sinatra with the velvety voice, to the brink. By 1958, Miller returned to Nashville with another batch of songs and convinced cowboy star Rex Allen to record one of them for Decca Records. Ray Price, on the other hand, undeterred by Miller's erratic talents on the road, recorded his song "Invitation to the Blues" and soon Miller got a job for twenty-five dollars a week writing songs for Tree Publishing under the tutelage of Buddy Killen. Killen plugged one of his songs to Ernest Tubb. Faron Young hit Top Ten with a Miller tune, and then Jim Reeves, one of Nashville's biggest stars at the time, scored No. 1 and No. 2 hits with "Billy Bayou" and "Home" respectively.

It was time for Roger to try again as a solo artist. From 1959 to 1963, Miller recorded for Decca, then RCA, and came up empty on both counts. By 1964, starved for fame, he decided on a different strategy. When Jimmy Dean guest-hosted *The Tonight Show* for Johnny Carson, Miller convinced Dean to book him as a guest. His goofy style and clever showmanship made him highly compatible for television,where he skewed his music more as comedic novelty tunes and less as country songs.

Next he appeared on *The Merv Griffin Show*. By then, after Phillips and Mercury Records passed on inking Miller to a recording deal, an executive from a noncountry subsidiary called Smash Records showed interest. Miller agreed to join Smash's hodgepodge roster; they had also just signed James Brown, Jerry Lee Lewis, and the Left Banke. Roger arranged to enter the studio for two sessions for an advance of $1,600, which he planned to use for his relocation to Los Angeles to become an actor.

Smash counted on getting 16 finished sides over two days, which would justify Miller's advance at $100 per song. That meant they would have ample material to release singles and one album. Mercury executive Jerry Kennedy was brought in to produce the sessions. Miller and Kennedy first cut three songs with a full orchestra on the evening of January 10, 1964. The three tunes, "Why," "Less and Less," and "Ain't That Fine," were considered as potential singles.

The next morning, Miller showed up at the studio where Kennedy had assembled a five-piece band. Although Roger had caught only a few hours' sleep, he was creatively energized. That's when his career was sealed and the essence of his sound was conceived. With 12 songs in his satchel, Miller and crew counted off one song after another. They cut "Chug-a-lug" and "Dang Me." The band was kickin' and snappy. Miller experimented with scatting vocals and the band's sound centered on his funky, note-bending acoustic guitar accompaniment.

Beneath a goofy, affable show-biz exterior,
Roger Miller was an intensely driven spinner
of verse and rhyme. Songwriters hung around
Roger carrying notepads to jot down any stray
witticisms that might turn into a song.

Afterward Miller left for Los Angeles and moved into a room above Lee Hazlewood's garage. "Dang Me" flew right to the top of the Top 40 charts. Country radio followed along, since programmers were already familiar with Miller's past records. "Chug-a-lug" and "Do Wacka Do" garnered the same enthusiasm. Roger was in the creative driver's seat. One day while driving outside of Chicago, he spied a sign: "Trailers for Sale or Rent." He liked the rhythm of the words. "King of the Road" was born. It became Miller's biggest record of his already booming career.

Other Miller novelties like "England Swings," "Walkin' in the Sunshine," "Kansas City Star," and "You Can't Roller Skate in a Buffalo Herd" fared very well. While Miller's hit singles flew out the doors of the record stores, his finest, more philosophical work was equally remarkable. Turning his razor wit inward to more serious material was the coup de grace, and was what ultimately endeared him to today's contemporary fans of American roots rock.

Miller offhandedly referred to "One Dyin' and a-Buryin'" as "that suicide song" but to date, nobody has ever scored such a monster hit using suicide as a main theme. Half spoken, half sung, "One Dyin'" sounds like a harmless offshoot of "Streets of Laredo." But closer listens reveal a narrator eaten up by passionate love turned to hate. The only way to peacefully reconcile his predicament "and to be free" is to have six pallbearers carry his body to the cemetery. At just over two minutes total, it's a song that begs to be played over and over and over.

When "Husbands and Wives" was recorded in 1966, it could have been a frank testimonial to Miller's own failed track record at marriage. (Roger was married three times.) As usual, the instrumentation is jazzy and sensational, pivoting around a nylon-string guitar, a string bass, spare piano fills, and a tap on the drummer's high hat. Miller's vocal is brilliant and relaxed as he professes simply that stubborn pride is the chief cause of divorce between couples (a hot topic among Americans).

What made Miller's bonanza chain of hits so impressive was that it was done *during* the British Invasion, when groups like the Beatles, the Animals, and Herman's Hermits dominated the American pop scene, while top American acts like the Four Seasons and Elvis Presley fell short of the top ten.

"The Last Word in Lonesome Is Me" and "Train of Life" were laidback, front-porch country chestnuts, minus the knee-slapping, screwball antics that characterized Miller's radio and television persona. As Miller's hit potential wound down by 1969, he used his established fame to help launch Kris Kristofferson as a songwriter by covering "Me and Bobbie McGee" in 1969. He also cut an early 1967 version of Mel Tillis's powerful, chilling Vietnam era ballad, "Ruby (Don't Take Your Love to Town)," two years before it broke pop with the First Edition.

Miller was a talent of limitless possibilities and he rarely left a creative stone unturned. In 1985 he scored no less than a full-scale Broadway musical called *Big River* (based on the writings of Mark Twain), which won seven Tony awards, one of which went to Miller for best musical score.

Up until his death in October 1992 from throat cancer, Roger Miller was a lovable, cuddly figure in American pop culture. Yet one sensed a moody side to him. Insiders claimed that Miller's high highs and low lows often forced him to struggle and finish writing songs at the last minute. Yet he could whip up a tune in the studio control room in four minutes flat.

Behind the madcap photos of a happy/sad guy wearing a skinny tie and a sharkskin suit jacket and making scrunched-up faces for the camera, lurked a genuine songwriting genius—a bright mid-'60s square hipster who fit right in with the inimitable, chug-a-luggin' conga line of Newbury-Hartford-Hall-Miller, the proverbial Nashville Rat Pack.

Download This!

Songs from Tootsie's Orchid Lounge, Over a Bowl of Chili and a Glass of Beer . . .

The best way to wrap your arms around the sounds of Newbury, Hartford, Hall, and Miller is to pick up Tom T. Hall's *Storyteller, Poet, Philosopher* (a two-CD box set) and Roger Miller's *The Genius Of . . .* (a three-CD box set). Then there's a comprehensive Australian import anthology of John Hartford's best RCA works, a single disc on Raven Records, called *Natural to Be Gone 1967–1970* (available online). To take the Newbury plunge, *The Mickey Newbury Collection* of all his works is available for a hefty hundred bucks, also online. All that is expensive, so here's our pick of the pack.

1. "Old Dogs, Children, and Watermelon Wine"—Tom T. Hall (Mercury).
   This is the crown jewel of Tom T. Hall tunes, as poignant as puppies and as wise as old bikers. The opening line of the song is "'How old do you think I am?' he said." Simply a masterpiece and arguably Hall's best song.

2. "Down at the Mall"—Tom T. Hall (Mercury).
   Prior to its appearance on Tom's box set, this tune (one of his last major label works) was cut in 1986 and was available only as a single. Plus, it wasn't even written by Hall. But it truly captures his essence, so that's why he cut it. One of our personal favorites.

continued on the next page

Songs from Tootsie's Orchid Lounge, Over a Bowl of Chili and a Glass of Beer . . . *continued*

3. "Faster Horses"—Tom T. Hall (Mercury).

Hall discusses the philosophy of life with an old cowpoke, has a disagreement, and soon feels the cold steel of a blade on his neck. It's the second knife reference in Hall's discography, if you include "Salute to a Switchblade."

4. "Old Five and Dimers Like Me"—Tom T. Hall (Mercury).

When Tom cuts a track he didn't write, you know darned well it's made from the best cloth of country songwriting, like this song written by Texas songwriter Billy Joe Shaver.

5. "Spokane Motel Blues"—Tom T. Hall (Mercury).

This tune was cut in 1973, just as the outlaw country movement began gaining steam. Hall mentions Willie, Waylon, Kris, Bobby Bare, Billy Joe, and Dolly in this homesick ode.

6. "Husbands and Wives"—Roger Miller (Mercury).

Miller's best tunes have that definitive all-male, pre-hippie '60s, sharkskin suit, Jack Lemmon/John Cassavetes vibe. This is one of the best songs ever written about divorce. The dull pain and resignation in his voice is persuasive.

7. "One Dyin' and a-Buryin'"—Roger Miller (Mercury).

A suicide song that became a pop/country/MOR hit. Who would have bet?

8. "King of the Road"—Roger Miller (Mercury).

The Proclaimers, a Scottish twin brother duo, had a hit with Roger's anthem in 1990. It has songwriter imagery so economic yet illustrative, it's like something Jane Austen would describe.

9. "(Ruby) Don't Take Your Love to Town"—Roger Miller (Mercury).

Miller cuts an early version of a Top 40 hit, and you can hear how the Kenny Rogers and the First Edition version borrowed heavily from his arrangement. Or was it the other way around?

10. "Tall Tall Grass"—John Hartford (RCA).

A rolling, laidback piece from Hartford's very first album, *Looks at Life*. Chet Atkins signed Hartford and handed the producing reigns over to Felton Jarvis.

11. "Gentle on My Mind"—John Hartford (RCA).

Hartford's version is, of course, purer and more straightforward, cut before Glen Campbell's giant rendition.

12. "A Simple Thing as Love"—John Hartford (RCA).
If Hartford could be accused of trying to pen a sequel to "Gentle on My Mind," this would be the song.

13. "I Would Not Be There"—John Hartford (RCA).
Everybody's life is the product of a string of crazy coincidences. This lyric is structured as one complete run-on sentence.

14. "San Francisco Mabel Joy"—Mickey Newbury (Mercury/Elektra).
Mickey's melodramatic opus appears on at least three records in his catalog, maybe more. Newbury was fond of repeating performances on record.

15. "Write a Song a Song/Angeline"—Mickey Newbury (Mercury).
From *It Looks Like Rain,* the first record that really dug into the seriousness of Newbury's presentation. The only instrument that sounds dated is the occasional electric sitar buzz. But hey, 'twas 1969.

16. "Lovers"—Mickey Newbury (Elektra).
"Lovers," in our opinion, is *the* heartbreaker of Newbury heartbreaker songs.

17. "An American Trilogy"—Mickey Newbury (Elektra).
Mickey's surgical composition of three great American anthems joined into one classic song. Elvis singing it in his white Vegas jumpsuit may have spoiled the fundamental nature of the tune for some. We disagree. Now, don't be messin' with the King.

18. "How I Love Them Old Songs"—Mickey Newbury (Elektra).
This is the opening tune on the *Live at Montezuma Hall* broadcast that became its own album. So upbeat and sweet, it's quite a contrast from Mickey's usual sullen presentation.

19. "Heaven Help the Child," "Good Morning Dear," "Sunshine"—
Mickey Newbury (Elektra).
The peaceful chirping of birds precludes the beginning of "Sunshine." These tunes represent the most powerful one-two-three punch of Newbury's career, from 1973's *Heaven Help the Child.* Newbury finds the pot, but, typically, there's no gold inside. The country and orchestral nuances are spare but powerful.

chapter 6

Kris Kristofferson

Lonesome Coyote Survives

The heart is really what matters," said Kris Kristofferson in his charac-
teristically subsonic drawl.

"I learned that by fighting in the Golden Gloves. I was talking to this old
Mexican guy who had just climbed off the canvas. He was knocked down
seven times in one fight. I admired him so much for it. I had just gotten
knocked out myself. He said, 'You know, Mexican men will keep trying.' I saw
what he meant, and I was not the same after that."

Kris Kristofferson's career has probably seen as many ups, downs, and
crucial bouts as that Mexican boxer. Kris has "climbed off the canvas" many
times, triumphant and beaten, throughout the lean and successful years of
his life. Whether he was fighting to break through as a songwriter, fighting
the battle as a "user and abuser" of alcohol, or trying to navigate a schizo-
phrenic film career, Kris Kristofferson is one of America's most unlikely and
resilient success stories.

He's been a poet, a career service man, a scholar, and a music and movie
superstar. He's tasted good and evil on several creative fronts, and if you
haven't delved deeply into the man's work, there are a few key entry points
from which to approach America's finest songwriter, next to Bob Dylan and
Hank Williams.

"I feel like one of the luckiest people on the planet. I've had many opportunities, going back to the Rhodes scholarship, being airborne, being a helicopter

pilot working in the Gulf of Mexico. I worked construction jobs in places like Alaska and Wake Island."

Musically, the best starting points are his first two records, classics *Kristofferson* and *The Silver Tongued Devil and I*. The 1970 self-titled Monument debut (lovingly reissued in 2001), reigns supreme as a songwriting monument, indeed. It's crammed full of future standards that became the cornerstone foundation of the Kristofferson legacy, including tunes like "Help Me Make It Through the Night," "For the Good Times," and "Sunday Mornin' Comin' Down." And those are just the big hits.

The Silver Tongued Devil and I is another story. It's a no-brainer in terms of quality, imagination, and innovation when, in 1971, it served as the lynchpin between the slick and conservative country music that was being churned out in Nashville versus the revolutionary shots being fired elsewhere in America by such luminaries as Mickey Newbury, Guy Clark, Lee Clayton, Billy Joe Shaver, and Townes Van Zandt.

Much the same way the film world was being transformed by movies such as *Easy Rider* and *Five Easy Pieces*, country music was also experiencing a cultural shakedown by the young Turks at approximately the same time. The outlaw movement with Waylon and Willie had yet to begin when Bob Dylan first visited Nashville's Music Row in 1966 to record a countercultural explosion, *Blonde on Blonde*. For the coup de grace, guys like Kristofferson made a concentrated push into the country mainstream. By the start of the '70s the race was on, and the table—already being set by Johnny Cash, Waylon Jennings, and Willie Nelson—would soon transfer country music artists and listeners into a pills-pot-and-whiskey-fueled state of bliss. Traditional country tunes now had to compete with Kristofferson's more convincing and emotionally raw songs, which documented the more realistic affairs of the heart.

"In the '60s, Nashville was in darkness," songwriter Chris Gantry once said. "When Kris arrived, the lights went on."

"I felt closer to Dylan than to any of the country acts," Kristofferson remembered. "When I started out, I didn't work in any of the country clubs. I started working the Troubadour [in Los Angeles] and the Bitter End [in New York], and backed into the country market."

The year 1970 was a fertile time for music in general, let alone an explosion for country. Nashville was not unlike Greenwich Village during the early

'60s, when writers like Dylan, Joan Baez, and Mimi and Richard Fariña were tilling fresh soil. Even more similar is Paris of the '20s, when legends like F. Scott Fitzgerald and Ernest Hemingway were gaining steam. Granted, Tootsie's Orchid Lounge in Nashville as a destination was a lot less glamorous than the Café de Flore in Paris, but it was no less significant. Kristofferson's earliest output beautifully emulated Hemingway's macho prose as set to music, which stemmed from the time he actually ran into the famed novelist while bumming around Spain with his brother during the '50s. It's an archetypal Kris tale.

"It was at a bullfight," Kristofferson recalled. "I was following Luis Miguel Dominguin and Antonio Ordonez, who were having a series of *mano a mano* fights to determine who was the number one. This younger guy, Ordonez, was pressuring Dominguin. Ironically, Dominguin was once the young guy who was pressuring Manolete in the *mano a mano* when Manolete was killed.

"Anyway, at this particular fight, Dominguin was taking some unnecessary chances. He was caught up against a horse and gored in the groin. We were waiting downstairs, outside of the plaza, to see how he was. Then I looked up and there was Hemingway. It was not too long before his death. His face was so ravaged that it was a shock to me. Hemingway was probably as big a hero as I had at the time because I wanted to be a novelist. I was trying to live like him. I was running in front of the bulls in Pamplona, anything Hemingway-esque I could do.

"Anyway, he looked like he was dying. I don't know whether what I was thinking showed in my face, or what, but we locked eyes. It was the strangest thing. He was looking at me, then he just wheeled around, jumped in his Volkswagen, and sped off. I remember my brother saying something like, 'That old son of a bitch didn't look too friendly.' I could never understand why Hemingway did that. It was a non sequitur."

Kristofferson would later have a similar intuitive experience when he ran into a "great and wasted" Johnny Cash in the hallway of CBS Studios. That meeting resulted in one of his best and earliest songs, "To Beat the Devil." It wasn't long before Kristofferson himself would experience the "ravaging" excesses of drinking.

"I can still see Hemingway. Later, when I'd been through more in my life, I thought about Hemingway committing suicide. I got to wondering how much the booze might have been to blame for his mental condition. I know as a user and abuser of that particular drug that it can cause depression that gets close to suicidal."

As a soldier on leave in the early '60s, Kristofferson visited Nashville, attended the Grand Ole Opry, and first met Johnny Cash while still in uniform. He submitted tapes of songs he'd written and recorded while stationed in Germany to Marijohn Wilkin, a relative in the Music City publishing biz. By 1965, at age 29, Kris Kristofferson had officially left the service. He gave up a plum assignment to teach literature at West Point (he'd originally volunteered to go to Vietnam) to pursue a less lucrative art in Nashville. With a wife and child, he was walking the high wire without a net.

"Scared my family to death. My wife just about divorced me. She came out and tried to make a go with me, but of course I didn't make money at it for a long time. My father, a major general in the air force, thought I'd gone crazy. They were very upset when I first came."

Kris Kristofferson (pictured here during the esteemed 1971 Silver Tongued Devil and I *sessions) helped make Nashville songwriting earthier and more sensual.*

By 1966, the same week producer Bob Johnston brought Bob Dylan to Nashville to record *Blonde on Blonde*, Kristofferson landed a menial job at CBS Studios on Sixteenth Avenue. Security police surrounded the locked-down studio when Dylan arrived one day, as Kristofferson was emptying trash-cans and jockeying tapes. He called himself Dylan's "janitor." (Sidekick Billy Swan remembered their roles as engineering assistants.) It was a pivotal experience that placed Kristofferson in the intimate proximity of history.

"I was the only songwriter in Nashville allowed to be with him. I was in heaven. The sessions went all night long. The doors were locked. The musicians would sit and play cards while Bob Dylan went out, sat at the piano, and wrote.

"It was the strangest session I'd ever seen. The guys in Nashville ran 'em through, three songs in three hours, just like machinery. Then this guy came in and closed the studio up. Of course he was our hero. I just sat and watched him through the glass, sitting there at the piano with dark glasses on, all by himself in this huge studio. At the end of the night, he'd come up with a song and they'd just knock it out."

After securing a publishing deal with Roy Orbison's producer, Fred Foster, and Combine Music, Kristofferson's fame burst through the previously closed doors of Music Row. While his family fell apart, his first Monument album, *Kristofferson*, initially sold a modest 32,000 copies—not too bad for an unknown. Underground FM radio guru Tom Donahue championed the record. But by the time Kris started his second effort, *The Silver Tongued Devil and I*, the first album was reissued with a fresh front cover photo featuring a beard Kristofferson had grown in the hospital while recuperating from a bout with pneumonia in 1970. He was hoping the beard might add a few years to his baby face. With its new cover, *Kristofferson* went gold just as *Silver Tongued Devil and I* reached the record store shelves. Kris was now on an unstoppable roll.

Years later, on "This Old Road," an autobiographical song he wrote for the 1986 album *Repossessed*, Kristofferson pondered the young man who made the quantum leap from part-time bartender on Seventeenth Avenue to "songwriting janitor" at CBS Studios. Kris was now the guy who rivaled Williams and Dylan as America's purest songwriting voice, even though, in his words, he "sings like a bullfrog."

"I felt pretty autobiographical when I was writing that song. I got the idea when somebody gave me a photo of myself back when I was a bartender at the Tally Ho Tavern. There's this clean-shaven guy with a cigarette hanging out of his mouth, looking like James Dean, smiling, obviously drunk. It was a different person."

By the '70s, Kris Kristofferson's star had risen. He'd played Billy the Kid to James Coburn's Pat Garrett for film director Sam Peckinpah. In Martin Scorsese's 1976 *Taxi Driver*, Robert De Niro's Travis Bickle buys an LP in order to impress Cybill Shepherd's character, Betsy. It's a copy of *The Silver Tongued Devil and I*. Ironically, Kristofferson became a leading man in a subsequent film by Scorsese called *Alice Doesn't Live Here Anymore*.

Come the '80s, Kristofferson's dual career as a singer-songwriter and actor started to wobble. He hit the wall when he signed on to appear in director Michael Cimino's 1980 film *Heaven's Gate*, one of the biggest financial film disasters of the 20th century. *Heaven's Gate* effectively ended the "era of the director" while Kristofferson's status as an icon seemed to go down with Cimino's sinking ship. After *Heaven's Gate*, the scripts stopped arriving. Kris signed a recording contract with Mercury Records after Monument Records went down during the mid-'80s. Just like that Mexican boxer, Kristofferson would have to get back up off the canvas if he was to continue to fight. While the marketplace would knock him around the ring for the next several years, Kristofferson would stay hungry and tough enough to leave behind an impressive legacy of songs and films.

For better (securing his artistic integrity) or worse (scaring the daylights out of the blue-collar portion of his fan base), left-wing politics would rule Kristofferson's musical roost from the '80s onward. During the decade spanning 1986 to 1995, Kristofferson would travel the world, stopping in places like the Soviet Union and Central America. Those experiences would inspire him to record three controversial albums that would once again define him as an idealistic songwriting force. If Kristofferson had been "shipwrecked in the '80s," he would raise eyebrows singing about it in graphic detail, bearing his sociopolitical soul in the process.

Repossessed marked the 1986 return of Kristofferson's "shoulder ghost," the Silver Tongued Devil and his road band, the Borderlords. This time the Devil was peddling contra-counter-revolutionary war in Central America, which Kristofferson addressed with "Shipwrecked in the Eighties." Written for the Vietnam veterans, Kristofferson sings this song to this day.

"It's a tale of personal isolation. I happened to be in Hawaii, standing there in the surf. This guy came up to me. He looked like a real blasted case. He said he had done some hard time in Vietnam and had had trouble with agent orange. He was telling me that a song of mine had gotten him through his mental recuperation from Vietnam. He showed me his old underlined Bible. That all came into the second verse, 'like an old Holy Bible that you clung to through so many seasons'."

At the time, in 1986, Kristofferson's label was promoting "They Killed Him," a song about Gandhi, Martin Luther King, the brothers Kennedy, and Jesus Christ. Kris wryly recalled the uphill country radio promotion process.

"When you've got people who say, 'The only trouble was there ought to have been four more bullets in the gun,' it gets hard to communicate."

Kristofferson wouldn't release a follow-up until 1990's *Third World Warrior.* But like that stubborn Mexican boxer, damned if he would put a damper on his politics. While the content seems dated today, the spirit isn't. He still sings "Sandinista" and his latest theme song, "Don't Let the Bastards Get You Down," at concerts.

Producer Don Was took the helm for 1995's *A Moment of Forever.* While not as politically didactic, the production is sturdy and the material stays consistently strong. Kristofferson is in fine voice and the band is cooking while the material finds its rightful balance between life, liberty, and pursuit of happiness. There's mention of Baghdad and Waco in "Slouching Toward the Millennium," and "Shipwrecked" makes a return visit. The album ends powerfully with a tribute to Sam Peckinpah, "Sam's Song (Ask Any Working Girl)." It's clearly Kristofferson's most commanding collection, second only to *The Silver Tongued Devil and I.*

After recording his clench-fisted "radical trilogy," Kristofferson would get up off the movie canvas, this time, to make John Sayles's *Lone Star* in 1996, an art house classic that would rescue him from the sting of cinema misfires and direct-to-video stinkers. In *Lone Star,* he portrayed Sheriff Charlie Wade, a murdering racist Texas lawman, chilling (then thawing) the hearts of the Hollywood film casting community. *Lone Star* was a powerful vessel that would re-establish his career as an actor who could hold his own in any acting ensemble. He would soon make an esoteric string of art films and big-budget flicks. Kristofferson's repertoire now includes Merchant and Ivory's *A Soldier's Daughter Never Cries, Payback* (a violent film noir with Mel Gibson), Sayles's *Limbo,* Tim Burton's remake of *Planet of the Apes,* and a major sci-fi role in *Blade* followed by a lucrative string of *Blade* sequels.

Today, pushing 70 years old (a milestone Willie Nelson beat him to by three years), Kristofferson's face is filled with character, not the image of the "ravaged" Hemingway he locked eyes with at the Spanish bullring. Like Hemingway, though, Kristofferson has made a tireless living being a "man's man." A recent live concert CD released on John Prine's Oh Boy! label is peppered with songs from his "radical trilogy" past, including, yes, "Shipwrecked in the Eighties."

Kristofferson remains a bold voice, taking "unnecessary chances" by standing against the 2003 Iraqi invasion while the silence of dissent following 9/11 was dangerously in force. While being honored recently with a humanitarian award in Nashville, Kris sang "Don't Let the Bastards Get You Down" and scorned George W. Bush's occupation of Iraq.

Kris Kristofferson has not been good at keeping his mouth shut or toning down his politics. Like the character in his famous song "The Pilgrim—Chapter 33," he has claimed his rightful birthright as a poet, a picker, a prophet, a pilgrim, and a preacher. And today, he's still pushing the message of peace, anti-interventionism, and activism with equal and ageless fervor.

Download This!

Silver-Tongued Selections

Here's a list of vital Kristofferson songs, sticking close to Kris's own interpretations plus a few cool covers thrown in for good measure.

1. "The Pilgrim—Chapter 33"—Kris Kristofferson (CBS).
   The role is called up yonder with a fresh list of bad influences. Chris Gantry, Dennis Hopper, Johnny Cash, Norman Norbert, Funky Donnie Fritts, Billy Swan, Bobby Neuwirth, Jerry Jeff Walker, Paul Siebel, and Ramblin' Jack Elliot. Off *The Silver Tongued Devil and I*.

2. "Casey's Last Ride"—Kris Kristofferson (Legacy/Monument).
   This dark tale is singer-songwriter James McMurtry's favorite Kris song, found on the debut.

3. "Stranger"—Johnny Duncan (Columbia).
   We prefer Johnny Duncan's hit version to Kris's own. It's those mariachi horns and the marimbas. Also, Johnny (and Janie Fricke) nailed the mood.

4. "Billy Dee"—Kris Kristofferson (CBS).
   Characters are Kristofferson's strong suit. Here's a sad tale of struggle and drugs.

5. "Sunday Mornin' Comin' Down"—Kris Kristofferson (Legacy/Monument).
   Kris's version of one of his biggest songs is dark and looming, unlike Johnny Cash's version, which is uptempo and reinforced with strings. What man couldn't relate to grabbing for your "cleanest dirty shirt"?

6. "To Beat the Devil"—Kris Kristofferson (Legacy/Monument).
   Kris meets the Devil in the bar, drinks his beer for nuthin,' then rips off his song.

7. "El Coyote"—Kris Kristofferson (Mercury).
   Kris's band, the Borderlords, pushes him convincingly through this song, one of the best tracks off 1986's *Repossessed*.

8. "Slouching Toward the Millennium"—Kris Kristofferson (Justice).
   Don Was has worked with the best—Waylon, Willie, and Dylan individually, and Johnny Cash with the Highwaymen.

continued on the next page

Silver-Tongued Selections *continued*

9. "Me and Bobby McGee"—Kris Kristofferson (Atlantic).
   In 1999, Kris released *The Austin Sessions*, perfect for those on a budget. All his best songs are sparsely and convincingly re-recorded with guests such as Jackson Browne, Steve Earle, Alison Krauss, Mark Knopfler, and more.

10. "I Can Help"—Billy Swan (Monument).
    When Billy Swan got a small organ keyboard as a Christmas present, he wrote this song and cut it with Kris's band. It became a huge pop and country hit in 1974.

11. "When I Loved Her"—Kris Kristofferson (CBS).
    Buried toward the end of *The Silver Tongued Devil and I,* this is a beautiful song filled with sadness and regret.

12. "Shipwrecked in the Eighties"—Kris Kristofferson (Oh Boy!).
    From his live album, *Broken Freedom Song,* Kris cuts and releases "Shipwrecked" for the third time. Live at San Francisco State University in July 2002, Kris was one of the few dissenting entertainers standing up against Gulf War II, aka Operation Enduring Freedom.

13. "Don't Let the Bastards Get You Down"—Kris Kristofferson (Oh Boy!).
    A live rendition originally recorded for the *Third World Warrior* album. It's since become a theme song of sorts that cuts across all of Kris's fan base, from the lefties to the few remaining rednecks.

14. "Help Me Make It through the Night"—Sammi Smith (Sony Music Distribution).
    Up to this time, country writers wrote more about cheatin' than sensuality. Sinatra inspired this one while Sammi Smith sang a smoldering version and scored a hit in 1970 after Kris taught it to her.

chapter 7

Steve Earle

The Rumble and Torque of Copperhead Road

Steve Earle is known for having rehabilitated himself from a life of fast living and nasty habits. As the famous Hell's Angel Sonny Barger once remarked, "Doesn't rehabilitation mean going back to the way you were before they threw you in jail?" Grounded with a 12-step spiritual base, Earle is widely respected in musical circles today for putting his heart and his politics to song.

Post 9/11, Earle tweaked the noses of the cable news channels singing about John Walker Lindh, the reviled American Taliban soldier. Then he kept the embers of anti-war dissent glowing with an outspoken and unpopular public opposition to Iraqi War II. Since, Earle has published short stories, written a novel (and is working on another), composed haiku, and staged a play based on Karla Faye Tucker, the female inmate on death row in Texas who was executed under then-Governor George W. Bush's watch. He also tends bonsai and has acted on the hit cable show, The Wire.

Earle can do pretty much anything he puts his mind to. "It's really important to do stuff outside of your core craft," he once told a Washington Post writer. "I think it keeps you fresh in your core craft."

Earle is a hard-hitting contemporary songwriter with a far-reaching discography, ranging from country to southern rock, bluegrass, folk, hard rock, Bakersfield twang, rockabilly, and more. He is accustomed to being in the eye of the storm. In the earliest days of his career, Earle was best known for his predilection toward adding hard rock elements to his country recordings.

Whether it was through personal addiction problems or butting heads with the system, Steve grew accustomed to staring down the precipice. In 1995, he independently released an important acoustic album, Train a Comin', when his career was in the balance. At the time, Earle narrowly escaped hard prison time, instead completing a year in a rehab center on a heroin possession charge.

By 1996, Earle was back in the major label game. Warner Bros. distributed his next two releases, in 1996 and 1997. I Feel Alright and El Corazón, both ensemble-oriented albums influential enough to inspire Lucinda Williams to scrap and recut her Car Wheels on a Gravel Road into a pre-millennium classic (with the help of Earle himself). In 1999 he cut a bluegrass record called The Mountain with the Del McCoury Band.

Earle stands up for his right to politicize his music and talk about social issues on stage.

"Johnny Cash once wrote a letter that was published in a country music magazine," Earle told us. "He stated that artistic people have a responsibility to stand up for what they believe in, whether what they're saying is popular or not, whether people agree or not. It's a line I have to walk all the time."

That said, one cannot discount the impact of Earle's best work, his first three breakthrough MCA recordings—Guitar Town, Exit 0, and Copperhead Road—cut between 1986 and 1988. With those three records, he blazed a trail not unlike what Waylon, Willie, and Tompall Glaser accomplished during the '70s outlaw country movement. The only difference was that Steve Earle walked the line alone.

Like many artists who have conquered substance abuse, there's a line of demarcation between the works of a reckless user and the enlightened music of someone on the path of sobriety. In Steve Earle's case, we prefer the music he made when he was out of control and on his way to prison. While half-cocked and crazy, his vision was clear and courageous, and he was breaking exciting new ground. From 1986 until 1991, Steve was the Nashville Rebel.

It's 1988 and Steve Earle is on wife number God-knows-how-many. Maybe number four. He's standing near the lip of the stage of the famed Fillmore

Auditorium, wielding an electric axe with his rock 'n' roll band, the Dukes, touring on *Copperhead Road*. Steve's hair is shoulder length and straggly. His band looks more like a police lineup, a collection of Dixie dregs who might have rolled in on choppers instead of a tour bus. They could easily be mistaken for bikers, Outlaws MC with a capital O.

The embroidered image on the cover of the *Copperhead Road* CD could signify one of two things: either a motorcycle or a military patch. There's an aura of peril surrounding *Copperhead Road*, an ominous swirl of nonconformist imagery on both the cover art and inside the song lyrics.

In 1986 and 1987, Steve Earle's first two MCA releases, *Guitar Town* and *Exit 0*, dealt a one-two punch of countrified rock aimed at country radio. Years ahead of their time, both records carried the same curse: too rocky to twang, too twangy to rock, and a Duane Eddy guitar-bending twang at that.

On the cover of *Guitar Town*, a lean and hungry Steve Earle, not unlike a young Waylon Jennings before him, is captured standing in front of a guitar store window. A case-less acoustic is slung over his shoulder. *Guitar Town* was one of the first all-digital recordings, co-produced by Emmylou's original Hot Band bassist Emory Gordy, Jr., and MCA label exec Tony Brown. At the time, Brown had championed many a rock wannabe trapped in Nashville, and to this day, he's considered one of the most open-minded executives on Music Row.

The power of *Guitar Town*'s material is formidable. It's one of those rare records where every track is a keeper. The guitars are skillfully woven and layered, and the vocals are unpolished but expressive on songs like "Hillbilly Highway," "Someday," "Fearless Heart," and "Good Ol' Boy." Bucky Baxter's steel guitar howls like a runaway freight train. Even now, after nearly two decades, *Guitar Town* is arguably Steve Earle's finest record.

Guitar Town set the stage for an even bolder and broader follow up. *Exit 0*, badly in need of re-mastering, now falls victim to early cold digital technology. Yet the drums rumble and the guitars resonate, as *Exit 0* benefited mightily from Earle's road-tested band, the Dukes. The lyrics and the music itself retain an unyielding connection to the highway. (Earle swore that they actually ran across a real Exit 0, as in zero, out on the road.)

"A writer once explained that *Guitar Town* was more of a rock record than *Exit 0* was," Earle said. "Yeah, *Exit 0* was slicker and bigger, more produced, but the song 'Guitar Town' had a straight rap cadence that ran all the way through it, just like Dylan's 'Subterranean Homesick Blues.' Woody Guthrie wrote hundreds of talking blues songs while Townes Van Zandt had done several, too.

"I grew up in Texas and lived in Tennessee," Steve recalled, "so I was exposed to lots of country. I don't understand how anybody got the idea that country and rock were necessarily mutually exclusively terms. That didn't make sense to me. The Everly brothers and Roy Orbison were examples of rock 'n' roll and country staying on the same path."

Thematically, *Exit 0*'s spirit extols a colorful cache of rural themes, such as Farm Aid, domestic flux, tricked out, American-made hot rods, and small town Texas high school football heroes. *Exit 0* was (and still is) the embodiment of Dust-Bowl-Meets-Sun-Belt America.

Although Steve Earle was born in Virginia in 1955, he was raised in Texas, outside San Antonio. As a wild seed, he dropped out of school with barely an eighth-grade education. But he showed a keen proficiency for music, the arts,

A rugged Steve Earle smashes hard rock and country boundaries during his Harleys-and-hellraising Copperhead Road *era.*

and drama. Like Joe Ely and Jimmie Dale Gilmore in Lubbock, Earle wore his hair long and rallied against the Vietnam War in conservative Texas. At 18, he settled into the Houston area and developed his songwriting abilities by personally reaching out to songwriters like Townes Van Zandt and Jerry Jeff Walker. Then he made the inevitable pilgrimage to Music City.

"I got to Nashville in 1974 and the way I survived was with three different publishing deals," said Steve. "My first job was a $75-a-week draw against future royalties. That's how I made ends meet from 1974 until *Guitar Town* came out in 1986."

Earle obediently packed his lunch box and his guitar and wrote songs by day. By night, he thumped bass with Texas songwriter Guy Clark. Soon Earle grew frustrated with Nashville and headed back to Texas where he formed the Dukes. But soon after, he experienced a change of heart and returned to Nashville to give songwriting one last shake.

"I went into the office every day at nine o'clock," Earle said, "and I wrote eight songs every day. I was getting farther away from what I liked to write, but I learned about structure and I learned about brevity and keeping to the point. After *Guitar Town* came out, I went back to writing the kind of songs I wrote before I came to Nashville, folkier and more story-oriented songs that were a little more adventurous rather than just 'personal relationship' songs."

By the time *Copperhead Road* was released in 1988, Earle had officially flown the country-music coop. He longed for rockier pastures, changing label mastheads within the giant Universal label conglomerate from MCA to UNI, the latter a refurbished rock imprint formerly home to acts like Strawberry Alarm Clock, Desmond Dekker and the Aces, and Neil Diamond.

When *Copperhead Road* hit the streets, Earle had given up on evangelizing his brand of country-rock to country radio programmers. That battle had already been fought and lost.

"I felt like I did something for country music, but I don't feel my efforts were fully appreciated. I changed what you could get away with *sonically* on country radio. But what didn't change was what you could get away with *saying* on country radio."

Soon it was goodbye to competing with artists like George Strait for his record company's affections and a slot at the bottom of country radio's over-researched playlists. Instead Earle competed with Bob Seger and Bruce Springsteen for the hearts and ears of rock audiences. Album rock radio programmers seemed only slightly receptive.

Copperhead Road stands as a gritty masterwork. "The Devil's Right Hand" is an Earle anthem if ever there was one. He treats the subject of firearms and pistols with reckless abandon. A Colt .45 blows a card cheat out of his chair. On his way to the gallows, the protagonist is asked who pulled the trigger. Blame it all on Satan. After all, a pistol is the devil's right hand.

The remaining songs are liberally spiked with references to guns, Vietnam flashbacks, and forbidden marijuana fields, all set against a backdrop of mistrust and paranoia. "You belong to me," Steve sings to his woman, as if she were, in biker lingo, "property of . . ."

On "Johnny Come Lately" Earle delves aggressively into his earliest Celtic music influences. Not the mystical New Age blends of early Clannad, mind you. Instead, Earle enlists the two-fisted drunken accompaniment of the Pogues, the earthy, Joycean blend that might be heard in a pro-IRA pub on the rowdier side of Dublin. Earle was one of the first to understand that the simpatico of raucous Celtic, rock, and country made musical sense. Just as the Clash took a shine to recording and touring with Joe Ely, Earle enlisted the Pogues for the same instrumental and spiritual support on *Copperhead Road*.

"Celtic is where country music came from in the first place," Earle explained. "Modern country music comes from Appalachian music. And Appalachian music was originally Scottish and Irish folk songs that were brought over, played on different instruments. Pipes gave way to banjo, mandolins, and a few other instruments. I was surprised that the Pogues used five-string banjos. That's definitely an instrument invented on American soil. After all, we are a nation of immigrants."

Thanks to the artistic success of *Copperhead Road* and heavy touring in territories like Ireland, Australia, and the United Kingdom, today Earle enjoys critical success and a large fan base all over Europe and down-under.

"Songwriting is a viable form of literature," said Earle. "If kept to a certain level, it's literature you can consume in your car. You can convey emotions the same way novels and poetry does. Bob Dylan elevated songwriting to that level of literature."

Earle, like many American roots musicians, freely admits his country roots.

"I am a country singer," confessed Earle. "I stole more licks from Merle Haggard and Hank Williams than from rock singers.

"I didn't grow up in Butcher Hollar listening exclusively to the Grand Ole Opry. Economics dictated how I started out. I couldn't afford a guitar and an amp and because I couldn't make my guitar sound like the Beatles or Jimi Hendrix I gravitated toward acoustic music. I could duplicate a Tim Hardin or a Tim Buckley record because they were solo recordings. The good thing about that was that it got me interested in songwriters. I started emulating them."

Far be it for us to assert that a man's best work may have occurred when he was on his way down the darkest spiritual path of his life. But looking back, *Copperhead Road* is the cerebral equivalent to riding a rigid-framed Harley Panhead. It's loud and mean, absorbing every bump on the road. Named after one of America's deadliest snakes, *Copperhead Road* contains all the basic ingredients of a great Southern rock record with smarts.

While *Guitar Town*, *Exit 0*, and *Copperhead Road* may only represent a small body of Steve Earle's total output, there's a strong case to be made that they are his most essential works. This is music that harkens back to a bygone era when the US economy was shaky, when there was war in Iraq, and George Bush was president of the United States. In other words, it's music that speaks loudly today.

Download This!

El Corazón de Steve Earle

Here's a collection of a few "crossroads" Steve Earle stood at before wandering down the paths of country, rock 'n' roll, folk, bluegrass, rockabilly, and beyond.

1. "Pilgrim"—Steve Earle and the Del McCoury Band (E Squared/ADA).
   This song, included on The Mountain with the Del McCoury Band,

continued on the next page

El Corazón de Steve Earle *continued*

also appears on the soundtrack CD from the Kenneth Lonergan film, *You Can Count on Me.*

2. "Guitar Town"—Steve Earle (MCA).
   The ultimate Steve Earle single. Twangy in a Duane Eddy fashion, *Guitar Town* the album, although initially considered too rockin' for country, became a milestone Nashville release. It was re-mastered and punched up in 2002, like a country classic ought to be.

3. "Fearless Heart"—Steve Earle (MCA).
   Hard to believe, but in 1986 you had to have a fearless heart to release this brand of country music in Nashville. This song illustrates Earle's best use of pedal steel.

4. "Nowhere Road"—Steve Earle & the Dukes (MCA).
   Exit 0 could use the same re-mastering face-lift *Guitar Town* enjoyed. It contains lots of radiant guitars, shiny steel, and Steve's wonderful, breaking voice.

5. "The Rain Came Down"—Steve Earle & the Dukes (MCA).
   One of Steve Earle's Farm Aid staples off *Exit 0.* It tells the story behind farm subsidies and corporate conquest of the food industry. Farmers aren't just getting shut down, experiencing falling prices, or losing subsidies; they're losing their farms to the auctioneer's gavel.

6. "Copperhead Road"—Steve Earle (MCA).
   The most menacing use of mandolins in a song. The album *Copperhead Road* is rife with images of Vietnam and firearms.

7. "Johnny Come Lately"—Steve Earle (UNI/MCA).
   Steve, ferociously backed by the Pogues, combines the spirit of Johnny Reb and Michael Collins. It's a look at heroes as an American dream goes slightly awry.

8. "The Devil's Right Hand"—Steve Earle (UNI/MCA).
   One of Steve's earliest tunes, recut. A love song to a cap and ball Colt pistol.

9. "You Belong to Me"—Steve Earle (UNI/MCA).
   The most lovey-dovey track off *Copperhead Road* maintains an edge.

10. "Billy Austin"—Steve Earle & the Dukes (MCA).
When we saw Steve perform this song in 1990, he seemed to be hanging by a thread. He managed to include this ode to the death penalty on *The Hard Way* disc.

11. "Goodbye"—Steve Earle (Winter Harvest).
An exquisite acoustic "anti-MTV-unplugged" album, *Train a Comin'* was originally released independently after Steve Earle got out of the joint. "Goodbye" is a contrite song that was beautifully recut by Emmylou Harris on her *Wrecking Ball* album.

12. "More Than I Can Do"—Steve Earle (E-Squared/Warner Bros.).
Clearly off the substances by 1996, Steve hits his stride combining *Rubber Soul* with a wheezy harmonica.

13. "You're Still Standin' There"—Steve Earle with Lucinda Williams (E-Squared/Warner Bros.).
An uptempo precursor to the touch and feel of Lucinda Williams's *Car Wheels on a Gravel Road*.

14. "Christmas in Washington"—Steve Earle (E-Squared/Warner Bros.).
El Corazón (1997) is right up there with *Copperhead Road, Guitar Town*, and *Exit 0* as Steve Earle's best collection. This song is a sad and pessimistic Christmas card featuring a lone acoustic guitar and a harmonium.

15. "Telephone Road"—Steve Earle (E-Squared/Warner Bros.).
A funky backbeat with guitars, churchy organ, a blast of baritone sax, plus the Fairfield Four on backing gospel vocals. Not to be confused with Rodney Crowell's song of the same name.

16. "Texas Eagle"—Steve Earle and the Del McCoury Band (E-Squared/ADA).
Possibly the most rockin' bluegrass album cut with acoustic instruments. Railroad buffs will love this song.

17. "The Galway Girl"—Steve Earle (E-Squared/Artemis).
The beginning of the Artemis era and a continuation of Steve Earle's edgy romance with Celtic music.

continued on the next page

El Corazón de Steve Earle *continued*

18. "Over Yonder (Jonathan's Song)"—Steve Earle (E-Squared/Artemis).
Death penalty ode "Billy Austin" sparked a correspondence with Texas inmate
Jonathan Nobles, whose 1998 execution Earle witnessed.

19. "Amerika v. 6.0"—Steve Earle (E-Squared/Artemis).
From 2002's *Jerusalem* release, Earle returns convincingly to the big-room
rock sound of *Copperhead Road*.

20. "John Walker's Blues"—Steve Earle (E-Squared/Artemis).
Steve's verboten character study of the American Taliban who twisted the
kishkas of the 24/7 cable news net-nerds.

21. "Time You Waste"—Justin Earle (E-Squared/Artemis).
The next generation. This is the final track from Steve Earle's *Just An American
Boy* live soundtrack album. Son Justin recalls the stark beauty of his father's
"Goodbye."

chapter 8

"More Red"

Revved-Up Jug Band Music
and Hums of the Lovin' Spoonful

R eleased in November 1966, could Hums of the Lovin' Spoonful be the first American roots rock classic? We think so. In February 2003 when BMG Heritage beautifully reissued the 1966 effort, Peter Buck of R.E.M. called its re-release "criminally overdue." In the evolution of American roots rock classics, Hums is a groundbreaker, predating Dylan's John Wesley Harding LP by a whole year (November 1966 to December 1967), and nearly two and a half years before "Lay Lady Lay" laid across Dylan's big brass bed on Nashville Skyline. As rootsy as Hums sounds, its staying power stems from its musicianship and influences, from Ma Rainey to Fred Neil to George Gershwin. The production by Erik Jacobsen and engineer Roy Halee is steady but adventurous. The blend and tones of the guitars—acoustic, electric, 6- and 12-string—are fat and resonant. Another pleasant surprise on the reissue is the extra tracks, which are not throw-aways, but quite extraordinary. They include a solo demo of John Sebastian performing "Darlin' Companion," plus instrumental versions of "Full Measure," "Voodoo in My Basement," and "Rain on the Roof." And, of course, there's "Summer in the City." Digitally spruced up, it's Hums' shimmering tour de force of guitars, vocals, trashcans, and traffic.

In the early '60s, aside from the small, dank clubs in places like Greenwich Village where bands struggled through their salad days and cultivated their earliest fan base, there was no underground media or FM radio to buoy the credibility of rock 'n' roll musicians. A record deal with radio airplay was your only ticket to ride. In 1965 even the hippest bands of their time—the Beatles, the Rolling Stones, Bob Dylan, the Byrds—had to secure Top 40 hits in order to be taken seriously. Free-form FM rock radio wouldn't start until April of 1967, when radio pioneer Tom Donahue launched KMPX in San Francisco. In the interim, the top bands stood at the mercy of "boss radio" programmers like Paul Drew (who controlled the powerful RKO radio chain) and Bill Drake in order to gain enough meaningful airplay to generate sales and word of mouth.

The earliest traces of Nashville influences among contemporary American and English bands surfaced in 1965. In the summer, the Beatles covered Buck Owens's country hit "Act Naturally," which appeared on the UK version of the *Help!* soundtrack. By year's end, the Rolling Stones closed out their *December's Children* LP with a crude version of Hank Snow's 1950 hit, "I'm Movin' On." Also that winter, the Byrds' *Turn! Turn! Turn!* album ventured beyond folk-rock and included a version of Porter Wagoner's "A Satisfied Mind."

Bob Dylan's 1965 album releases, *Bringing It All Back Home* and *Highway 61 Revisited,* only remotely dabbled with countrified guitar licks. When Nashville session master Charlie McCoy visited Manhattan and dropped by Columbia Records to pick up a couple of free Broadway tickets, he was handed an acoustic guitar by producer Bob Johnston and invited to play along on a new tune Dylan was cutting. In a single take, Dylan, McCoy, and a string bass player polished off the timeless, socio-politico 1960s anthem "Desolation Row."

The ascension of back-to-rural-roots rock is indeed associated with Dylan, as in 1967 he added a sensual pedal steel guitar to "I'll Be Your Baby Tonight" during the *John Wesley Harding* sessions. But a year prior, another essential album release came from a band that also nursed a long string of Top 40 hits, garnering teen appeal along the way.

In November 1966, the Lovin' Spoonful devoted their third album to chasing down vital American roots and pinching influences ranging from Bessie Smith and Robert Johnson to Tennessee pickers like Chet Atkins and indigenous jug bands like Jim Kweskin's. That album was called *Hums of the Lovin' Spoonful.*

John Sebastian, Zal Yanovsky, Steve Boone, and Joe Butler entered the studio in the summer of 1966 to begin work on *Hums*. At that juncture, the band's career already enjoyed the momentum of three bona fide hits in 1965 ("Do You Believe in Magic?," "You Didn't Have to Be So Nice," and "Daydream"), all derived from a wacky concoction of late '50s rock styles fused with homegrown Appalachian mountain music.

John Sebastian, the band's primary songwriter and front man, reflected on the band's early roots.

"In the beginning we were a cover band playing the Chuck Berry songbook and mixing it with revved-up jug band music. The Spoonful was all about combining the energy of rock 'n' roll with sped-up old jug band tunes. Also, we were exploring ideas like, what if a song like 'Heat Wave' were done in double time?"

The quartet continued on a creative tear. Even before the November 1966 release of *Hums of the Lovin' Spoonful*, the band was blessed with *two more* hit singles. "Summer in the City" had catapulted to No. 1 and stayed there for three solid weeks. By September, Sebastian and his crew scored another Top Ten hit with "Rain on the Roof" (fully titled "You and Me and Rain on the Roof").

Looking back and studying all ten songs on *Hums* shows how pop-rock bands during the mid-'60s civil rights/pre-psychedelic/pre-Summer of Love era absorbed their roots, then spat them back out onto an unsuspecting young audience. It was a simultaneous process of imitating and adulating, whether it was the music of Howlin' Wolf, Mississippi John Hurt, the Supremes, or Tim Hardin.

"The way we enjoyed our music" said Sebastian, "was through impersonation sometimes entailing mild caricature. It was an accidental process. Part was the bliss of discovery. Part was sheer imitation."

By 1966, the Lovin' Spoonful was determined to create a fully realized collection of album cuts on the scale of the Beatles' *Rubber Soul* or the Rolling Stones' *Aftermath*. Sebastian remembers the mission as not being particularly ego-driven.

"With *Hums*, we were saying to our audience, 'We're glad you like the mainstream pop stuff, but we want to show you that we don't sound like the same band all the time.'"

Like McGuinn and Hillman of the Byrds, Sebastian and Canadian guitarist Zal Yanovsky were folk accompanists. Zal was a member of the Mug-
wumps with Denny Doherty and Cass Elliot, before Denny and Cass were
in the Mamas & the Papas. Sebastian was known in New York music circles as a studio harmonica wiz. Headquartered in New York's Greenwich
Village, the Spoonful tightened their chops during an extended residency
at a local tavern.

"We were attracting teenagers to a club on West third street called the
Night Owl Café," said Sebastian. "In the early stages, the Night Owl was
a local drinking establishment that mostly drew from the Beatnik set."

Although their radio hits earned them a worldwide following, the Lovin'
Spoonful exhibited a zany image unlike many of their British or Los Angeles counterparts. The Beatles, Byrds, and Stones posed seriously on their
album covers. The Spoonful, conversely, while deadly serious about their
music, came across as screwball and slapstick. The Spoonful seemed content to pick and grin.

"By the middle to late '60s, the Beatles were the worthwhile competition.
Beyond the screaming teenagers, they set the mold for rock 'n' roll to become
more self-indulgent. We didn't have much interest in that. We wanted to be
the band you listened to, danced to, and snuggled up to. The Spoonful wasn't
about pointing inward. The songs on *Hums* were pointing outward. 'How
about those Nashville cats? YOU and me and rain on the roof. Lovin' YOU!'"

At the time, Yanovsky was accumulating many unorthodox methods of
pickings, tunings, and pickup and amplifier settings that inspired other guitar players. He did so with a pronounced irreverence.

"Zal had sarcasm to his style," Sebastian explained. "Very often he took
the mickey out of guys who would get up and posture. Zally could throw off
some incredible guitar licks, but he'd do it with his eyes crossed and make
a complete parody out of it. That was what people misunderstood about his
style, that terrific sense of self-deprecation."

The roots recognition, songwriting skill, and musicianship that perme-
ated *Hums of the Lovin' Spoonful* were anything but a joke. Although it may
have been fun laying it all down in the studio, producer Erik Jacobsen (well
known for his work with Tim Hardin and, much later, Chris Isaak) and en-

*Pegged pants and Beatle boots: The Lovin' Spoonful
appear on a television soundstage. Left to right: Steve
Boone, Zal Yanovsky, John Sebastian and Joe Butler.*

gineer Roy Halee (known for his studio work with Simon & Garfunkel) were creatively paving the road as they traveled it.

Hums was made in two conventional hit factories in New York City, Columbia and Bell Sound studios, with additional recording done in Los Angeles. As the band's material gelled, Hums (assembled 18 months before *Sgt. Pepper's Lonely Hearts Club Band*) became a rock precursor to the full-album listening experience.

"We were very conscious of that," Sebastian admitted. "As album buyers ourselves, we often bought records that had only one or two viable tunes on them, unlike LPs by folks like Little Richard, where every tune had something."

While the Beatles had their creative "Fifth Beatle" in producer George Martin (although New York DJ Murray the K was named with that distinction), Jacobsen and Halee served as the Spoonful's honorary fifth and sixth members. The band ran their new tunes through a kaleidoscopic prism of diverse influences that included Mississippi John Hurt (whose lyrics to the song "Coffee Blues" inspired the band's name), folk-rock singer Tim Hardin, and the ultimate blues guitarist, Hubert Sumlin. Erik and Roy were in charge of translating the band's nonconformist panoply of rock/jug/blues/country sound concepts to the crew-cutted crew of iron-fisted, white-coated Union studio engineers.

"We were coming in with a style that was essentially guitarists trying to imitate ragtime pianists," Sebastian noted. "How do you sound like Huey 'Piano' Smith on a guitar with a finger picking style? Or what do you do when Zally came in with this uncanny ability to combine this Elmore James howl with a Floyd Cramer piano style he transposed by using banjo techniques?"

Hums opened with "Lovin' You," a song inspired by a country blues shuffle in the style of Mississippi John Hurt. Singer/actor Bobby Darin covered "Lovin' You" in 1967 after trading in his Copacabana sharkskin suit for a Levi denim jacket. While recording *Hums*, country blues could give way at any time to country-pop imitations.

Perhaps *Hums'* most impressive gift to the Nashville country establishment was John's composition "Darlin' Companion." Not only did the tune sport authentic country licks, it was later added to the road show revue of one of country music's greatest performers, where it became the country equivalent to Sonny and Cher's "I Got You Babe."

"Johnny Cash picked up 'Darlin' Companion' after he performed it live on his *At San Quentin* record," Sebastian recalled proudly. "It became a theme piece for both him and June Carter onstage. It was very often the first tune they played when the two walked out together. For me, in terms of musical contributions, when I first heard about that, I was floored."

For inspiration, Sebastian, Yanovsky, and the band continued to experiment with the country idiom. When *Hums* was finished and released, the first single would be a humorous spoof on country pickers called "Nashville Cats."

"Zal grew up in Canada and heard more country music than I did in New York. We had already been down to Nashville and felt comfy with the musicians. But as songwriters, we were looked at as outsiders. Remember, we had long hair and this was back in 1966, during that odd time when Northerners were Northerners and Southerners were Southerners and concert promoters threw us on the road in the South with the Supremes.

"A pedal steel guitar was sitting in the studio because the instrument rental company hadn't picked it up from a previous session. I sat down and strummed the strings and pushed the foot pedals down. I messed around with it."

Sebastian and Yanovsky played the pedal steel guitar by committee. For tunes like "Rain on the Roof" and "Nashville Cats" the band didn't have the luxury of hiring a seasoned steel player. Instead, John noodled around with the basic notes while Zal added his own fills.

"Zally actually owned a guitar that had a pedal steel pickup in it. I would do all the moving tones that involved three or more strings. When we wanted to reproduce standard pedal steel licks in the songs, it was both Zally and I masquerading as this third guy."

As a hit songwriter, John Sebastian had his predecessors and contemporary influences.

"There were guys who went over the foxhole first and took the bullets for us younger guys," he said. "People like Tim Hardin and Fred Neil figured large in our tiny Greenwich Village sphere. The song 'Coconut Grove' came completely out of my friendship with Fred Neil. Coconut Grove was a district in Miami like Greenwich Village, except it was a fashionable suburb that had greenery and lots of privacy. I wrote part of that tune on Freddie's boat, feeling the motion of the waves. The mood of it is very Fred Neil, this jazzy waltz over a 12-string guitar. Zally's reverb-drenched part was so great. He co-wrote the tune with me."

Unconventional instruments gave *Hums* its unmistakable organic flavor. A slide whistle, a Jew's harp, banjo, and hootenanny-claw-strummed guitars fueled old-timey songs like "Henry Thomas" and "Bes' Friends."

"The model for "Bes' Friends" was Ma Rainey and early Bessie Smith. They would sing tunes like 'I Hate to See That Evening Sun Go Down.' If you find Bessie Smith's original version of 'Best Friends,' you'll hear it."

The live-in-the-studio edge of "Four Eyes" is a flailing, raucous mini-jam, with cruel lyrics about a gawky adolescent kid growing up wearing glasses. But on closer inspection, it's much more.

"It was Robert Johnson electrified. I had been listening to the *Delta Blues* album by Robert Johnson on tape with Johnny Hammond. John [son of the famous Columbia record executive John Hammond, Sr.] had it on his father's tape recorder and we played it over and over back in 1964, a couple years before it came out on Columbia. Johnny and I listened to it and looked at each other and said, 'Is it our imaginations, or is this the greatest thing we've ever heard?'"

Another shining aspect of *Hums of the Lovin' Spoonful* was its inherent groundbreaking production technique. Sebastian credits producer Erik Jacobsen.

"When Erik recorded Tim Hardin in 1963 or 1964, there were no road maps to guide him and it was his challenge—and eventually his success—to figure out a way to record music that was so experimental and expressive for its time.

"I remember when Zally was recording during the early stages of *Hums* and the engineers came out en masse. 'I'm sorry, Mr. Yanovsky, but the way you're playing, we're all into the red on the VU meters. This isn't going to translate well onto vinyl.' Then we'd march into the control room and it would sound great. The next day, Zally would play and they'd ask him, 'How's the sound?' and he'd answer, 'More red.'"

It was a landmark era of discovery; Jacobsen and the band were creating nontraditional sounds within restrictive two- or three-minute song structures. There were no 8-, 16-, or 32-track machines. Capturing revolutionary new sounds meant packing each track with as many unusual combinations as possible, "bouncing" instruments across to another track, and filling each track with an unpredictably compressed mishmash of odd instrumentation. Jacobsen prodded Sebastian and the band to experiment with extreme amp and guitar settings, and to figure out unusual combinations of instruments—autoharps, zithers, steel guitars, dulcimers, banjos, Wurlitzer pianos, clarinet, antique and exotic stringed instruments, and vibraphone—to fill each track.

"Within a session, Zal and I would finish a tune and quickly trade guitars. We knew the next song would put a different emphasis in different places on different instruments."

Although "Summer in the City" clocks in at just two minutes, 45 seconds, with its three separate movements, it's a masterpiece. What started off as an innocent pop tune by John's 15-year-old brother Mark became a twentieth-century pop classic in the tradition of George Gershwin's *An American in Paris* and Richard Rodgers's *Slaughter on Tenth Avenue*.

"In the beginning Mark wrote a song that was about summer in the city. You know, it's gonna get hot and the shadows of the buildings are the only shady spots. But at night, it's a different world.

"I said, 'Whoa, whoa, whoa. What chord did we just go to?' The feeling suddenly shifted. I remember at the time 'California Dreamin' by the Mamas & the Papas did that. It changed key, which made you perceive some sort of transition.

"Then Zally tried beating a trashcan on the two and four. We flew that idea before on six tunes and it hadn't worked. Too big a sound. The seventh time, it worked on 'Summer in the City' and became that huge backbeat you hear on the record.

"Writing 'Summer in the City' took a group effort," said Sebastian. "There was my brother's chorus, my overlay of the verse and the piano figure, and Steven's middle-eight section that we felt sounded like Gershwin where we added the traffic effect and the car horn. When we finished, we knew it was going to be a huge hit."

Hums of the Lovin' Spoonful was released on the Kama Sutra/MGM label and became an instant success. Today it is one of the finest rock experiments of its era. But it was to be the last important contribution from the Spoonful. After one more LP, John Sebastian left the band in 1968 to pursue a successful solo career.

Through *Hums of the Lovin' Spoonful* the group joined the "full-album" elite. They were among the very first 1960s rock bands to experiment with a wide cross-section of divergent American roots music forms. *Hums* blazed many trails on many levels, making it one of the earlier—if not the earliest—American roots-rock classics ever.

Download This!

Land of the Giants:
The Masters Who Influenced *Hums of the Lovin' Spoonful*

These songs, as well as the artists on this list, represent the key determining influences that made *Hums of the Lovin' Spoonful* such an important American roots-rock recording.

1. "Misty Roses"—Tim Hardin (Verve Forecast).
    Known for songs like "Reason to Believe" and "If I Were a Carpenter" (also a Bobby Darin cover hit), "Misty Roses" is in a class by itself, a folk-rock gem.

2. "Other Side of This Life"—Fred Neil (Capitol).
    Fred Neil, a forceful songwriter, was the dean of Greenwich Village troubadours during the early '60s. He wrote, "Everybody's Talkin'," a hit cut by Harry Nilsson, and "Candy Man" by Roy Orbison.

3. "St. Louis Blues"—Bessie Smith (Columbia).
    Bessie Smith duets with Louis Armstrong's trumpet, backed by an eerie "reed organ" on this 1925 vintage recording. "Don't you hate to see that evening sun go down?"

4. "Ma Rainey's Black Bottom"—Ma Rainey (Yazoo).
    Like Bessie Smith, Ma Rainey was another blues diva who sang with blues, jug, and jazz bands. She recorded throughout the 1920s performing such standards as "C.C. Rider."

5. "I've Been Abused"—Howlin' Wolf (Chess).
    Some fantastic singing by Howlin' Wolf and some torrid funky guitar licks by Hubert Sumlin, topped with some mighty fine harmonica by Wolf. A major influence for Sebastian and Yanovsky.

6. "Blues in the Bottle"—Jim Kweskin Jug Band (Vanguard).
    A Jim Kweskin song covered by the Spoonful appeared on Kweskin's 1967 Vanguard recording called *See Reverse Side for Title*. The lineup includes Geoff and Maria Muldaur, washtub bassist Fritz Richmond, and future religious folk cult leader Mel Lyman on harmonica.

7. "Preaching Blues"—Robert Johnson (Columbia).
This Robert Johnson classic comes from the *King of the Delta Blues Singers* album that thrilled so many young rock players. Even today, John Hammond opens his acoustic solo shows with this tune.

8. "Last Date"—Floyd Cramer (RCA).
Floyd Cramer was an old-school country pianist whose phrasings are clearly evident in Zal Yanovsky's guitar techniques. Cramer was the house pianist at RCA Studios Nashville under producer/guitarist Chet Atkins.

9. "Madison Blues"—Elmore James (Chess).
A swinging tune from Elmore James, America's consummate slide guitarist.

10. "Rockin' Pneumonia and the Boogie-Woogie Flu"—Huey "Piano" Smith (Demon).
You know you're a hot player when the instrument you play is your actual nickname. A major player in New Orleans R&B, Smith was as wacky as the Spoonful and even led a backup band called the Clowns.

11. "Richland Woman Blues"—Mississippi John Hurt (Vanguard).
Mississippi John Hurt, a dexterous, finger-picking sharecropper, was discovered and brought to prominence by the 1950s–1960s Greenwich Village folk set.

12. "Darlin' Companion"—Johnny Cash (Columbia).
The Man in Black included this Spoonful tune on his second live prison LP, *At San Quentin*. Cash the country statesman brought young deserving rock talents into closed Nashville circles. In turn, Cash's Tennessee Three twanging guitarist Luther Perkins influenced the Spoonful.

13. "Butchie's Tune"—The Lovin' Spoonful (BMG/Buddha).
Zally's glassy, Floyd Cramer-like tremolo guitar lines beautifully offset a brooding vocal by drummer Joe Butler.

chapter 9

Bernie Taupin

West Coast
Tumbleweed Connection

It was dawn in Nashville on a Sunday morning when Bernie Taupin decided to jump in his car and take a break from recording. He and Elton John were hard at work on an album called Peachtree Road, recorded not far from Elton's residence in Atlanta, Georgia. That morning, on a whim, he re-stocked his car's CD changer with fresh music and opted for a drive on the Natchez Trace Parkway, a beautiful scenic trail that extends 450 miles from Nashville, Tennessee, to Natchez, Mississippi, by way of Tupelo. Tupelo, of course, is known worldwide as the birthplace of Elvis Aaron Presley.

"The Natchez Trace is one of America's most beautiful roads," Bernie explained, "going through the epitome of what you would expect from the old South—cotton fields and back roads. The road hasn't changed much over the years. A small portion cuts through Alabama on into Mississippi.

"Driving into Tupelo, it's as if you're entering a time warp. It's Sunday and nothing's open, nobody's on the streets, and all the signs on the business doors read, 'Gone to church.' It was like being in a ghost town."

Taupin hadn't visited Elvis's birthplace since way back in the early days when Elton and the band first toured America during the early '70s.

"Even though I'd been through Tupelo years ago, I had to see Elvis's birthplace again. It's a tiny place, practically a shoebox. You can't believe four people actually lived there. But when I got there it was closed, nobody around. Not that there was much to see inside anyway."

It was a beautiful day, and on the porch of the house where Elvis was born hung an old-style porch swing.

"I was sitting on the porch swing when this mini van pulls up and an entire family pours out of the van. I know right away these people are from England. They're white-skinned and sun burnt and I'm sitting on the porch swing.

"A guy walks up, puffing. He looks at the sign on the door that reads 'Closed,' and in the broadest Northern English accent shouts out,

"'I don't fucking believe it. I've come five thousand fucking miles and it's closed.'"

A song was born that day, the second track on Peachtree Road, a tune called "Porch Swing in Tupelo."

Readers might find it puzzling to associate an Englishman like Bernie Taupin with the likes of Gram Parsons and Lucinda Williams. But Bernie and Elton's early body of work, particularly Tumbleweed Connection, Madman Across the Water, and Honky Chateau can be arguably considered sturdy American roots rock classics. Yes, the players are all British, but each album, particularly Tumbleweed Connection, resonates with songs and lyrics filled with Americana images of the frontier, cowboy gunfighters, railroad trains, rural farmhands, and Mississippi riverboats. Each track is augmented and flavored with the sounds of steel guitar, fiddles, mandolins, and other acoustic instruments. To add to the authenticity, many of Elton's piano melodies and chord progressions are reminiscent of early American protestant hymns.

While writing this book about American roots rock, we spent hours listening to Elton John's Songs from the West Coast. The songs resonated America, particularly the lone prairie and barbed-wired images of "American Triangle," a song that dealt with the 1998 murder of Matthew Shepard in Wyoming.

The lyrics of Songs from the West Coast prompted us to hook up with lyricist Bernie Taupin. We wanted to speak with him not only about his and Elton's creative process, but how American culture influenced such a long and influential string of worldwide hit songs. While the premise of this book was to feature American singers and songwriters, we felt the need to temporarily break away from that premise. Some rules are made to be broken.

As it turns out, Taupin has been an American citizen for well over 20 years. When he's not writing, he spends his time tending to his Southern California ranch, riding horses, herding cattle, hanging out with cowboys and ranch hands, and hitting the road showing his horses. During the mid- and late '90s, in addition to his work with Elton, he sang and wrote with the Farm Dogs, a band of veteran English rock 'n' roll musicians. Their album Immigrant Sons, recorded in 1998, is well worth seeking out.

"I'm very proud of the Farm Dogs," said Bernie. "We achieved exactly what we set out to do, which was to recreate the music we were raised on."

Since then, Willie Nelson has covered two Farm Dog songs, "This Face" and "Last Dam," as well as "Mendocino County Line," a duet later written with producer Matt Serletic that Willie sang with country star Lee Ann Womack. We met Taupin at an elegant hotel bar in Beverly Hills. Bernie was in a talkative mood, wearing a snazzy dark urban straw hat pulled low across his face, ragged jeans, and a loud, colorful cotton shirt. Once we reiterated the premise of our interview, Bernie was off and running.

Here are his words.

The Big House in Putney

I raised myself on music. By that I mean I found music dialing through stations on the radio. It was music that brought me to America in the first place. I longed for the historical side of America. There was musical history in America that I really needed to discover—music I grew up listening to that we tried to recreate years later by forming the Farm Dogs.

I was born in a small town in Lincolnshire in the North of England, located in the Alabama of England, so to speak, the Deep North as opposed to the Deep South. As a young child, I would come south to stay with my dad's relatives in London. They had this big house in Putney with dozens of kids, a huge phonograph, and lots of 78s. Lonnie Donegan became my first great influence. Lonnie Donegan would take Woody Guthrie, Huddie Ledbetter, and Jimmie Rodgers songs, songs like "Grand Cooley Dam" and "Muleskinner Blues," and turn them into skiffle tunes that became big hits in England. In Putney, I would dig out all those 78s of the original songs, and for hours, play them over and over again, thinking they were Lonnie Donegan songs. Through Lonnie, I discovered Woody Guthrie, Leadbelly, and Sonny Terry and Brownie McGhee. So while everybody else was listening to the Beatles, I couldn't get enough Woody Guthrie.

As a result, everything I've done musically has been an attempt at telling stories and writing on a cinematic scale. The oar that I've tried to put into the water of rock 'n' roll, if any, is that I've tried to bring the storytelling side back to pop music. If someone were to ask me what I've contributed in the canon of my work, I hope I've added a little more intelligence and story into the three-minute pop song. And for that, I credit Marty Robbins's "El Paso" and *Gunfighter Ballads and Trail Songs,* an album I wore out as a kid and an album I still play today. That was my Bible. "Big Iron" and "Running Gun" sound like mini-movies to me. Marty Robbins, Johnny Cash, and especially Johnny Horton songs like "North to Alaska," "Sink the Bismarck," and "The Battle of New Orleans." They were major epics to me.

When I was just a child, my mother read me narrative poetry like *The Rhyme of the Ancient Mariner* by Samuel Coleridge, Thomas Babbington Macaulay's *Lays of Ancient Rome,* and *Lochinvar* by Sir Walter Scott. They were amazing stories, epic poetry. Having loved those poems, by the time I heard Woody Guthrie, Johnny Horton, Johnny Cash, and Marty Robbins, something clicked. It was like someone singing epic poems, a meeting of rhythm and the written word. That's when I first started writing.

I didn't attempt those types of songs straight away. In order to get where I wanted to go, to America, and to make some success of myself, I had to emulate what was going on at the time. That was psychedelia. So the first songs that Elton and I wrote were knock off versions of things like "Lucy in the Sky with Diamonds" and "A Whiter Shade of Pale." We were writing these awful, pseudo-pop, psychedelic songs.

If you listen to the very first album we did, *Empty Sky,* it contains a lot of references to Nordic mythology and some very odd stuff. Nothing happened. Then we did the *Elton John* album, which had mythic and romantic references like "the king must die" and "sixty years on." For the most part, those songs were based on English literature and mythology.

Empty Sky and the *Elton John* album were both very English-sounding records, except for tunes like "Border Song" and "No Shoestrings on Louise."

Once we tasted success, and we knew we were on solid ground, next we did *Tumbleweed Connection* and *Madman Across the Water* back to back, which are total American-sounding records.

My whole focus in life was to get my feet on American soil. Not only was it music, but to this day, 19th-century American history has been my passion. My library at home is made up of books about America in the 1800s. I wanted to get here not just so I could be engulfed in American music, but I needed to be engulfed in American history and geography as well.

Tumbleweed Connection was written and recorded before I'd set foot in America. But I was listening to the Band, and Robbie Robertson's writing was a huge influence on me. There's no denying that the Band heavily influenced a lot of people from England. The great thing about Robbie was that his material was timeless. "King Harvest" and "The Night They Drove Old Dixie Down" may have been great, but there was also this surreal, Appalachian thing happening. The Band *looked* like a bunch of hillbillies and played really good, but every one of them sang like angels. From day one, from when I was eight years old listening to Lonnie Donegan in the big house in Putney, my passion has always been American roots music.

Songs from the West Coast

Our 1997 record, *Big Picture*, truly was a horrible album. The production was so synthetic. Everything was done by machine. Plus it was done in England. Not only did I have to be in England for God knows how long, which drove me fucking batty, but I had to sit in the studio and listen to a lot of goddamned machines all day, which was soul-destroying.

So when Elton and I planned to return to the studio in 2000 to make our next record, I was determined that it had to be much more organic and stripped down. Elton and I hadn't been apart so much as we just hadn't made a record in three years. So I went over to Europe to spend time with Elton in the South of France to think the record out.

Gold by Ryan Adams had come out. Ryan inspired Elton, which really helped the cause. It was an extra elbow nudging us to keep things simple. I also have to credit Pat Leonard who produced *Songs from the West Coast*. He did a good job keeping us on course.

The ball was in my court from the very beginning as far as subject matter. On a personal level, I'd just gotten divorced, which makes for good material, so songs like "Dark Diamond" and "I Want Love" were kind of autobiographical, while "Ballad of the Boy in the Red Shoes" was an imaginary tale about a dying ballet dancer seeing images of himself from his death bed.

The album did extremely well in Europe. "American Triangle" was one of the album's most talked-about songs. While it's supposedly about the killing of Matthew Shepard in Wyoming, I've tried not to succumb to tunnel vision when I write, meaning I don't like being nailed to one subject. I like having peripheral things happening, like for instance, in a song like "Candle in the Wind." "Candle" doesn't have to be about Marilyn Monroe. After we wrote that song, especially after it became a hit, people assumed I was this huge Marilyn Monroe fan. They sent me all kinds of memorabilia. Truth was, I've never particularly been a Marilyn fan. Rather, the whole idea of the song was about how death projects people onto different plateaus. Dying young is better than dying old. Elvis Presley, Jim Morrison, and Billy the Kid all now live in the same place.

And while "Candle in the Wind" isn't just about Marilyn Monroe, neither is "American Triangle" about one needless killing. It's about what truly lives in the hearts and minds of people. Yes, it was an American triangle, two killers and one victim, but everyone suffered all around. One person lost his life because of two people's ignorance. Two people lost their lives because of that same ignorance. What is ingrained in people stays ingrained unless someone comes along and shows us a different way. I tried to portray more than a senseless killing. It's more about what your parents teach you and that we're all accountable and that the circle never ends.

Unlike most of the critics, I didn't feel that *Songs from the West Coast* was a throwback to the so-called "classic years." A lot of reviews called it "classic Elton and Bernie." They even stamped "the classic years," literally, on our older CDs. What's classic Elton and Bernie to me is when we *write* a good song as opposed to a song we wrote 25 years ago. If you asked me for a short list of my favorite Elton and Bernie songs, not only would you possibly not know them, but also they'd probably change in a week's time.

The Process

I'm uncomfortable with the moniker of "songwriter." I don't feel like a song-writer in the traditional sense of the word. Two people sitting around a piano, their ties undone, throwing ideas around, that's a songwriter to me. Me, I ride horses, so I guess I'd rather be a cowboy.

Writing songs is not a difficult process. I'm all about titles and pieces. If I know Elton and I are going to make a record, I'll start writing long before we go near a studio. I'll collect single lines. The other day I was at a horse show and there was this funky old lady in one of the booths lying back on a Barcalounger. It was such a great picture, Grandma in her Barcalounger. That was it. A line. I wrote it down and slipped it into my pocket. All those bits go in a box, so when I feel like writing, I'll pull them out and see what goes with what.

When I write, I sit in my office in front of a huge old picture window with a big valley in front of me with that box containing the ideas I've col-lected over the months. Since I collect song titles, I have to have a title that's interesting. Or sometimes I'll totally go the other way around. For example, "I Want Love" is such a mundane title, but when you hear the song, it's not what you're expecting at all.

I write lyrics with a guitar, and I need that guitar like Linus needs his blan-ket. I can't just sit with a pad of paper because, to start with, lyrics aren't po-etry. If I was going to write poetry, and I've written poetry, I sure wouldn't use a guitar. I'll play chords. I'll sing to myself. I'll feel the rhythm of the words. Then when I have a whole bunch of stuff on a pad of paper that I can't figure out, I'll transfer it onto the word processor so I can see it.

I like how words work together. I like to feel the rhythm of words. The syn-copation of words is very important. I love putting something complex next to something really simple. I like the author Cormac McCarthy. He'll write a sentence that goes on for six lines. Then the next sentence will be really mun-dane, four words. I love putting a complex line next to something simple.

I'll submit a stack of lyrics. If Elton can't write a melody to one of my lyrics in ten minutes, it's on to the next one. Elton is all about instant grati-fication. What he writes melodically is usually right in the pocket with what

I've originally imagined. If there's a lyric that I really feel that he should stick with, or if he says, "I can't get that one," I'll sometimes say, "You really should try and go back to that one."

What Elton likes me to do is to give him points of reference. Like, "This song is Ray Charles." I was thinking in terms of "I Can't Stop Loving You," not that we're ripping off the song. It's a vibe, a feel. I'll make notes on the side. "Think Tom Petty." He really likes me to do that.

When we did *Songs from the West Coast*, Elton had a hundred sets of lyrics to work from that I had written over several years, and a lot of them were obsolete as far as I was concerned. But he took them all and we recorded about 25 tracks and whittled it down to an even dozen.

With *Peachtree Road*, we started with a lot less. I didn't have as much time, so Elton had about 30 lyrics and wrote about 18 songs. After that, we'll go through them and pull some.

Originally with *Peachtree Road*, we hadn't planned on going in and making a Southern-styled record, but the atmosphere of Atlanta overwhelmed us. Elton lives down there. We love music that's emanated from the South, whether it's Ray Charles or the Allman Brothers. There's pure country on this record where Elton's piano sounds like Floyd Cramer blended with George Jones. It's also a bit like old Leon Russell, except a little more filled out. The album is very spiritual, positive, and uplifting.

What's This Song About?

There's a legendary story about the song "Daniel" that has become Elton folklore now. Originally there was a last verse to "Daniel" that explained what the song was about. "Daniel" was a Vietnam song, about a vet coming home. But as it was recorded, the song didn't mention anything about Vietnam. But it did in the last verse, which for some reason is lost in time. We don't know where it went. It's gone.

I like to prod Elton sometimes. It might take him a while to even realize what a song is about. I agree that sometimes I'm a little cryptic. At the same time, he could ask, "What's this song about?" But he rarely does.

There was this one song that Elton does all the time onstage. I wish I could remember which one. It was written years ago, a song from way back in the seventies. Anyway, years later, one night I was standing on the side of the stage. Elton was just coming off the stage and as he passed me he said,

"You know, I just realized what that song's about."

Lonnie Done Gone

Lonnie Donegan really hasn't been given the credit he truly deserves. John Lennon once said that he started playing because of Lonnie Donegan. Lonnie influenced the Quarrymen, the skiffle group Lennon was in when he and Paul McCartney first met.

The last time I was in England, which is once in a blue moon, was when Elton and I received a British Music Award. It's a very special award, a very big deal, so we both went over because they'd assembled this huge tribute film with testimony from all these people. For me, the most important person on it was Lonnie Donegan, who said something like,

"Bernie, I haven't seen you in a long time. I hope to see you again, soon."

Besides writing lyrics for Elton John's music, Bernie Taupin's passions include American history, his California ranch, and showing horses.

He died the day after he filmed that. It was so sad. Lonnie is definitely an unsung hero. So many English people to this day, both my peers and predecessors, owe him a great debt of gratitude. Many British musicians would not have known about American roots artists had it not been for Lonnie Donegan. I wanted to write a trad-blues thing for *Peachtree Road*, so we wrote a song called "Lonnie Done Gone."

Years ago, when I first started out, someone asked me, if I could choose anyone to sing one of our songs, who would it be? My answer was, George Jones, Nina Simone, and Ray Charles. Well, I'm one for three because Elton recorded a duet of "Sorry Seems to Be the Hardest Word" with Ray Charles. It turned out to be the last song of the last session before Ray Charles died.

I consider that an honor.

Download This!

Immigrant Son Burns Down the Mission

Here's a lineup of songs that might exemplify what makes Bernie Taupin tick musically.

1. "El Paso"—Marty Robbins (Columbia).
   In 1959, radio played the full four-minute version of this Western epic. Sonny Barger trivia question: Why was the cowboy in the song hunted down and shot by the posse? Because he killed a man in a bar over a woman? Answer: No. The other guy drew first. The cowboy was killed because he stole a horse when he tried to escape. Horse thieves were considered lower than killers.

2. "Rock Island Line"—Lonnie Donegan (Pie).
   A transformed Leadbelly song that became *the* seminal skiffle hit of Great Britain in 1954.

3. "Does Your Chewing Gum Lose Its Flavour on the Bedpost Overnight?"
   —Lonnie Donegan (Pie).
   Recorded on a famous live British LP in 1957. A huge novelty North American hit, too.

4. "Foreign Windows"—Farm Dogs (Sire).
Taupin compares the antiquity of Europe with the relative modernity of the United States. Guess which region wins out? From the *Immigrant Sons* record.

5. "American Triangle"—Elton John (Rocket/Universal).
Taupin and Elton use the 1998 murder of a gay man in Wyoming to explore the far-reaching tragedy of sexual bias in America.

6. "The Hanging Tree"—Marty Robbins (Columbia).
A Johnny Cash-inspired tune that came out in 1958 as a single, but appears as a bonus track on the CD reissue of the great *Gunfighter Ballads and Trail Songs.* An archetypal campfire favorite in the tradition of film director John Ford.

7. "Ballad of the Boy in the Red Shoes"—Elton John (Rocket/Universal).
More Chekov and Dostoevsky than George Jones and Billy Sherrill, but it's a pleasant blend of tasteful acoustic instruments and masterful orchestration by Paul Buckmaster.

8. "Burn Down the Mission"—Elton John (Rocket/Universal).
The cinematic showstopper steeped in an 1800s American frontier plotline. "My wife cried as they came to take me away . . ." The melody and lyrics merge as one.

9. "Distance to the Mountain"—Farm Dogs (Sire).
The Farm Dogs were Bernie Taupin, Jim Cregan, Robin LeMesurier, Tony Brock, and Tad Wadhams—expatriated Englishmen singing and playing rock 'n' roll as American as an old Little Feat album.

10. "Ballad of Dennis Hopper and Harry Dean"—Farm Dogs (Discovery).
This is an acoustic, Sonny Terry and Brownie McGhee-ish salute to two "men's men," actors Dennis Hopper and Harry Dean Stanton. A wealth of harmonica, dobro, and strumming guitars from the Dogs' debut CD, *Last Stand in Open Country.*

11. "Big Iron"—Marty Robbins (Columbia).
Live by the iron, die by the iron. In the tradition of Louis Lamour, Robbins sings one of the finest gunfighter ballads ever written and recorded.

continued on the next page

Immigrant Son Burns Down the Mission *continued*

12. "Tiny Dancer"—Elton John (Rocket/Universal).
One of Elton and Bernie's most famous songs recently made even more famous in Cameron Crowe's classic music movie study, *Almost Famous*.

13. "This Face"—Farm Dogs (Sire).
Also cut by Willie Nelson, Taupin writes and sings an introspective ballad of a man growing old.

14. "Battle of New Orleans"—Johnny Horton (Columbia).
A spine-tingling tune from 1958 glorifying Andrew Jackson's famous battle with the British during the War of 1812. Ultimately, Yankee ingenuity wins out over British tradition.

15. "Sink the Bismarck"—Johnny Horton (Columbia).
Yet another historical Johnny Horton epic that made a huge impact on pop radio in 1960.

16. "Down by the Riverside"—Sonny Terry and Brownie McGhee (Varese).
Sonny Terry and Brownie McGhee, a premier Southern folk and blues duo, were as respected on the Greenwich Village scene as players like Josh White, Blind Boy Fuller, and Woody Guthrie.

17. "Hotel Yorba"—White Stripes (SFTRI).
This is from the *White Blood Cells* release, cut before the White Stripes signed their major label deal with Virgin. Jack and Meg White are rocking out American style, stickin' it to the man!

Love is Rock N Roll/
Rock N Roll is Hell

Picking Up the Pieces and Reassembling the Fractured Brilliance of Ryan Adams

Depending on whether you listen to his music or read the music magazines detailing his rambunctious behavior (talking shit in concert, raising tantrums after being mistaken for Bryan Adams, or falling off the stage into the orchestra pit and breaking his wrist), Ryan Adams is either the Crown Prince or Clown Prince of roots rock 'n' roll.

Some fans prefer Ryan Adams's first solo album, the beautifully understated *Heartbreaker*, made after his five-year stint (1994–1999) with Whiskeytown. *Gold*, as polished as it may sound to Adams's purist "alt.country" constituency, is an extremely impressive collection of tunes, released on September 11, 2001, the day of the Twin Towers tragedy. The crafted nature of songs like "La Cienega Just Smiled" and the confident nine-minute "Nobody Girl" places him in the big leagues alongside giants like Van Morrison and Elton John (the latter credits Ryan as an inspiration for his *Songs from the West Coast*). But it was "New York, New York" that seemed well on its way to becoming a huge, post-9/11 hit. Unfortunately, Ryan was unable to totally capitalize on the mood of the nation and on the song's strong airplay on radio, MTV, and a well-timed appearance on *Saturday Night Live*.

If Ryan Adams becomes the assured star he ought to be, *Gold* will brave the elements of cynicism and take its proper place next to such classics as

Neil Young's *After the Gold Rush* or Rod Stewart's *Gasoline Alley,* two efforts from which *Gold* seemed to have gleaned generously.

How Adams chooses to widen his potential as a singer and songwriter hinges on the next few critical releases. He's already an anachronism of sorts. He records and composes at a rapid clip, a pace far ahead of what major labels today are willing to absorb and release to the public. His fans are finicky as he stands on the precipice between being an indie darling and a mainstream player.

As satisfying as *Gold* was, it was officially followed up in 2002 by *Demolition,* a disorienting mishmash of ho-hum super demos. Adams continued on his usual songwriting spree, churning out four albums worth of material in 12 months and bouncing from studio to studio in California, Tennessee, and Sweden, using three different producers not counting himself. The first few minutes of *Demolition* sounds promising. The opening track, "Nuclear," roars out the chute with an elevated, unabashed blend of pedal steel and power chords, hard rock, and modern country blasting through verse and chorus. After "Nuclear," *Demolition* merely winds down, ultimately lacking the songwriting dexterity of *Gold.*

If rock 'n' roll songwriting is about accumulating a significant body of work, so is it about maintaining momentum and a steady vision. However, the end of 2003 and early 2004 saw three separate Ryan Adams discs released a few months apart. The *Rock N Roll* album and two EPs, *Love Is Hell* and *Love Is Hell Part 2,* became the "Great Compromise" that did just that: further compromised Ryan Adams's potential as an impact artist.

If *Demolition,* culled from several different sessions, typified a lack of focus, then the three-disc *Rock N Roll/Love Is Hell* release scheme was equally baffling and confusing. The reviews were mixed for *Rock N Roll* while the "label-rejected" *Love Is Hell* EPs ("too dark") actually garnered much better notices. Fan reaction was dazed, confused, and defused. The indie rock set seemed poised to cut him loose.

Ryan Adams's talents as a rock 'n' roller and as an introspective and cerebral stylist (two disparate reasons we like his music so much) were separated like oil and water. The rocking and the atmospheric elements were disastrously segregated.

Why? The aural gerrymandering of releasing one full CD and two EPs had all the earmarking of commerce colliding with art. Rock or roots? Four-on-the-floor pounding tracks or cerebral musings? Who said the two couldn't mix? It worked on *Gold*. After recording a collection as superb as *Gold*, hadn't Adams earned a little leeway to color outside the lines?

The ultimate irony is that the individual ingredients of all three *Rock N Roll/Love Is Hell* discs represented some of Adams's finest studio recordings. The problem lay in how the songs were released. What if the 14 *Rock N Roll* songs that sounded so reminiscent of early U2, Kurt Cobain, and Neil Young were meshed with the 15 stark, acoustic mood pieces and jangly Smiths-sounding band songs released as *Love Is Hell* and *Love Is Hell Part 2*?

Did anybody think about combining the two? If *Gold* was Ryan's *Sticky Fingers*, couldn't *Rock N Roll/Love Is Hell* be his *Exile on Main Street*?

Welcome to Roots Rock Science Lab 101. Here's how we solved our Ryan Adams conundrum. First we laid our money down and supported the artist by purchasing all three discs. Then what?

Simple technology came to the rescue, the very same technology that makes the Recording Industry Association of America (RIAA) shiver and quiver in fright. We're talking about the common CD burner that lives inside most home computers. So when one writer reviewed *Rock N Roll* and *Love Is Hell* and suggested that "all this music would have made a great double album," it set our minds to wonder: what would the music sound like in a wider context if it was combined and re-sequenced in the grand tradition of double-set albums like *Blonde on Blonde*, *Exile on Main Street*, the *White Album*, *Physical Graffiti*, or *Being There*?

We began our quest. As luck would have it, we were already writing this book. So we used these pages as a forum to give 29 songs the credibility and space they are due. Granted it shouldn't be up to the consumer to repackage or re-sequence every album, but if you think about it, sometimes being a music fan in the 21st century involves a little extra interactive elbow grease. Then again, it's fun to put on your A&R hat, experiment, and take advantage of how home technology can bend and shape the enjoyment of music.

It was time to reconsider Ryan's CDs as software and not just as vinyl substitutes. It's been the RIAA's ironclad, law enforcement-like view that those of us who still buy CDs ought not to have full rights for how we choose to use that music. Absurd devices like copy-control have been added to some commercial CDs so that the digitalized music information cannot be duplicated onto CDRs or even listened to on a computer. How arrogant is that?

Has it occurred to the corporate recording industry that consumers who buy their products might want to reconfigure the music their own way? Also, has it occurred to the label lawyers that CD burners can be used for something other than "stealing" what we've already paid for? Lastly, if CD burners are outlawed, would only outlaws have CD burners?

Rifling through our own digital disc collections, we pulled out some key points of reference. We spread them out in front of us like a cornucopia. Exhibit One, Two, Three, Four, and Five. There was Bob Dylan, photographed all blurry, one hand in his pocket on the cover of Sony's newly and gorgeously refurbished *Blonde on Blonde*. A few years back, the Beatles' *White Album* was also sleekly re-mastered back to its original form, and cleverly repackaged in a tiny cardboard cover like a mini-album, complete with the (now shrunken) posters and photographs from the 1968 original vinyl edition. Ditto *Exile on Main Street*. During the mid-'90s, Virgin Records repackaged *Exile* as a single disc housed in a miniaturized cardboard cover, looking just like its original 1972 release. Then we had Led Zeppelin's *Physical Graffiti,* housed in a deluxe hardbound cover from a complete works box set. Wilco's *Being There* represented a modern band well capable of releasing a double-set album in the spirit of the aforementioned classics. Donna Summer's *Bad Girls*? Perhaps another time.

The suspense was building in our lab. Here was one corporate consolidation that might work. Would Ryan Adams's *Rock N Roll/Love Is Hell* hold up alongside the great double sets of the past? Would the 29 songs create the necessary flow?

We had to figure out what made these other classic releases so special. Besides being huge stars of the 1960s and 1970s, what entitled acts like Dylan, the Stones, and Led Zeppelin to indulge themselves in *four* sides of music as

Ryan Adams shares an introspective moment as a member of Whiskeytown during a September 2000 gig in North Carolina.

opposed to two? The proof was entirely in the content and the segues that dictated flow.

Bob Dylan had a helluva lot to say and sing about in 1966. Producer Bob Johnston had just brought him down to Nashville. He sat alone in CBS Nashville studios, writing songs from scratch, keeping the Nashville studio musicians waiting all night, sleeping on cots, and playing ping-pong in the dayroom while he mapped out musical history. That's when *Blonde on Blonde* swelled to four sides. Fourteen songs bobbed and weaved like a graceful football running back, culminating with "Sad Eyed Lady of the Lowlands," a single-sided opus that ran even longer than Marty Robbins's "El Paso." Imagine! (Interestingly, "Sad Eyed" was the very first song Dylan cut during those sessions.)

The Rolling Stones were in the midst (thanks in small part to Gram Parsons being nearby the studio) of mixing country music with their own hybrid of rock 'n' roll and blues. The extra space on *Exile* afforded the band the opportunity to stretch out and experiment, not only with country chord changes but also with more electric blues.

Physical Graffiti was a Led Zep album that allowed the band to reproduce inside the studio the heat and energy they generated onstage. Conversely, extended tracks like "In My Time of Dying" became live staples for the band several years later.

As for *The Beatles* (or the White Album, as it came to be known), well, that was another story. The Beatles had an arsenal of material from three excellent and capable songwriters. Paul McCartney, John Lennon, and George Harrison were all arguably creating at the height of their prime. It was a wonderful plateau of A-, B-, and C-grade songs. (After all, the best double-set albums require all three ingredients.) In 1968, with three dynamic personalities bursting at the seams with fine material, there was zero chance that just two sides of vinyl could possibly contain such a creative explosion.

There were some interesting conclusions to be drawn from listening to these spectacular double-set albums. We found that these bands weren't afraid to turn on a dime in arranging the order of their songs. While a few of the song transitions could be abrupt, the arrangement is what made these extended efforts so intriguing. For example, "I Want You" into "Stuck Inside of Mobile with the Memphis Blues Again." "Sweet Virginia" into "Torn and Frayed." "The Rover" into "In My Time of Dying." "The Continuing Saga of Bungalow Bill" into "While My Guitar Gently Weeps." Trance-like jams like "I Don't Want to Talk About Jesus, I Just Want to See His Face." The more material an act had to work with, the more interesting the sequences became.

After a few test runs on the old Dell Victrola, and after a few laps around the CD burner, and after a few simple song tweaks and switcheroos, we came up with our final sequence of Ryan Adams tunes. The result was a solid, 29-song package that truly enhanced the impact of *Rock N Roll*'s rock tracks while enlarging the importance and subtlety of the softer and more delicate spaced-out songs on the *Love Is Hell* EPs. Our newly expanded edition sounded more dynamic, especially as the rockers contrasted nicely with the softer and deeper textural material.

Surprisingly, many of the songs from *Rock N Roll* dovetailed beautifully into the acoustic *Love Is Hell* songs. Plus, there were lots of quirks and surprises. What looked funky on paper sounded glorious in the air. All in all, we could hear no appreciable mismatches or gaffs.

Our experiment was a success. Renamed *Love Is Rock N Roll/Rock N Roll Is Hell,* Ryan Adams's material stands up nicely as a classic double-set album. Check out the "Download This!" below for our sequence. In the spirit of our experiment's celebrated predecessors, we've split up CD one and two into sides one, two, three, and four. We've also identified the original disc of each song—see the song legend provided.

Download This!

We found that by combining Ryan Adams's *Love Is Hell* and *Rock N Roll* sessions into a two-CD, four-sided vinyl configuration, what you get is an old-school double album in the vein of *Exile on Main Street* or the *White Album*.

Consequently, in our sequence we purposely included quite a few "train wreck" segues. For example, "So Alive" into "Luminol" into the Noel Gallagher-approved acoustic cover of Oasis's "Wonderwall" shows Adams's depth as a writer and interpreter. Conversely, the edgy intimacy of "Shadowlands" flowing into "Anybody Wanna Take Me Home" shows beautiful contrast. *Love Is Hell*'s "English Girls Approximately" into "Rock N Roll" lights up the potential of both songs. Like the songs on the 2001 *Gold* release, on our version of *Love Is Rock N Roll/Rock N Roll Is Hell*, Ryan Adams's rock songs and ballads co-exist peacefully.

Disc One: *Love Is Rock N Roll*

Side One	Side Two
1. So Alive*	**1.** Political Scientist+
2. Luminol*	**2.** Love Is Hell+
3. Wonderwall+	**3.** I See Monsters#
4. City Rain, City Streets#	**4.** English Girls Approximately#
5. This House Is Not for Sale+	**5.** Rock N Roll*
6. The Shadowlands+	**6.** The Drugs Not Working*
7. Anybody Wanna Take Me Home*	**7.** Hotel Chelsea Nights#

Song Legend: * *Rock N Roll*   + *Love Is Hell*   # *Love Is Hell Part 2*

Disc Two: *Rock N Roll Is Hell*

Side One	Side Two
1. This Is It*	**1.** Boys*
2. Wish You Were Here*	**2.** Shallow*
3. Afraid Not Scared+	**3.** Thank You Louise#
4. Do Miss America*	**4.** 1974*
5. Avalanche+	**5.** She's Lost Total Control*
6. Please Do Not Let Me Go#	**6.** World War 24+
7. Note to Self: Don't Die*	**7.** Burning Photographs*
	8. My Blue Manhattan#

Song Legend: * *Rock N Roll* + *Love Is Hell* # *Love Is Hell Part 2*

(Note: On May 11, 2004, both *Love Is Hell* EPs were re-released as a single CD with the original sequences butted up against each other, along with a bonus live version of "Anybody Wanna Take Me Home.")

There are a couple of lessons to be learned here. First, the RIAA should not assume that technology in the hands of music lovers necessarily spells doom for the recording industry and its artists. With the advent of single-track downloading and digital storage pods, how music is individually programmed will soon turn into a competitive art form. Listeners not content to randomly shuffle songs will want to arrange, store, or burn their own version of CDs or DVDs (or whatever the next delivery system is) beyond the simple concept of a multi-artist mix tape or CD. Secondly, there's the lesson that "context" is important in pop music. Packaging and sequencing can make or break a listening experience.

Sooner or later, music delivery systems will be sophisticated enough so that it will be impossible for the labels to suppress music-on-demand. The quicker and easier music is available, the faster consumers will want to play around with it. Plus, as corporate commercial radio remains conservative and tight-playlisted, and as labels continue to discount the tastes of music customers over the age of 35, a larger collection of individual songs will become more readily available online. The result? An important percentage of discriminating, trendsetting listeners will be more interactively involved with their music again. The sooner that happens, the sooner contemporary music can return to a popular culture forefront and regain its place alongside masterpieces like *Blonde on Blonde* and *Exile on Main Street*.

The Ballad of Ramblin', Gamblin' Chip Taylor

One of the basic tenets in writing novels and short stories is to include characters that possess a certain "wow" factor. Chip Taylor falls into that "wow" category. He's a songwriter of famous international hits. He's (literally) a rambling, gambling troubadour. He says what he means in a song and means what he says in a verse. He's complicated, soft-spoken, assured, smooth, driven, and is an onstage charmer. Chip has a propensity to completely master whatever it is that interests him.

He's probably best known as the composer of the timeless garage anthem, "Wild Thing," which was a smash Top 40 hit in 1966 by the British band, the Troggs. A year later, the Jimi Hendrix Experience delivered the song to the rock underground when Hendrix blazed his way through it at the Monterey Pop Festival.

Another one of Chip's hits was the cerebral, sexual ode "Angel of the Morning," recorded by Merrilee Rush in 1968 and modernized by country pop singer Juice Newton in 1981. Taylor also co-wrote "Try (Just a Little Bit Harder)," one of Janis Joplin's showstoppers, and "I Can't Let Go" by the Hollies. Other "Chip hits" include "Son of a Rotten Gambler" (recorded by Anne Murray), and "Sweet Dream Woman," cut by Waylon Jennings in 1972 during the height of the outlaw country movement.

After serving time as a productive tunesmith in the Nashville/Tin Pan Alley tradition, Chip inexplicably, but voluntarily, shelved his music career for 13 years. By the time Juice Newton had resurrected "Angel," Chip, whose real name is James Wesley Voight, was gone, headed for much stranger pastures.

We first saw Chip perform in 1993 as part of a traveling troupe of song-writers singing their wares. Along with Midge Ure, Darden Smith, Rosie Flo-res, and Don Henry, Chip strummed his guitar and recounted the tall tales that lurked behind his country and rock 'n' roll hits. At the time, Taylor was officially on the musical sidelines. But he seemed ready to come back. Three years later, he made his official re-entry with a homegrown cult classic titled The Living Room Tapes. *By 1996, Chip had fully resurrected his muse, this time as a performing singer-songwriter in the modern American roots rock genre, recording with writers like Lucinda Williams and Guy Clark, two of his close associates.*

Chip has created a new and notable singing and writing style. When he performs his songs, he'll sometimes insert those dramatic pauses—just like the ones in "Wild Thing"—or else he'll speak the lyrics in a soothing North-eastern burr. After originally making his mark with clever, catchy lyrics, his current material is grittier and much more stream of consciousness. His songs often unfold into dusty narratives filled with the names and places of actual people he's visited and met along the way.

Since his return to music, Chip has released and reissued five full-length, solo albums on his own Train Wreck label. In 2001, Chip expanded his reper-toire and hooked up with a talented young violinist named Carrie Rodriguez. The pair forged a close musical partnership after Taylor convinced Rodriguez, then only a player, to sing with him onstage. Her untrained voice sounded as naturally country and hillbilly as the Blue Ridge Mountains. He invited Car-rie to tour Texas, Europe, and the United States with him as a duo act. By 2002, Chip and Carrie released their first duet project, Let's Leave This Town. *A subsequent effort,* The Trouble with Humans, *was released in 2003.*

To fully appreciate the saga of Chip Taylor, we need to start from the very beginning. Taylor was born James Wesley Voight on the poor side of Yonkers, New York, in 1940. His father worked as a golf pro back in the days when a resident golf specialist was tantamount to being a country club servant. Yet his father was a dreamer and an inveterate storyteller around the house. He encouraged Chip and his two brothers to take chances in life. Taylor's boy-

*Chip Taylor has written huge pop and country
hits spanning five decades. He currently
co-stars on stage and CD with gifted Texas
violinist and singer Carrie Rodriguez.*

ish face, now framed in a full head of silver-gray hair, emits a wide grin at the
memory of his father.

"Dad was a real character, a frustrated actor and singer. Depending on his
mood, he carried himself around the house like Cary Grant or Bing Crosby.
At night he told us stories. He swore us to secrecy, telling us that his golf pro
job was merely a ruse. He was really an undercover FBI agent who worked
the docks spying on thieves and rumrunners."

When Chip was in grammar school, his father, who worked weekends,
convinced the school principal that Mondays were Czechoslovakian holy days
and that Chip should be let off early from school to attend religious services.
Every Monday at noon, the family car rolled up to the school entrance. Chip's
mother would have sandwiches packed and the family would escape to the
movies for double features and other daytime family activities.

All three Voight brothers went on to become high achievers. Brother Jon
is one of Hollywood's most successful actors, starring in such movies as *Midnight Cowboy*, *Deliverance*, and *Mission Impossible*. Chip's other brother,

Dr. Barry Voight, is a geosciences professor known in geological circles for his work in predicting volcano eruptions around the world, including the famous 1980 Mount St. Helens blast in Washington state.

Like his brother Barry, Chip excelled in mathematics, but scored higher marks in creative writing. He realized his artistic side as a young boy, and two major events would steer him forever toward a life of music.

"Even today I get a physical chill when I'm inspired," said Taylor. "The first time it happened was when I was eight years old and my parents took me out to a Broadway play. My brothers were away from home, and my parents had no babysitter and an extra ticket. They forced me to go to this play, *My Wild Irish Rose*. I remember sitting in the fourth row feeling really angry that I had to go.

"All of a sudden the music started and I got this inspirational chill. I couldn't believe it. I was mesmerized. During the ride home I couldn't speak. I sat in the back of the car as this chill ran through my body. I remember thinking, I was going to play music for the rest of my life."

"The big chill" soon returned when Chip heard his first dose of country music on a faraway, late-night AM radio airwave.

"My dad and mom let me stay up late at night and listen to the radio. I heard this country music station from Wheeling, West Virginia. Up until then, I had only listened to pop music.

"I sang and listened to country music all through high school. I had a ukulele. At age 14 there was a country band whose lead singer had left town. Two of my high school friends in the band told me that if I learned to play guitar by Thursday, I could be their lead singer.

"We cut demos and sent them out to all the pop labels. Everybody said no, and I thought that was it. Then my guitar player, Greg Richards, walked into King Records and played our demo for their A&R guy, Henry Glover. We had a rockabilly sound. It wasn't very good, but Henry loved the songs I'd written.

"We were signed by King Records, the same label James Brown and his Famous Flames recorded on. We were the only white artists on the label in 1956: Wes Voight and the Town and Country Brothers."

The label proposed changing the lead singer's name after Voight was deemed too difficult to pronounce.

"I had the nickname 'Chip' from my golfing days at my father's club. The pros dubbed me Chip because I was pretty good around the greens. I couldn't hit the ball half as far as they could, but I was real good at chipping and putting. So Chip became my nickname.

"The label needed a name that went with Chip, and settled on 'Taylor.' I've been Chip Taylor since 1956. Before that, my father called me Jamie. My mom called me Wes, but as soon as the record company changed, my whole family changed, too."

When Taylor graduated from high school he had a choice to make: go to college, pursue a vocation in golf, or carry on with his music.

"I really wanted to remain in the music business in New York, but instead I went off to Mobile, Alabama, to go to college and play golf. I had the King Records deal, but I was a real good junior golfer, too. Later I decided to take my shot at music. I left Mobile, headed home, and attended the University of Hartford so I could drive down to New York and make records. I had a song that got to No. 80 on the national charts called 'Here I Am,' but it went to No. 1 in Connecticut and a couple other places."

At the time, a struggling singer didn't make much money. So Chip tried his hand at songwriting. He was excited about the prospect of other artists interpreting his songs. He phoned up numerous publishers in New York without much success. He walked into a song plugger's office, guitar in hand and no appointment. He waited in the lobby for hours.

"The publisher walked out and saw me waiting. I told him I had called him ten times and that I would wait forever outside his office if I had to. After he got back from lunch, I sold him my first song, 'Just a Little Bit Later on Down the Line.' Bobby Bare recorded it. Then somebody took another of my songs to Willie Nelson, a tune called 'He Sits at My Table,' and all of a sudden I was a writer."

Chip's next big break came when Chet Atkins heard one of his songs and contacted the small-time publisher who was representing him. Atkins had no idea who Chip Taylor was, but admitted it was hard to imagine this writer being from New York. He told the stunned publisher that he wanted to hear every "country" song Chip had written.

"That's what did it for me," said Chip. "After that, every publishing company wanted to sign me up. Instead of selling each song for a $30 advance, and trying to make a hundred bucks a week, I got a job with CBS's new publishing company, April Blackwood Music. I was one of their first staff writers. For $250 a week, I could write whatever I wanted."

It was at April Blackwood that Chip composed an unusual, lustful, pop ditty that would become the next garage band theme, second only to "Louie Louie."

"April Blackwood had a deal with Dick James Music in England to send them new tunes," Taylor recalled. "I was a little embarrassed by 'Wild Thing.' I heard the demo. I had played it so seriously; I was self-conscious by its outright sexuality. I took the actual acetate demos out of the 'W' section, got up on a stool, and hid them on the top shelf so nobody could find them. But somehow they made their way to England where the Troggs heard it and cut the tune."

Chip's next hit was in 1968 when Merrilee Rush scored with his urgent love ballad called "Angel of the Morning." Like "Wild Thing," "Angel" as a Top 40 hit dabbled overtly with blatant sensuality. This time the subject implied premarital sex. Chip recollects the creative process.

"With 'Angel of the Morning,' the first line of the song took two hours to come up with. 'They'll be no strings to bind your hands, not if my love can't find your heart.'"

Then he composed his next line.

"'There'll be no need to take a stand, for it was I who chose to start.' Once those two lines hit, I thought, 'Whoa.' I was floating. And that wasn't even the hook or the chorus. I don't normally think about hooks, so that part came later.

"I'm a stream of consciousness writer. I don't think about what I'm going to write. I want to feel some magic attached to my songs, that same chill I felt seeing *My Wild Irish Rose* or my first listen to country radio. I pick up my guitar, float around, and hum some things to myself. As soon as something gives me a chill, I try to identify what it is."

Taylor wrote a solid follow-up tune for the Troggs, a pleading piece called "Any Way That You Want Me," which was also covered by the American Breed. Then he struck more gold, co-writing "Try (Just a Little Bit Harder)" with Gerry Ragovoy for Lorraine Ellison (the definitive recording of this song was later made by Janis Joplin). For the country genre, Chip composed for Anne Murray and Waylon Jennings. Dusty Springfield picked up a couple of his tunes. But as Chip continued his streak of hits on the radio, he immersed himself in another time-consuming hobby—handicapping thoroughbreds at the Belmont Racetrack out on Long Island.

"I met this acting teacher who taught in the morning and went out to the racetrack in the afternoon. He'd show a profit every year. I asked him if I could hang out with him at the racetrack. I promised to buy him coffee and keep my mouth shut. I just wanted to catch his vibe. So I cut out papers and charts for him and he started teaching me. I read the *Thoroughbred Guide to Handicapping* and was soon tabulating my own spreadsheets at night."

As Chip got the hang of the horses, he started devising his own theories and systems for picking winners; which race to focus on and what horse was due to win big.

"My winning percentage was phenomenal," said Chip. "It was freaky good. I had my music career going, but I also knew I could beat this horse racing game. So I wrote songs during the day and picked up the *New York Post* at night and worked on my spreadsheets for the next morning. I'd place one horse race bet every day. It supplemented my income. Then I made bunches of cash."

Chip knew he was on to something big when the local bookies stopped taking his bets.

"The first bookie I used was a small-time guy in Westchester. He dropped me after I won ten weeks in a row. The next bookie dropped me, too. I went to Meyer Lansky's bookie and won 53 out of the next 56 weeks. His guys brought me gifts every Christmas.

"I guess I was naïve. I didn't realize what was going on. 'George,' I asked the guy. 'Tell me. I've been playing with you guys for three years now and I've done very well. You're polite to me. You pay me on time and every Christmas you bring me a bottle of champagne. I don't understand it.'

"George looked at me and laughed. 'Do you think we're stupid, Chip? My boss is a very smart guy. We've had a thing on you since the third or fourth week. Every cent you make at the racetrack, we make ten times more. You're our biggest moneymaker!'"

Chip's unbelievable luck and sheer passion for gambling continued as he entered the bright lights and casinos of New Jersey. Chip soon became one of the gambling industry's first notorious card counters.

"A book came out called *How to Beat the Dealer*. I read it over and over until I learned how to count blackjack cards. I practiced for a week and found out I could do it really easily. I wouldn't stare at the cards as they came out. I'd sit back, nurse a drink, and count the cards until I knew exactly when to play my hand."

Chip rolled into Atlantic City winning big. At first, the casinos suspected nothing. Chip was considered just another high roller. Soon every gambling palace on the boardwalk rolled out their red carpet.

"I was an action player. I got invitations from places like Bally's and Caesar's Palace in Atlantic City. They'd give me free rooms and airfare, comp my dinners. One weekend I called this guy from the Playboy Club. He was excited to hear from me.

"'Hey, Chip! You coming down to visit us? We'll have a suite of rooms for you, dinner, and whatever you want. When you coming down?'

"Most high rollers played for about three days maximum because if they stayed any longer, they'd get killed at the blackjack tables. I told him I'd stay for two weeks.

"Back then you needed to give the casino four hours of action at fifty dollars a hand in order to be comped. I made it a point to win very little at whatever place put me up. Then I'd go across the street to another casino, count cards, and beat their brains out."

Chip's counting system went on for a couple of years until the casinos got wise, clamping down on card counters' huge scores at their tables.

"I was in Atlantic City playing at the Regency casino when somebody walked up and tapped me on the shoulder.

"'Mr. Taylor, would you please step back away from the table?'

"They read me some legal wording from a sheet of paper, 'We have deemed that you are a card counter. From now on, you are allowed to play any game of chance in the house except blackjack. Please leave the blackjack floor immediately.'

"I went over to Bally's. Within a few minutes, the same thing happened. My picture had been passed around the boardwalk and within a week's time,

I was banned from every casino except one. I showed up there with a bunch of my friends for a final 'banning' party. We played two monster rounds of cards before they banned us there, too. That was the end of it."

Chip Taylor's casino days were over just as the music side was beginning to perk up again. He recorded an album in 1972 called *Gasoline*, his first solo project, on the Buddha label. After his deal ran out with Buddha, Warner Bros. Records stepped up and made him a multi-record offer.

"I locked myself away in Boston with a band and recorded the album I always wanted to make, a country album called *Last Chance*," said Chip. "Even today, it's one of my favorite records."

Throughout the seventies, Taylor recorded three albums for Warner Bros., one for Columbia, and another one for Capitol. But like many contemporary rock and pop artists heavily influenced back then by country and folk, his music fell through the promotional and marketing cracks. Since Chip hadn't recorded in Nashville, country label reps hesitated to promote his records to country radio stations. In the final analysis, it didn't matter. Because of his undying passion betting on the horses, Chip rarely toured in support of his records anyway. He was prosperous and independent because of his hit record royalties and gambling winnings. Music drifted more and more into the background.

"Throughout the seventies," Chip recalled, "I only did a couple of tours because the gambling urge was so strong in me that I couldn't leave town. I wanted to be near the racetrack."

As his solo career wound down, so did Chip's desire for writing songs. By 1980, the big chill had dissipated, and music took a permanent back seat to handicapping the ponies. His office became racetracks like Belmont and OTB (offtrack betting) sites. Unlike his aborted blackjack action in New Jersey, OTB parlors in New York couldn't give a hoot who won or lost. They'd earn their money by taking a slice from the entire betting pool.

By the early '80s, Taylor partnered with Ernie Dahlman, known as one of the biggest moneymakers of all time in horse race betting. The two merged in 1983 and continued their association as successful gamblers until 1996.

"We had so much fun over that 13-year period," said Chip. "Every morning I couldn't wait to drive out to Long Island. The place we wagered at gave us our own room and our own replay system. We had our own private teller taking all of our bets. It was wonderful."

Rarely did anyone see Dahlman and Chip fraternizing with the regulars, drinking or consorting at the turf clubs.

"Ernie and I were loners. We didn't want to be around other people. We used scientific approaches and worked very hard to learn more about betting horses than anybody else. And we did."

During the 13 years Chip spent playing the ponies, he rarely dabbled in his music. He did, however, co-write a song in 1991 with Billy Vera, who, as a young pop singer in 1968, had cut two of Chip's tunes on Atlantic—"Country Girl, City Man" and "Storybook Children" with singer Judy Clay. Chip's luck on the track soon spread back into his music. That 1991 song with Vera became "Poppa Come Quick," which appeared on Bonnie Raitt's *Luck of the Draw* record. By 1993, Taylor had embarked on a one-shot acoustic tour of the United States with four other singer-songwriters, beginning at New York's Bottom Line. Then he returned home.

In 1995, Taylor's mother was dying of cancer. One day, instead of going to the racetrack, he picked up his guitar to spend the day singing to her. As he played her a few songs he'd written, without warning, the big chill for singing and writing songs returned.

"I had a great day, which was supposed to be for her. But it ended up being an emotional release for me," said Taylor. "I loved my mom. The music brought us closer in a way we hadn't been in a while. For the next week or so I started writing songs again in the living room. They became an album called *The Living Room Tapes*.

"A couple weeks later, I called up Ernie, my racetrack partner. 'You're not going to believe this, but I'm quitting gambling.' I had to stop. My heart was totally back into making music."

With his fresh outlook and a new batch of songs, Chip didn't know exactly how he would re-enter the music business. He checked into a new scene called Americana. It was a radio format that featured songwriters like him who held a special reverence in their music for country and folk influences. He promoted *The Living Room Tapes* in the US as best he could, but the reaction was scattered and limited. He had been out of the limelight for almost two decades. For a possible breakthrough, he looked overseas to a small European fan base. Then Chip made a savvy move that rekindled his career.

"I saw this little ad in a British music magazine that said for $300 you can send out a song on a compilation CD that reaches over 3,000 country DJs in Europe. I called the guy up. 'How much if you sent out my whole CD?' $2,000. Out went the CD. I didn't think much about it until one day a nice stack of mail came in."

The responses were magnanimous. "'Chip, it's great to have you back. We thought you'd died.' I read these wonderful reviews from all these European DJs."

Taylor's next break came when he cold-called Paul Fenn, a British booking agent, on the advice of a songwriter friend, Guy Clark. Based on the success of his promotional CD mailing, Taylor embarked on a series of live shows in Europe. He then secured overseas distribution of *The Living Room Tapes*.

Back in the United States, Guy Clark and his wife Susanna staged a listening party in Texas for *The Living Room Tapes*. It was there that Chip met Lucinda Williams, who was a big fan of his work.

"I hadn't met her before, but I loved her music. I saw her play a couple of times, so I asked her, 'What are you doing here?'

"'I wouldn't have missed this party for the world,' she told me. It was during the time when she was making some difficult decisions about *Car Wheels on a Gravel Road*. She asked me to listen to the tapes to get my opinion. Later that night, I had dinner with Lucinda.

"At dinner that night, I was awaiting word to see if my record had charted on the Gavin Americana chart. When we found out it had debuted at No. 37, it was the first time I had been on the charts in 35 years. Lu and I were so excited. She was happy for me and I was crying. Afterward, we went to her gig and she got up onstage and announced, 'Tonight I'm hanging out with the best fucking songwriter who ever lived. He's back on the charts again, and we're gonna rock this place.' We did a version of 'Wild Thing' that went on for seven minutes."

Chip Taylor was back. Word continued to spread stateside. Doors that were previously closed now popped opened. His own label, Train Wreck Records, secured distribution for his records in the US. Over the next few years and into the new millennium, Chip released a steady run of quality CDs including the delightfully low-tech double disc *The London Sessions Bootleg*.

With an impressive new body of work on his Train Wreck label, Chip teamed up with a young violinist named Carrie Rodriguez in 2001.

"Lucinda's ex-boyfriend Richard Price brought Carrie to my attention," Chip explained. "Carrie was playing fiddle down at South by Southwest. Richard brought her over to see my show at this little place I was playing. He introduced us before the show. I thought she was charming and lovely. I was hoping she was a good player. That night I was up on the stage singing all my songs to her.

"The next day I asked if she would go on tour with me, playing fiddle. I also asked her if she could sing. She said she didn't sing but she would try to sing background. So the next time we played live, I put a microphone up in front of her. We sang more and more harmonies each night. I loved the way our voices blended together.

"Carrie gets all the attention at our shows because she's so pretty. We had done some shows in Holland when we first got together. For the opening half of our show, she just played fiddle. Then we started the second half with 'Storybook Children,' the Billy Vera song I wrote. Carrie walked over to the microphone to sing lead. The whole house erupted with applause. It was so loud we had to stop the song and start again. The audience went crazy."

Chip retooled a bunch of songs for them to sing together. In 2002, the duo released *Let's Leave This Town*. A year later the chemistry gelled farther with their next record, *The Trouble with Humans*. That album hints at a complex relationship brewing between the two musicians—as close friends, perhaps as lovers—intertwined throughout the music.

"*The Trouble with Humans* has a lot to do with the relationship between Carrie and I, how it's developed and the honesty surrounding it. It's not easy, but Carrie and I have a wonderful way of digging in when things get tough. This album is a slice of what's going on between us."

Currently Chip Taylor and Carrie Rodriguez spend about ten months of each year on the road. Their remaining time is spent recording. Home for Chip these days is an apartment in midtown Manhattan. As for his gambling, like he did with his music, Chip keeps it on the back burner. He and Ernie are close friends and once a year the two put their heads together at the racetrack for a two-week binge. Ernie keeps the data updated so that when Chip sits in, he doesn't lose his shirt. But after the last race is run, Chip can't wait to return to his music—cutting tunes, playing live, writing songs, and waiting for the big chill to guide him through the next exciting phase of his ramblin', gamblin' life.

Download This!

Taylor-Made Oldies and Roots Rock

Chip Taylor's musical output is evenly divided between his hit record phase and his more organic American roots rock music, which started in 1996.

1. "All the Rain"—Chip Taylor and Carrie Rodriguez (Train Wreck).
   Chip's in his sixties, and Carrie is, uh, 38 years younger. Here's a song that confronts the volatility of their relationship. It brings up gambling, horses, and feminine stubbornness.

2. "The Healer"—Chip Taylor (Train Wreck).
   Chip likes to bring real folks into the plotlines of his tunes. This song is about a girl named Shelly he met at the Sandman Hotel in Calgary.

3. "Head First"—Chip Taylor (Train Wreck).
   That's Lucinda wailing in the background as Chip's dire lyrics remind us that when life is the pits, it *can* get worse. "Did you hear my story? Does it sound like nonsense?"

4. "Angel of the Morning"—Merrilee Rush (Bell).
   A teen ballad deals with promiscuity and premarital sex. Hard to visualize today, but imagine the awkwardness in 1968 when it played on the radio with your parents in the car.

5. "Wild Thing"—Jimi Hendrix Experience (Reprise).
   Besides being one of the greatest guitarists that ever lived, Hendrix loved to cover radio hits with his own inimitable style. Performed live at Monterey Pop.

continued on the next page

6. "Let's Leave This Town"—Chip Taylor and Carrie Rodriguez (Train Wreck).
   The title track from Chip and Carrie's first duo CD sounds like genuine Texas roots music. Mandolins, guitars, fiddle, and Carrie's twangy vocals.

7. "I Guess the Lord Must Be in New York City"—Harry Nilsson (RCA).
   Can't resist playing the Voight brother card here. This Harry Nilsson tune was written in response to Fred Neil's "Everybody's Talkin'," which eventually became the theme song for the film *Midnight Cowboy* after the use of Bob Dylan's "Lay Lady Lay" fell through. Anyway, the movie starred Chip's brother Jon Voight. Under repeated listening, Nilsson's song could have been written by Chip.

8. "Grandma's White LeBaron"—Chip Taylor (Train Wreck).
   This tune off *The Living Room Tapes* is a sentimental, Taylor-made piece from Chip's re-entry into full-time songwriting.

9. "I Can't Let Go"—The Hollies (Imperial).
   This was one of many 1960s hits for the Hollies, written by Chip and longtime songwriting partner Al Gorgoni.

10. "Country Girl, City Man (Just Across the Line)"—Billy Vera and Judy Clay (Atlantic).
    Long before Billy Vera was known for his modern soul hit "At This Moment," he and Judy Clay were perhaps the first interracial R&B duo. "Country Girl, City Man" and "Storybook People," their two hits on Atlantic, were both co-written by Taylor.

11. "Sweet Dream Woman"—Waylon Jennings (RCA).
    When country and western audiences first started grooving to outlaw country tunes like Willie and Waylon's "Good Hearted Woman," "Sweet Dream Woman" was also on the set list.

12. "Holy Shit"—Chip Taylor (Train Wreck).
    A man looks at himself in the mirror and hates what he sees. Sometimes Chip has a bleak, dark side and, holy shit, this is it.

13. "Sweet Tequila Blues"—Chip Taylor and Carrie Rodriguez (Train Wreck).
    Here's a fine rollin'-down-the-road song off Chip and Carrie's first record. A unique partnership: the resonance of Chip's voice and Carrie's soulful fiddle playing. It doesn't get much better than this.

Jackie Greene vs. the Mooks and Midriffs

If it were any time other than today, singer-songwriter/multi-instrumen-talist Jackie Greene would already be signed to a major label and hard at work on his second record. But in 2003, one of the majors rented out the Viper Room nightclub in Los Angeles in his honor, where the label's legend-ary president embraced Jackie and declared him 'part of the team.' Two weeks later, the label stopped returning Jackie's phone calls. There were ru-mors that the record label was to be dismantled, derailing Jackie's quest for a deal. Temporarily.

The timing could not have been worse for Greene's search. The music industry had been severely roughed up with significant double-digit drops in CD sales. Every stockholder-driven label conglomerate was up for play, whether through merger, joint venture, or acquisition. After deep financial cutbacks, large-scale roster reductions, and massive layoffs, no A&R person was brave enough to open his or her checkbook to take a chance. As a result, the bold artist development strategies that had signed the artists who fueled the record industry's creative/economic boom from 1965 to 1999 seemed to be on life support.

But Jackie, in his youthful vigor, pressed on with his own progress. As of this writing, the 24-year-old singer/guitarist/keyboardist is busy composing, recording CDs and a DVD, and playing cross-country gigs large and small, racking up on-road experiences musicians twice his age would envy. While the recording industry is forced to re-examine an aged business model, Jackie's future burns bright.

This chapter on newcomer Jackie Greene operates on two levels. First, it gauges how American roots rock is perceived through the eyes of a young performer born in 1980. Second, it asks a rhetorical question: what happens to a young, evolving American roots rock artist when major labels are more anxiously in search of fast bucks and tabloid-friendly pop acts?

When roots rock song stylist Rita Coolidge joined A&M Records in 1971 (and eventually delivered a string of successful LPs a few years later), she described her initial enthusiasm at being offered a deal. "A&M was the label that I wanted to be on," Coolidge said. "When I first met [A&M co-founder] Jerry Moss, he said, 'We don't bring artists in for one or two records, we're about longevity.' That gave me a lot of security, not feeling like I was gonna be tossed if I didn't have a hit right away."

The question remains, has the major label nurturing system run its course? During previous decades, labels like A&M, Warner/Reprise, and Elektra/Asylum were guided by visionaries like Herb Alpert and Jerry Moss, Mo Ostin and Lenny Waronker, Jac Holzman and David Geffen, men who patiently fostered singer-songwriters toward prosperity and wide bodies of work, creating catalogs that to this day are literally worth billions. Who is out there now rounding up the future Jackson Brownes, Bob Dylans, or Laura Nyros? The answer to that question is what young performers like Jackie Greene would like to know.

A quick visit to Jackie Greene's official homepage at www.jackie-greene.com demonstrates the depth of a young musician's roots and influences. The proof is in the online music samples. All five tunes come from his indie CD, *Gone Wanderin'*, recorded in 2002 when Greene was a mere 22-year-old lad. Each song is distinctive.

The opener, "Gone Wanderin'," is a bouncy, upbeat mixture of folk and rural blues; a knee-slapping, uptempo song with strumming acoustic guitars and Dylan-esque harmonica. The next piece, "Tell Me Mama, Tell Me Right," shifts to a grittier eight-bar blues accented with dashes of fiddle. The third tune, "Mexican Girl," is a light boogie shuffle in the spirit of the early Doobie Brothers. On the fourth piece, called "Judgment Day," Jackie moans in the hellhound tradition of rural bluesman Leadbelly. The final clip, "Travelin' Song," is an earnest acoustic ballad lamenting the rigors of living on the road, which Jackie has experienced a lot lately.

In one clean sweep, Jackie Greene embraces a full spectrum of roots rock influences. But originally, Jackie's singing voice resonated towards the sweeter side. His earliest musical aspiration was to play piano and sing, à la Billy Joel's "Piano Man."

"I started writing in high school," Jackie explained. "At first I didn't even like Dylan. Instead I played and sang Elton John ballads like 'Levon' and songs from *Tumbleweed Connection*. I wanted to write like Elton and Bernie Taupin, and perform like Paul McCartney, mainly piano stuff like 'Hey Jude' and 'Let It Be.'

"My first big problem was that I couldn't finish a song. That's been my personality since I was a child. I remember one time I wanted to design roller coasters, so I learned everything I could about roller coasters. Then I wanted to draw and design my own comic books. Then I wanted to write songs. After high school, I disciplined myself to finish tunes and then to start on new ones. It was a matter of discipline.

"I kept notebooks filled with songs I started and cool chord changes. Then I got into songwriters like Leadbelly, Hank Williams, and Bob Dylan. Their music had a little bit of everything that I liked—the blues, country music, bluegrass, folk, and rock 'n' roll. I was also partial to balls-to-the-walls rock 'n' roll."

Jackie Greene was born in Salinas, California, in 1980. He was raised in Cameron Park, a small settlement ten miles outside of Placerville near the Sierra foothills, nestled in California's Gold Country. His dad was a chiropractor, his mom a homemaker. When Jackie was nine years old, his father left the household, leaving his mother alone to raise him, two younger brothers, and a little sister.

"We lived in a small house in Cameron Park on government assistance for a while," recalled Jackie. "I didn't know it at the time. I just remember my mother being thrifty and budget conscious. We had a TV, but it broke. I had to entertain myself somehow, so I plugged in the record player and figured out how to work it. That's when I started listening to my mother and father's old vinyl record collection. Ray Charles was the first record I put on the turntable. It was one of my dad's favorites. I immediately thought Ray Charles was cool."

The next day, much to the displeasure of his mother, Jackie tacked his parents' album covers up on the wall of his bedroom. To this day he keeps the collection safe in his closet. It was from the same stack of records that a young Jackie Greene heard the indelible croon of Hank Williams.

"I was 17 when I first put on a Hank Williams record. I remember thinking how great the guy was. His songs were only two minutes long, yet he really wrapped it up, so short and perfect. Next, I realized I had already heard a lot of contemporary versions of his songs, tunes like 'I'm So Lonesome I Could Cry' and 'Your Cheatin' Heart.' That really did it for me."

Jackie Greene's love affair with American roots rock began. It also collided with the usual "mooks and midriffs" type of music his friends and classmates listened to at school.

"When I entered high school, Britney Spears and the boy bands really started taking off, music I associated with cheerleaders and popular kids. Even if my friends listened to it, that shit really turned me off."

It was through a teacher in high school that Jackie's appreciation for acoustic music blossomed.

"My foreign language teacher played fiddle in a bluegrass band," said Jackie, "and he kept acoustic instruments in his classroom. Mandolins, banjos. I was already fairly proficient on guitar. But banjo? How fucking cool was that? Mandolins were tuned differently. The teacher made me a bunch of mix tapes and introduced me to players like Doc Watson. On break, instead of going out to lunch, I'd sit in his classroom and learn how to play. I was probably the only kid in his class who showed any interest in bluegrass. Most kids thought it was hick music. But as a musician, it was music that was difficult to play, so to me it was challenging. I learned to pick out the solos.

"Thank God for Tom Gunnerman, my Spanish teacher," Jackie smiled. "The guy who introduced me to bluegrass music! He still teaches public high school. Actually, my little brothers are in his class. We're friends.

"He lives in the Northern California foothills where there's a thriving bluegrass community. He hosts picking parties, which is where I learned to

Jackie Greene, in his early twenties, extensively tours the U.S. playing folk rock acoustic guitar with harmonica, electric blues, piano ballads, and even boss organ.

flat-pick. It was 'Sink or swim, kid,' and man, those guys kicked ass. Those influences clearly show in my music today, especially when I do a lot of two-step, train-type music. Tom played fiddle on my first two records."

In addition to bluegrass and country, Greene grew interested in the blues and explored the many different styles and genres of blues the same way music fans of his parents' generation did.

"When I first listened to music before I was a teenager, the hot bands were Nirvana, Pearl Jam, and Metallica. The whole Seattle thing was exploding. I love Nirvana and Pearl Jam. In high school I also listened to classic rock. Led Zeppelin, the Beatles, the Stones, and from there I ventured backwards. I got into electric blues like Stevie Ray Vaughan, B.B. King, Freddie King, and Albert King. Then I kept moving backwards toward the acoustic stuff.

"As I got more interested in playing and writing, I learned through liner notes that a lot of the blues guys were singing the same songs. I checked my Led Zeppelin albums. Who wrote all these songs? Who the hell was Willie

Dixon? Well, Robert Johnson seemingly wrote fifty percent of them, but who the hell was he? So I bought a Robert Johnson collection. At that point, I was used to listening to modern recordings, so it was a shock."

At first, the scratchy Robert Johnson recordings from 1936 sounded strange to Jackie's young ears, but he soon recognized Johnson's essential lines, structure, and phrases from the classic rock records he enjoyed from his parents' LP stash.

After graduating high school, Jackie passed on the opportunity to advance his education by attending college. Instead, he chose to walk the high wire and become a full-time songwriter and musician. He dabbled with a backup rhythm section, sorted through his notebook of tunes, and created a set of live material.

"Since I was 18 years old, I knew this is what I needed to do," said Jackie. "My friend played the drums and I had been through several bass players. After high school I started playing coffee shops around Placerville. I performed my own songs at open mic nights. I played at one club in Citrus Heights outside Sacramento called the Time Out Tavern for a year. Every week they paid me forty bucks for four hours' work. That was cool, except they made me stand outside during breaks because I wasn't yet 21."

The life of becoming a musician seemed risky, especially to Jackie's hardworking but supportive mother. "When I decided to become a musician, my mom advised me that I should have something to fall back on. But all parents say that. I told her, 'Listen, if you want to make it in this business, you have to choose to do it or don't.' You can't have something to fall back on. If you do, you'll never lean forward and make the leap."

As Jackie struggled in clubs in and around Sacramento, by October 2001 he'd recorded a homegrown CD called *Rusty Nails*, which he sold at his live shows. Six months later, Greene met his current manager, Marty DeAnda of DIG Music. DeAnda had left a lucrative business in real estate to operate an independent label in Sacramento. The two became fast friends. DeAnda secured a few more gigs around Sacramento for Jackie's trio while he furiously wrote more new tunes. By November 2002, DIG Music had released Greene's second CD, *Gone Wanderin'*. In the studio, Jackie had the knack for cutting his tunes mostly as first takes. The *Gone Wanderin'* sessions ran smoothly and cheaply. The songs proved to be an accurate representation of how far Jackie had progressed by his twenty-first birthday.

"I had a large assortment of songs, so Marty and I just picked them out and cut them. It didn't take that long. I was writing a lot. Most of the time I'd sit in the bathroom and write because I could hear myself better and it felt like I was onstage. 'Santa Fe Girl,' 'Travelin' Song,' 'Gone Wanderin','' and 'The Ballad of Sleepy John' were breakthrough songs.

"I wrote the song 'Gone Wanderin''' while I was delivering flowers as a day job. I went out in the morning on three delivery runs—morning, lunch, and afternoon. After the morning run, instead of going back to the shop, I parked on the side of the road and wrote 'Gone Wanderin''' in the delivery van. I didn't have my guitar, but I could sing the words in my head and soon it was done."

With a quality CD of tunes under his belt, Greene scored another career coup when Marty secured the services of a prestigious West Coast booking agency. In the summer of 2003, Jackie Greene signed with Monterey Peninsula Artists. Prior to sealing the deal, Monterey grilled Jackie's management thoroughly about financial goals, artistic direction, and strategic objectives. Soon their CD distributor, City Hall Records, saw increasing sales when Jackie won a California Music Award in 2003 for his *Gone Wanderin'* CD.

With the clout of a booking agency like Monterey Peninsula (which also handles prominent artists such as Aerosmith, Bela Fleck & the Flecktones, and Chris Isaak), Greene hit the road performing regularly in music halls across the US, both as a solo act and with his trio that sill includes longtime friends and stalwart band mates bassist Hence Phillips and drummer Ben Lefever. In addition to headlining his own shows, Jackie opened up for numerous American roots rock artists including Jonny Lang, Susan Tedeschi, Huey Lewis, B.B. King, George Thorogood, Taj Mahal, Dave Alvin, the Doobie Brothers, and the Blind Boys of Alabama. One time he assembled a band and backed Bo Diddley for an appearance. Typically, Jackie will tour for weeks at a time, opening a block of shows for performers like Chicago blues legend Buddy Guy.

When Jackie shares the road with veteran acts, some of the headliners, spotting his youth and exuberance (and possibly remembering their own days starting out), will take a somewhat parental interest in his career.

"Everybody has been super cool to me. Susan Tedeschi has been the nicest person. Her entire crew is great. She invited my road manager and me to ride on her bus for their whole tour. That meant I didn't have to pay for my car rental. She fed us while her roadies set up all my gear and took it down after each show.

"During the big 2003 power blackout in the Northeast, my band played the Newport Folk Festival. Then we were supposed to fly that day from Boston to Minneapolis to open for Susan. But because of the power outage, most of the flights to the Midwest were canceled. I didn't want to be a no-show at her gig so I spent a thousand dollars to fly by myself to Minneapolis on a one-way ticket. I showed up in a taxicab right before her gig. I played the concert, but Susan paid for my plane ticket out of her own pocket.

"Another time I was on a solo tour with Susan when all of our money was missing from the hotel lockbox. My road manager either lost it or left it in the room. Anyway, we lost three thousand dollars and she gave us that money. Susan just handed me over the cash. I was speechless. It's not like she's super rich. It's because she and her management team really care. Plus, every night she called me up onstage to play harmonica."

Jackie is accustomed to the lonely life of touring solo on the concert circuit, playing the difficult role as an acoustic opener. The advantage is that he can perform to a much larger audience than he customarily draws at the nightclubs where he headlines. But at every tour stop, Jackie must prove himself over and over again, often before acts he's worshipped as a young fan.

"I was so damned nervous opening up for B.B. King," Jackie confessed. "I was by myself in Louisville, Kentucky, at a 3,000-seater venue called the Palace, which is a pretty big place for me. I don't let myself get nervous before a show up until about 30 minutes before I hit the stage.

"After the show, Mr. King called me into his bus. I had a little sit-down with the man. He was very nice. He saw me without my coat. It was cold outside and he said, 'Put on your coat.' He warned me, 'You're going to catch a cold and you won't be able to sing.' Yes, sir."

Being an unsigned act on the road, far from home with no tour support, is no picnic for a struggling young artist.

"I can tell you it's tough, but it's also lots of fun. Fortunately," Jackie noted, "I like to travel. Being young, it's an eye-opener. I have my responsibilities back home. Pay the rent for the apartment. Learn to budget myself. The first couple of times I was out on the road, when I went to New York City, I spent all kinds of money. I bought clothes. I went to Nashville and bought more stuff there. Then I learned not to piss money away on the road on stupid shit."

With an eager manager and agents dispensing him across the country at a moment's notice, Greene has little time to fraternize with friends his own age at home. Between the touring, writing, and recording, developing his artistry is an all-consuming process.

"It is a job for me, same as everybody else," admitted Greene, "but it's a fun job. I'm a stranger in a strange town with no corporate label backing behind me. Truthfully, it can get aggravating. You have to find things for yourself; you're at the mercy of where you are. But mostly I've been lucky because the tours I've been on are with larger-name acts. Their shows are catered, so food is there, plus everybody shares."

The ritual of being the opening act can be a cruel baptism by fire. But, with Jackie's roots-oriented style, and with the headliners' crowds being on the sophisticated side, audiences are pleasantly surprised.

"Crowds don't pay attention to opening acts," said Jackie. "So my job is to make them listen. The trick is to be absolutely fearless. Do the best you can. I start off with a kicker. I give it everything I got. At the end, I really tear it up. Nine times out of ten I'll have gotten a standing ovation or at least an encore. It's pretty fucking scary to go out there all by yourself. Often times you don't have shit to hide behind or fall back on. No band, nothing. If you're playing at a venue like the Fillmore Auditorium in San Francisco and everybody is standing, a crowd can get a bit fidgety. In a theater setting it's easier to get across when people are comfortable sitting down. They're quiet and they'll pay closer attention."

Jackie often imagines what it was like in, say, 1964, when a young Bob Dylan doing the same thing, strolled out onstage armed only with a Martin guitar, a harmonica brace, and a couple of blues harps.

"When I walk out there, I'm nervous up until I at least get some response from the audience after a couple songs. If I don't get anything, I stick to it. It's like wrestling. You're out there, just two people, nervous. When that whistle blows, you start going at it, and it's balls to the wall. You don't pay attention to anything else. You do what you gotta do.

"To be by yourself onstage, you have to maintain a ballsy attitude. It's almost as if you have to pretend you're *better* than the crowd. 'I have something to say and you had better listen.' Lately, I'm more relaxed. For instance, I'm better at talking to the crowd. When I first started, I was hunched over and uptight. Now I've made progress and my body language has loosened up."

Watching Greene onstage, you notice his waifish appearance and youthful determination. He hides behind a thick, dark pair of sunglasses with his tussled early 1960s Dylan haircut. The girls dig him while their boyfriends find him nonthreatening. After the first couple tunes, the crowd realizes Jackie is no poser.

"I think because I'm young, younger people like my songs," said Greene. "Also, older people can relate to my style of roots music. It's a blessing. I see all ages in the audience, from five to 50 and everybody in between. One little six-year-old walked up to me after a show and described my music as 'farmy.' That was a great description.

"The Bob Dylan comparisons come because that's a lot of people's frame of reference. They don't know anybody else who plays harmonica in a rack. It's either Bob Dylan or Neil Young. They don't think about Jimmy Reed or John Hammond. There's a lot of other people.

"I love Bob Dylan and I don't mind the comparisons all that much. I know they say it's a curse, but I really don't care, because at one point, Bruce Springsteen was the new Bob Dylan and Bob Dylan was the new Woody Guthrie. You build your own house."

By remaining unsigned and playing loads of live shows, Jackie has the luxury to road test a lot of new material. He's devised conventional and unconventional methods in which to experiment and enhance his creative factor when writing.

"Beck said something really smart," Jackie observed. "He said that nowadays anybody can make a CD that sounds good in terms of studio quality just by using Pro Tools and all that available stuff. What matters now are the songs. It's come full circle since Hank. It used to be difficult and expensive to make music that sounded professional. Now any jackass with four hundred bucks and a CD burner can have a fairly decent studio sound. But *songs* are coming back around."

It's hard to believe there's such a thing as a "born songwriter," even with a talent as young as Jackie.

"I don't think people are born good writers or songwriters," Jackie agreed. "Everybody learns his or her own way. Every song I've written has been different in some respect. I don't necessarily write the music first; I don't always do the words first. Sometimes they both come around exactly the same time. Perhaps I'll have something going on with the music that I can't quite put words to for an entire year. Sometimes it's the other way around. Sometimes you write a song where the words don't work, so you put them aside and use them someplace else."

For Jackie, it's all about mixing and matching, and waiting for the happy accidents to occur.

"Sometimes if I'm working on more than one song, I'll switch lyrics. I'll graft lyrics from one song onto another or cut up the lyrics. Sometimes I'll do something technical and nerdy, like change the chord progression to exactly the negative. For instance, if it's a G-major, I'll make it a G-minor, just to fuck with it. Most times that doesn't work, but you *can* come up with some cool progressions. G-major, A-minor, and D-major becomes G-minor, A-major, D-minor. I'll take a song and give it a different time signature. I'll sing it as a waltz. I'll sing it in straight time. Tempo changes are easy to mess with."

Often it's down to simple tweaking, switching, and trying on different combinations.

"My favorite thing to do is relearn a song on a different instrument. If I wrote it on the piano, then I'll change over to guitar or organ. It helps to expand the possibilities of the song, especially when you go into the studio. You have a clearer idea of what kind of instruments should go where."

Sitting in his small Sacramento apartment while off the road, Jackie stubbed out a cigarette and popped a CD into the changer—the rough mixes of two brand-new tunes.

One song is called "Alice on the Rooftop," the other is "Miss Madeline (Three Ways to Love Her)." Coincidentally, Jackie noted, they're both waltzes. He penned "Alice" one night during the wee hours, unable to sleep. Since it's a rough mix, there's a whining Hammond organ way in the background, a line one might recall Al Kooper playing on Dylan's *Highway 61 Revisited*. The song is about a girl contemplating suicide. She stands on the edge of a rooftop, but chooses not to jump. The song is ultimately uplifting, but there's a darkness cast over the mood. It brings to mind Jackie's analogy of not having anything but his music to fall back on.

"Miss Madeline" is a dirgelike poem. Tipping-off his affection for the Beatles, the song swells into a dramatic buildup with a chord structure that suggests an oblique homage to "She's So Heavy" from the *Abbey Road* album. Miss Madeline, the song's protagonist, is "on the game"—a streetwalker, a common hooker. Rather than judging or condemning her, Jackie gives his character a voice, a point of view in the song.

"I'm drawn towards extremes—sad stories and joyous topics," Jackie explained. "Somewhere in the middle lies real life. Plus, I'm getting better at not being so self-conscious about sexuality. I recently wrote a song that's both sexy and whimsical. I know I'm a very young writer, but I'm discovering new things."

On closer inspection, perhaps Jackie's working-class characters recall the tough plight he and his mother faced when she scrimped and sacrificed raising four children. Jackie shakes his head in sadness.

"She rarely did anything for herself. She didn't buy anything for herself. She didn't have a boyfriend, no social life. She was too busy raising us kids. That image of a single mother . . ." he paused. "If you examine a lot of my songs, they do have that single-mother-against-the-world theme."

Jackie stubbed out his smoke and rolled up the sleeve of his shirt.

"I have a tattoo on my right forearm. The Virgin Mary. It's nothing religious, just a mother-and-child symbol, a touchy subject I guess because I've lived through it. I didn't realize at the time how fucking hard it was for my mother, and frankly, I don't see how she did it."

Inspired by prolific artists like Ryan Adams and Steve Earle, Greene feels the need to record as often and as quickly as possible, gauging his progress as he physically matures.

Besides enhancing his proficiency as a songwriter, Jackie is anxious to pursue his multi-instrumental skills. Onstage with his trio, he's a dynamic and forceful blues-based guitarist in the vein of Stevie Ray Vaughan. Or Tom Petty. Or Bob Dylan. He also plays organ with a decidedly jazzy flavor, in the spirit of Jimmy Smith or Charles Earland. Even as he relaxed in his apartment, Jackie sat perched behind a small portable organ and belted out funky phrases that would make Jimmy McGriff or Joey DeFrancesco grin. Jackie loves playing organ. It brings out his funky side.

The kid's goals are realistic. He wants to put out one album a year, and garner enough material for a second. Subsequently, while opening for larger concerts, as he generates more and more fans across the States, Jackie plans to set up his own mini headline-tours.

"The scary part is becoming the headliner," he revealed. "It's one thing opening for 45 minutes in front of a crowd of 3,000. It's another playing 90 minutes for a crowd who pays to see you. Seattle and Portland are warming up to me. I recently played Slim's in San Francisco as a headliner. It was packed to the walls. Then across town, the Great American Music Hall immediately followed up with an offer."

With a solid work ethic in place, Jackie is neither waiting around nor is he stuck at the crossroads. Like the song "Gone Wanderin'" says, Jackie is movin' on. As technology progresses, and as the business model for record labels shifts, anything can happen in the coming months or years. Jackie, however, knows one thing for certain.

"I'm going to make music for the rest of my life, whether I'm on a label or whether I'm just making my own records. I realized a long time ago I'd be creating songs for a living."

While major labels spin their wheels in "definite maybe" mode regarding Jackie Greene's future, the plucky unsigned talent soldiers on. He has already recorded 13 new songs, with 20 more titles knocking at the studio door. His manager sifts through offers from smaller, more independent labels. Both collectively ponder the next best moves. What new elements can be brought to the table in order to maintain momentum? He's just released *Broken Hearts, Dusty Roads*, a live DVD containing electric, acoustic, and piano performances.

"I'm trying not to get too caught up in it all. When you start doing that, you start questioning everything you believe in and stand for. There's an old mafia saying: 'Nothing hurts as bad as you think it's going to.' So I say fuck it, let's just do it."

Download This!

Music from the Vinyl Collection in the Closet

We asked 24-year-old Jackie Greene to list his favorite and most influential songs. The list started at ten then ballooned to 20 more. Much like his (parents') closeted vinyl record collection, the list (in no particular order) is a delightful assortment.

1. "Tom Traubert's Blues (Four Sheets to the Wind in Copenhagen)"—Tom Waits (Asylum)

2. "Visions of Johanna"—Bob Dylan (Columbia)

3. "Dead Flowers"—The Rolling Stones (Virgin)

4. "The Weight"—The Band (Capitol)

5. "Red Right Hand"—Nick Cave (Mute)

6. "Goodnight Irene"—Leadbelly (Palm Pictures)

7. "Devil Got My Woman"—Skip James (Shanachie)

8. "Got My Mojo Workin'"—Muddy Waters (Chess)

9. "(I Heard That) Lonesome Whistle"—Hank Williams (Mercury)

10. "Hey, That's No Way to Say Goodbye"—Leonard Cohen (Columbia)

11. "Brass Buttons"—Gram Parsons (Reprise)

12. "Going, Going, Gone"—Bob Dylan (Columbia)

13. "Christmas Card from a Hooker in Minneapolis"—Tom Waits (Asylum)

14. "Folsom Prison Blues"—Johnny Cash (Columbia)

15. "1913 Massacre"—Woody Guthrie (Smithsonian Folkways)

16. "Alice's Restaurant"—Arlo Guthrie (Warner Bros.)

17. "Highway Patrolman"—Bruce Springsteen (Columbia)

18. "Atlantic City"—Bruce Springsteen (Columbia)

19. "To Ramona"—Bob Dylan (Columbia)

20. "Amazing Grace"—Mahalia Jackson (Columbia)

21. "What'd I Say"—Ray Charles (Atlantic)

22. "Daughter"—Pearl Jam (Epic)

23. "Come As You Are"—Nirvana (DGC)

24. "Back on My Feet Again"—Randy Newman (Reprise)

25. "Maybellene"—Chuck Berry (Chess)

26. "Mercy, Mercy Me"—Marvin Gaye (Tamla/Motown)

27. "Homeward Bound"—Simon & Garfunkel (Columbia)

28. "Mama Tried"—Merle Haggard (Capitol)

29. "In the Good Old Days (When Times Were Bad)"—Dolly Parton (RCA)

30. "Don't Forget About Me"—Dusty Springfield (Atlantic)

chapter 13

Is "The Country"
Ready for Neko Case?

T he mysterious imagery woven through "Deep Red Bells," a penetrating Neko Case ballad, shows the singer's flair for the bold and unconventional. On the surface, it's pure twang, a fairly blue-sounding, modern country-rock ballad bolstered by a wall of electric rhythm guitars. The backup band sits tight in the pocket. The muffled upright bass thumps out a mild rolling bassline next to a rockabilly-style snare drum. A Duane Eddy "Forty Miles of Bad Road" kind of twangy lead guitar hovers over the arrangement. A haze of reverb blankets Neko's vocal, and the chorus punctuates a roadhouse pedal steel situated in the outer reaches of the mix.

"Deep Red Bells" depicts a mean, cold world. The song conjures a creepy setting of dark, desolate side roads and unsettling suspense—the same perverse intrigue director David Lynch used in Blue Velvet and Twin Peaks.

In fact, there is something disconcerting about Neko's song. Her lyrics document a chilling period in the recent history of the Northwest. But instead of finding a severed ear in the grass like in Blue Velvet, the city of Tacoma, Washington, faced a far more serious nemesis.

In the 1980s, a killer cruised the main drags of Tacoma and murdered 49 women, most of whom were alleged prostitutes and drifters. The "Green River Killer" roamed the road in a beat-up, green pickup truck. He strangled his victims, and their decomposed bodies were later discovered on remote Northwestern roadsides.

The murderer remained at large for two decades. As a teenager growing up in the Tacoma area, Neko Case walked to high school in the early morning on the same roadways where the killings took place. She carried a steak knife for protection.

In 1991, the Green River Task Force was whittled down to one lone investigator. To women's rights activists in the Northwest, the victims, mostly runaway girls soliciting sex acts on the main streets outside Tacoma, became faceless crime statistics.

In 2001, while sitting in an Arizona studio cutting her third album, *Blacklisted,* Case heard the news that Gary Leon Ridgway was arrested as the Green River Killer. Three days into the sessions, deeply distressed, she penned "Deep Red Bells." She wondered aloud: How could a monster like Ridgway get all the heavy media attention when so many women were murdered and forgotten? Why did it take 15 years to arrest a serial killer?

The song uses some poignant images. A bloodied handprint on a windshield resembles motor oil more than human blood. The murderer takes the time to fold up the victims' clothes. The lost spirits of the dead women roam the interstate while red bells toll like thunder. As if to memorialize the victims, Case intersperses images of her own childhood reminiscences—Popsicles, the smell of motor oil, and her blue-collar family—with all the disturbing metaphors of murder and violence.

"When I was a kid," she told the *Ottawa Citizen,* "we had broken-down cars in the yard. My dad was always working on them. He smelled like engine oil. We were very poor and that was [our] entertainment, to have Popsicles [in the summer]. So engine oil and Popsicles became one and the same for me."

For a thirty-something singer raised on punk rock who played drums in all-girl, independent bands, becoming a "country noir" singer was the most unlikely route out of the cynical world of Northwest grunge rock.

Born in Virginia, Case and her family rambled a while before settling in the Tacoma area where she was raised. At age 15 she ran away from home to join the Northwest punk scene as a drummer, where she beat the skins behind more than a few garage bands. In 1994, she migrated north to Vancouver, British Columbia, to attend art college where she played in an all-girl punk trio called Maow. As a neophyte musician, Neko found that punk soon played itself out as a viable outlet for her anger and aggression.

"In the early '80s, punk rock got really bad and super-macho and politically misdirected," Case told the *Arizona Daily Star*. "I wasn't really hearing any voices I could relate to as a girl. It just made sense to seek other things out. I found out that this other music was a lot more powerful than what I was listening to at the time."

That "other music" turned out to be pure roots country. As a girl, Case grew up listening to country and western with her grandparents.

"My grandmother was really into it," she said. "Jim Reeves was one of her big favorites along with Patsy Cline and Loretta Lynn and all the greats."

Neko soon discovered her passion for singing country, and in 1997, while an art student in Canada, released her debut record, *The Virginian*. In 1998, after her Canadian student visa ran out, Case returned to Washington, and by 2000, her commitment to playing unadulterated country deepened with

Neko Case, who comes from the punk side of the street, can belt out a vocal inspired by Tammy or Loretta.

Furnace Room Lullaby, released on Bloodshot, an independent label in Chicago. Case's gutsy singing style drew comparisons to the old masters, most notably Patsy Cline, Wanda Jackson, and, of course, the Coal Miner's Daughter herself, Loretta Lynn.

Case's dynamic vocal style is also reminiscent of the early Linda Ronstadt recordings, particularly her first two solo discs on Capitol—1969's *Hand Sown, Home Grown* and *Silk Purse* from 1970. Coincidentally, Case's *Blacklisted* was cut in Tuscon, Arizona, the same town where Ronstadt grew up singing as a teenager.

Neko's spirit draws from the more feisty female country singers of the '60s and '70s, when hitmakers like Loretta Lynn and Dolly Parton, both raised in poverty, were tough-minded, clear-sighted role models for modern ladies. Dolly's and Loretta's songs upheld morality and faithfulness; they challenged the "other women" who flirted openly with weak-willed husbands and wandering-eyed boyfriends. While Neko has avoided writing straight "cheating songs," Dolly and Loretta resound as inspirational influences.

"I never put much stock in role models until I realized that as a kid, if there wasn't Loretta Lynn and Dolly Parton, well, there wouldn't have been many women in the music industry for me to look up to."

Not being from the South has worked in Case's favor as she belts out melodies minus a clichéd country drawl. Rather, her confident rendering of her brand of country has left many critics genuinely impressed. Although her music is laced with modern independent rock influences, she's a welcome alternative to the pop currently canned and manufactured in Nashville under the guise of "new country."

Neko considers her booming voice an unpolished tool ("I get by on sheer loudness"), yet she has gained a growing, loyal following throughout the United States, Canada, and beyond. *The New York Times* and *Newsweek* have both written enthusiastically about her, and London DJ John Peel has featured her music prominently on his BBC radio show.

Through it all, Case refuses to shy away from her working-class upbringing as well as her love for both punk and country music. "They sound different, but they both have that same spirit. Country and punk rock comes from a place of poverty and dissatisfaction," she explained to the *Calgary Herald.* "It's passionate, dissatisfied music. Sometimes [punk and country] is the only thing that makes you feel like you're not under the boot heel of the world, or the government."

It wasn't until around 1999 that Case decided to eek out a living as a gigging musician. Today she tours with her backup band, a capable Toronto quartet called the Sadies. She spends large blocks of time traveling and playing live, and is in the studio recording on a regular basis. *Blacklisted*, released in 2002, gained her the most respect and kudos. In April 2004, while on tour, she recorded two nights in concert with the Sadies for a live record to be released sometime in late 2004.

It would be folly to believe at this stage that Neko Case would submit to becoming a malleable Nashville songbird pinned to a major label.

"I don't know if there's a deal out there for me," Case confessed to *Newsweek*. "Music is not supposed to be some mathematically formatted sound that is supposed to appeal to a certain demographic. It's what comforts people. That's what happened long ago with the great songwriters that I admired; their songs were timeless and not overly specific, but they're very empathetic. The major [labels] are having a hard time right now, but maybe they'll diversify. Perhaps there's room for someone like me and Faith Hill at the same time."

While major labels have approached Case about possibly signing a deal, the problem with aligning with a conglomerate is the fine lines of a record contract's boilerplate.

"I would've considered signing—and still would—if it were a fair deal," Neko revealed to the *Seattle Weekly*. "But the standard record contract is not a fair deal, and I don't want any part of it. I'm not willing to spend a year of my life touring to promote an album and recoup the album's costs with my royalties, only to find that I don't even own my own masters. That is totally insane! How were people ever convinced that was a good idea?"

In the meantime, Case has chosen her way—the highway—as the best means to advance her career. As word of mouth snowballs and radio sits idly on the sidelines watching, she continues to gain gradual momentum mostly through press and by expanding her current recorded body of work.

"A major label can get you things, or buy you things, but wouldn't you rather earn them yourself? Don't they feel more real or permanent that way?

I could sit around being sad that my music doesn't get played on mainstream radio, or I can look at it like I get to make exactly the music I want. I can play in an intimate setting and see the faces of my audience and talk to them after the show. That's enough for me."

The mere mention of the term "alt.country" sets her off. It's a term that haunts such acts as Wilco and Jay Farrar like a bad toothache.

Case explained to the *Calgary Herald* back in 2000: "Every time I'm interviewed, people ask me, 'What's up with alt.country?' and 'How come new country is such a problem?' I don't know. I don't care. You don't need to ghettoize something you love by calling it alt.country or insurgent country. I play country music. That's what it was called when I was growing up and that's what I play."

Four years later, Case is straight up about the music she champions: pure country. "I have nothing but the utmost respect for country music. I think it should be regarded as highly as jazz and blues as far as our cultural heritage goes. That's why the new country stations are the worst, because they discredit old country in order to get new listeners. It makes me so angry. You don't know how angry it makes me. To say old country is hick and lame is insulting."

With each record, Neko's songwriting improves exponentially, particularly with stylized tunes like "Deep Red Bells" and "Stinging Velvet" from *Blacklisted* or "Porchlight" from *Furnace Room Lullaby*.

But don't expect Case to become the next prepackaged Nashville diva, although stranger things have happened. Regardless of whether or not a large label is intuitive enough to sign her, she'll continue on, in her own brash and unconventional manner, doing stuff like recording EPs in her kitchen, touring the world with Nick Cave and the Bad Seeds, or continuing her association with Canadian group the New Pornographers. Until that glorious day comes, when fame catches up to her writing and singing skills, Neko Case can continue to aspire to the day when she takes her place next to the likes of Lucinda Williams, Emmylou Harris, Linda Ronstadt, Dolly Parton, and Tammy Wynette, under the unwavering and everlasting spell of Hank.

Download This!

Making a Case for Neko

Here's a mixture of Neko's best material, interplayed with songs by a few of her counterparts.

1. "Deep Red Bells"—Neko Case (Bloodshot).
   A roots rock classic, replete with mystery and twang.

2. "Stinging Velvet"—Neko Case (Bloodshot).
   Another quality track from *Blacklisted* with a pronounced honky tonk feel.

3. "Mood To Burn Bridges"—Neko Case & Her Boyfriends (Bloodshot).
   Flashes of early Lone Justice and Maria McKee? When the White Stripes' Jack Black produces Loretta Lynn at age 70, that's proof positive that country singers and indie rockers aren't such strange bedfellows.

4. "Lovesick Blues"—Linda Ronstadt (Capitol).
   When Linda Ronstadt arrived as a solo artist, she was an attractive brunette with a come-hither smile, clad in cut-off denim shorts. Compared to what the Byrds had endured at the Opry, when Linda sang traditional country like Hank's "Lovesick Blues," she faced no controversy.

5. "No Need To Cry"—Neko Case & Her Boyfriends (Bloodshot).
   This slow, sauntering, live-in-the-studio piece recalls Patsy Cline's "Walkin' after Midnight."

6. "Mass Romantic"—New Pornographers (Mint).
   Case hooks up with Canada's New Pornographers. This is the first track from the New Porn's first CD, which sold impressively in North America and earned a Canadian Juno award.

7. "Thrice All American"—Neko Case & Her Boyfriends (Bloodshot).
   An autobiographical ballad about the "rural" life, not in Oklahoma or Louisiana, but in working-class Tacoma. In spite of urban blight, guns, gangs, and crime, it's a place to be proud of.

8. "Still Time"—Ron Sexsmith (Interscope).
   Recorded in 1999 on a record called *Whereabouts*. Ron Sexsmith, a musical comrade of Neko's, hails from the Toronto scene. His most admirable personal trait is that he's an avid Gordon Lightfoot fan.

continued on the next page

Making a Case for Neko *continued*

9. "South Tacoma Way"—Neko Case & Her Boyfriends (Bloodshot).
    Neko returns to Tacoma to a friend's funeral. It's more of a slow rock ballad
    than the usual driving country stuff.

10. "Heavy Metal Drummer"—Wilco (Nonesuch).
    Jeff Tweedy pens a sweet reminiscence about the innocent, adolescent
    days of watching heavy metal bands and playing Kiss covers in stoned-out
    garage bands.

11. "Bowling Green"—Neko Case & Her Boyfriends (Bloodshot).
    On this 1997 solo debut, Case covers artists like Loretta Lynn. "Bowling
    Green," a duet with Carl Newman from the New Pornographers, is a spirited
    version of a minor 1967 Everly Brothers hit.

12. "Things That Scare Me"—Neko Case (Bloodshot).
    Blacklisted is a moody work. This opening song is an acoustic, Appalachian-
    style ballad. In her songs, Case's world is often a troubled, haunting place.

13. "All for Swinging You Around"—New Pornographers (Matador).
    Neko shows her power pop indie side. From the 2003 *Electric Version* release.

14. "Runnin' Out of Fools"—Neko Case (Bloodshot).
    A bluesy song that demonstrates Neko's tremendous vocal range.

15. "Feel Free"—Jay Farrar (Artemis).
    The Primitives begat Uncle Tupelo, which splintered into Son Volt (led by
    Jay Farrar) and Wilco (led by Jeff Tweedy). After Son Volt, Farrar became a
    spotlight shy solo act. This tune is from his 2001 solo debut, *Sebastopol*.

chapter 14

The Flatlanders
Flat-Out Love Texas

T he January 2004 release of the Flatlanders' Wheels of Fortune signifies to American roots rock fans more than just another high-quality collaboration by Joe Ely, Butch Hancock, and Jimmie Dale Gilmore, the three finest singer-songwriters to come from Lubbock since "Mr. True Love Ways" himself, Buddy Holly. It means that the ego-less triumvirate from West Texas will continue to appear onstage and in the studio as the Flatlanders for the foreseeable future. And that's good news.

In 1972 Ely, Hancock, and Gilmore completed their first LP together under the Flatlanders banner. But because of a contractual legal snafu—which also kept Jimmie Dale from signing another record deal for the next few years—the actual sessions didn't appear on vinyl until 1980 (and as a British import at that) and on CD in 1990. Several of their finest compositions were held prisoner because of that cursed debut, including Gilmore's "Dallas" and "Tonight I Think I'm Gonna Go Downtown."

In 1998, when director/actor Robert Redford contacted Ely to provide music for his film The Horse Whisperer, Joe called on Butch and Jimmie Dale and reconvened the Flatlanders in the studio. They wrote three songs in two days, and the keeper on the soundtrack was a tune called "South Wind of Summer," which also appeared on a full-fledged 2002 reunion album titled Now Again on the New West label. Because those sessions and a subsequent tour went so swimmingly, everybody decided to increase their commitment and produce another record, Wheels of Fortune, for New West in 2004.

After a 30-year gap (1972–2002) between
recordings, the beloved Flatlanders reunite three
premier Lone Star songsters. Left to right: Joe Ely,
Butch Hancock, and Jimmie Dale Gilmore.

As discussed in a previous chapter, the vast importance West Texas has
had on American roots rock music is incalculable. Good things happen in
threes in the region: Ely, Hancock, and Gilmore can stand tall in music history alongside a previous generation of West Texas icons and troubadours, including the Big Three—Bob Wills, Buddy Holly, and Roy Orbison. While
Gram Parsons, Chris Hillman, and the Burrito Brothers fused rock and country on the California West Coast, the Flatlanders were blazing similar trails
on the "Third Coast," East and West Texas. "We were fans of the Flying Burrito Brothers," admitted Gilmore, who was born one year before Parsons, "but
we were already on our way in Lubbock before their records came out."

Texas natives Joe Ely, Butch Hancock, and Jimmie Dale Gilmore no longer
live in Lubbock, the mid-sized Texas Tech University town they put back
on the musical map by launching their careers there. These days Ely and
Gilmore reside on opposite ends of town outside the Austin city limits. Joe
lives 15 miles south of Austin, while Jimmie Dale lives 20 miles west, not
far from Willie Nelson's compound in Spicewood. Butch, for the longest
time, lived right in the center of downtown Austin and maintained an art

studio and a music room. But since raising a family, Butch has spent a couple years away from recording, building a house in the dusty wilds of Terlingua. There's nine hours worth of flatlands between Terlingua and Austin, with no convenient airport nearby to land even a puddle-jumper.

Hancock and Gilmore were both born in 1945, and attended the same high school in Lubbock. Ely, the youngest, attended the same school later. Oddly, the three didn't connect creatively until after they all left high school.

"Butch and I were 12 years old when we first met," recalled Gilmore. "Butch was a jack-of-all-trades. He was a really good student, and even though he was short, Butch was a fine athlete and a scrappy member of the basketball team. We didn't have cars. We lived in different neighborhoods, but we were friends at school. All three of us attended Monterey High School in Lubbock.

"When we got to be college age, we started hanging out with each other more. I spent only a couple of years in college. Butch came within one hour of graduating with a degree in architecture at Texas Tech. One unit short.

"Joe went to the same high school but times got tough, so he didn't graduate. He and I were both born in Amarillo in the same hospital. We didn't know each other until Joe was 18 and I was 20."

Since Lubbock was a provincial town, it was only a matter of time until Joe, Butch, and Jimmie Dale hooked up.

Joe fronted live bands in the downtown honky tonks not far from where he grew up. Butch started composing tunes as a teenager while driving his daddy's tractor. Jimmie Dale brought the country roots to the group. All three wore their hair long and straggly under their cowboy hats. Just like Woody Guthrie, they hopped freight trains on the Rock Island Railroad. They hitchhiked (separately) to places like San Francisco's Haight-Ashbury and Berkeley's Telegraph Avenue where the action was. Each detested the right-wing brand of commercial country and western music served up by Nashville.

"My dad was a country guitar player," said Gilmore. "He learned to play back in the day when Jimmie Rodgers was a huge star. A lot of people don't realize it today, but Jimmie Rodgers, 'the Singing Brakeman,' was one of the first superstar recording acts in the United States, and he was particularly popular in the South. Then, as a 12-year-old boy, I saw Johnny Cash and Elvis Presley in concert. That was the turning point.

"If you liked rock, you weren't supposed to like country. But we didn't hate country music. Music had a lot more to do with lifestyle and politics."

As was typical of the Flatlanders, the three core members stayed close, but continued to roam and scatter away from Lubbock.

"Joe and I already had bands before," Jimmie Dale explained. "Joe went overseas to tour Europe with a theater troupe. Butch was out in San Francisco. I moved down to Austin for a year. I was also nomadic during that period. I spent a lot of time in California and in San Francisco. But in 1970, all three of us moved back to Lubbock close to the same time. That was the period where I introduced Joe and Butch to each other. Butch hadn't done any music professionally, but he had been writing a lot of great songs. When I introduced him to Joe, we reached a critical mass. I was the catalyst towards it all being a permanent association."

The three, along with Steve Wesson, a real-life cowpoke who played the musical saw, and a mandolin player named Tony Pearson, formed the basis of the Flatlanders in the summer of 1971. The name came from the topography of the area surrounding Lubbock. Texas can be flat as a pancake.

Gilmore, Hancock, and Ely each contributed specific genres to their new band. The Flatlanders started off as a local Lubbock phenomenon. But soon their influence would spread regionally. They represented a back-to-basics, youthful alternative fueled by underpinnings of classic country (Jimmie Dale), folk and blues (Butch) and rock 'n' roll (Joe).

All the while, Jimmie Dale maintained a reverence for the basic tenets of roots country music just like his father.

"When we first formed the Flatlanders, I was more into classic hardcore country than either Butch or Joe. Butch brought the folk and bluegrass aspect to it. Joe brought the rock 'n' roll. The three of us influenced each other so much, that sooner or later all of us became interchangeably involved with each other's musical experiences. That was the recipe for the Flatlanders. We couldn't be categorized. We weren't strictly country or folk because there was a lot of rock 'n' roll and blues in what we did."

During the formation of the Flatlanders, a chance meeting with a hitchhiking stranger ignited a spark.

Joe Ely was out riding around in his Volkswagen bus when he came upon a hitchhiker out in the middle of nowhere. Since he and his friends had all hitchhiked a lot in the area, Joe knew the guy was in a really bad spot to try to catch a ride. So he picked him up and gave him a ride to a better location. The hitchhiker carried with him a small backpack.

"Townes Van Zandt didn't have any clothes in his backpack, just a bunch of copies of a record he had just made," Jimmie Dale recalled. "He gave one of the records to Joe. Joe played it as soon as he got home. At the time, we hadn't yet done any music together. Joe called me up and told me I had to hear this record. We got together that afternoon and played the record again and again. I had the same reaction as Joe."

The experience was a kinetic inspiration for the two young players.

"Townes was doing what we wanted to do," said Gilmore, "combining folk, country, with a lot of blues influence. Two things happened as a result of that afternoon: Joe and I started running around together, and then we forged a lifelong, close friendship. Townes Van Zandt helped make this connection possible. It was many years before we got to tell Townes that story. He was a huge fan of Joe's when Joe was on MCA. My version of 'Dallas' was one of his favorite recordings.

"The quality of Townes's work influenced us tremendously. It demonstrated that high-quality writing wasn't just limited to Bob Dylan and Leonard Cohen. Here was writing of that quality coming from a Texan. It only validated what we were doing."

"We made a little money," recalled Ely. "The Flatlanders played the Kerrville folk festival and we played the bars in Austin. We went out to L.A. and back, playing wherever we could."

The Flatlanders were as much a concept and a state of mind as they were a band. They backed up Texas blues singer Marcia Ball. They played the Armadillo Beer Garden in Austin, or performed at private parties, goat roasts, and gigs at the Old Town Pub in Lubbock. Their association continued on a casual basis.

In February 1972, after cutting 17 songs at the Singleton Sound Studio in Nashville, the band broke up and scattered again like tumbleweeds. The three returned to Texas, hit the road separately, and made their own marks as solo artists.

"We didn't think of the Flatlanders as being much of a permanent fixture," admitted Gilmore. "That was part of the beauty of it. We'd done it out of love for the music and the fun of associating with each other. We didn't form the band as a commercial enterprise. It came together as a group of friends who liked each other's music.

"The core premise of the Flatlanders was a friendship between three men. People assumed we split up over some friction, but it wasn't about that. Too many smart and interesting people surrounded us. We all read books like *Meetings with Remarkable Men* [by the Russian mystic writer Georges Ivanovitch Gurdjieff], shared our ideas and interests, and turned each other on to lots of different things.

"We weren't exclusively devoted to music. Steve Wesson played the musical saw, but Steve wasn't only a musician. He was the *real* cowboy in the band. He'd been a carpenter, a rodeo rider, and a damn good artist and teacher. Lots of musicians have a one-dimensional quality to them. Visual artists can be extremely cliquish. Our gang of friends during the Flatlanders era was not just creative musicians. Some were novelists or philosophy professors at Texas Tech."

When the Flatlanders split up, Joe resumed his rambling ways, Butch relocated to Austin, and Jimmie Dale took a spiritual path via Denver to follow the teachings of a guru named Maharaji. The formation of the Flatlanders signaled a trend in Texas that the counterculture movement was on. Today, Ely, Hancock, and Gilmore are looked at as pioneers who made Austin and other small cities around it respected for fostering strong music and outlaw art traditions.

The influences of the band spread throughout Texas, from Lubbock to Austin, then to Dallas/Ft. Worth. To Jimmie Dale and the boys, Dallas and Ft. Worth marked the line of demarcation between East and West Texas culture.

"We've felt that if Dallas was East Texas then Ft. Worth was the beginning of West Texas," Jimmie Dale laughed. "If you accept that, then Townes Van Zandt, who was born in Ft. Worth, came from West Texas. Ft. Worth was about the dance halls while Dallas was about the country club. What Dallas called sushi, Ft. Worth called bait. I'm West Texas. My sympathies have been more with the dance hall crowd than with the country clubbers. But there's also an impressive list of people who came from Dallas and had tremendous influence on popular music including guys like Steve Miller, Boz Scaggs, and Jimmie and Stevie Ray Vaughan. Some of them came from the Dallas suburb of Oak Cliff."

The beauty of the 2004 *Wheels of Fortune* release is that it's seemingly devoid of ego. Unlike many all-star collaborations, Joe, Butch, and Jimmie Dale freely sing each other's songs interchangeably. It's a little like Abbott and Costello's "Who's on first?" bit. Jimmie Dale sings lead on Butch's "Wishin' for You," which originally appeared on one of Joe's records. But it was Jimmie Dale who turned Joe on to the song in the first place. Also, Jimmie Dale sings an old Ely composition, "Back to My Old Molehill," which had never been recorded. Conversely, Joe sings the Jimmie Dale-penned song, "Midnight Train," only because his voice better suits the bluesy grit of the piece. Finally, Butch sings "Deep Eddy Blues," written by Jimmie Dale. And so the wheel turns.

Wheels of Fortune was born after the group toured for almost two years on the preceding release, *Now Again*. The Flatlanders' road band included guitarist Rob Gjersoe (Gilmore's instrumental partner for years), bassist Gary Herman (who has played with Joe for a long time), and drummer Chris Searles (who gigs with Ely's band off and on). After the tour, everybody decided to continue the partnership, so a recording session with the road band was set up.

"There's something about our kindred spirit that we captured on the record. We were all fresh off the road when the band had congealed," remembered Gilmore. "Between us, Butch and Joe and I had this vast repertoire we wanted to record, so we just picked out a slice of time when we could all be there. The rhythm section was set up in one room, so we burned through and cut a whole bunch of songs."

The sessions took place at Ely's home studio, where he also served as producer of the project.

"It's a little more sophisticated than the term 'home studio' implies," Jimmie Dale noted. "It's a real studio. It's all Joe's equipment and he engineers a lot of the stuff. He's into it. Since I've known Joe, he's been really into sound—much more than Butch and I were. We also used a top-of-the-line recording and mastering engineer named Jim Wilson."

According to Gilmore, the sessions went fairly quick. Most of the songs on *Wheels of Fortune* were cut as first and second takes. All told, it took three full days plus one afternoon to record between 35 and 40 songs. Once the basic performances were laid down, background vocals and instrumental sweetening, mostly led by guitarist Gjersoe, polished up each tune. Another original Flatlander, Steve Wesson, reprised his role on musical saw.

There were extra appearances by familiar faces like Lloyd Maines on pedal steel and guitarist Mitch Watkins.

"Mitch is one of the very best musicians in Austin and has played on so many of our records. Lloyd played with Joe for years," said Jimmie Dale.

With three inexhaustible writers, the recording sessions yielded 14 tracks for *Wheels of Fortune* plus a stable of nearly 20 extra tunes available for a follow-up.

"I think there's a good chance that nearly everything we recorded at those sessions will show up sometime or another," predicted Gilmore.

Look for Joe Ely, Butch Hancock, and Jimmie Dale Gilmore to continue pooling their material for future projects, whether it's for future solo or band efforts. With Jimmie Dale and Joe currently both signed to Rounder Records, Jimmie Dale looks forward to assembling new tunes for future albums and cutting them at Joe's studio. And if Butch accumulates enough new material and decides to make more records of his own, he'll likely drop into Joe's compound and roll tape there, too.

For Jimmie Dale, the artistic and chart success of *Wheels of Fortune* (No. 1 on the American Association chart and Top 20 on the *Billboard* country sales chart), represents a high watermark over a long career.

"The popularity of the Flatlanders has outshone anything I've done," he confessed. "Joe may have had some better runs, but none of my records have done better than this newest Flatlanders CD. I haven't been as prolific as Butch and Joe. Maybe I'm a little too much of a perfectionist. But our careers as Flatlanders are still fresh. It's as if we're newcomers with the advantage of being old-timers."

Download This!

From Austin to Terlingua

Jimmie Dale Gilmore sneaks pure country into his progressive-sounding solo records. Butch Hancock is the sardonic folkie and more off-the-wall as a solo act. Here are a few West Texas chestnuts from each. (Flip back to chapter 3 for some of Joe Ely's rockin' tracks.)

1. "No Lonesome Tune"—Jimmie Dale Gilmore (Windcharger/Rounder).
   Jimmie Dale performs this Townes Van Zandt song from his best album to date, *One Endless Night.*

2. "Dry Farm Land"—Butch Hancock (Sugarhill).
   Between Ely, Gilmore, and Hancock, Butch's humor and wit are as dry as the summer breezes of Terlingua. Recorded back in 1978, this song is pure folk.

3. "Baby Do You Love Me Still?"—Flatlanders (New West).
   From *Wheels of Fortune,* Butch digs out some crazy one-liners for this song. "Is it androids or elephants that never forget? Have the East and West met yet?"

4. "Georgia Rose"—Jimmie Dale Gilmore (Windcharger/Rounder).
   Gilmore sings a pure "set 'em-up-Joe" honky tonk country crooner, complete with a mild twanging guitar.

5. "Dirt Road Song"—Butch Hancock (Sugarhill).
   From his debut album, *West Texas Waltzes and Dust Blown Tractor Tunes,* first released on his homegrown label Rainlight. It's country-folk—extremely Dylan-esque and rambling Woody.

6. "Defying Gravity + Ripple"—Jimmie Dale Gilmore (Windcharger/Rounder).
   More tunes from *One Endless Night.* Gilmore interprets Jesse Winchester and Jerry Garcia respectively and respectfully, with full band arrangements. Jim Lauderdale lends vocal support.

7. "Wishin' for You"—Flatlanders (New West).
   Jimmie Dale sings a famous Hancock tune that first gained popularity from a Joe Ely record.

continued on the next page

From Austin to Terlingua *continued*

8. "Tonight I Think I'm Gonna Go Downtown"—Jimmie Dale Gilmore/
Butch Hancock (Virgin-Australia).
This is a live solo acoustic version from an Australian import released in 1990.
The song originally appeared on the very first Flatlanders album, in 1972.

9. "One Road More"—Butch Hancock/Jimmie Dale Gilmore (Virgin-Australia).
Another live tune cut in Melbourne from the *Two Roads* CD of the rural blues
variety.

10. "Braver New World"—Jimmie Dale Gilmore (Elektra).
The most extravagant recording made by Gilmore is this 1996 record
produced by T-Bone Burnett. Tracks feature L.A. sidemen like drummer Jim
Keltner and guitar/keyboardist Jon Brion. Made during the dawn of the
alt.country movement.

11. "She Never Spoke Spanish to Me"—Texas Tornadoes (Reprise).
The late, great Doug Sahm and organist Augie Meyers from the Sir Douglas
Quintet join accordion legend Flaco Jimenez and country crooner Freddy
Fender to form the Texas Tornadoes in 1990, featuring this tune from their
self-titled debut record.

chapter 15

Rodney Crowell

*The Houston Kid
Gains Control . . . Again*

A spring night in 1975 turned out to be a landmark show. Rodney Crowell stood onstage with a shiny smirk on his face, strumming his guitar and blissfully singing harmonies. It was the very first public appearance of Emmylou Harris and the Hot Band—resplendent with legendary Elvis Presley band members James Burton and Glen D. Hardin, plus Emory Gordy, Hank DeVito, and other respected studio hired guns—now onstage together in a small San Francisco nightclub. Burton and Hardin were the same Elvis alumni that Gram Parsons tried but failed to take out on the road with him before he died.

After touring and recording as an original member of Emmylou's Hot Band in 1975 and breaking out later with nine solo albums between 1978 and 1995, Rodney Crowell didn't strike his most prolific iron until album number ten, 2001's The Houston Kid, a rich, image-filled work mined from vivid memories of Rodney's own childhood. Each song-tale candidly portrays a Texas slice-of-life and tackles tough issues like domestic violence, the AIDS virus, and hardened ex-cons, all depicted in Crowell's neatly hand-tooled Nashville style of verse and rhyme.

By raising the songwriting bar a few notches, "the Kid" kept his creative machinery intact and returned three years later with another excellent batch of 11 songs. Fate's Right Hand from 2003 is a brilliant companion piece to The Houston Kid. Less historic and more cerebral, Fate's Right Hand addresses Crowell's own mortality and spirituality. According to Rodney, it's far more philosophical and autobiographical. Regardless, both The Houston Kid and

Fate's Right Hand *make up the best one-two combination in American roots rock since Lucinda Williams's* Car Wheels on a Gravel Road *and* Essence.

As a songwriter, producer, and singer over the previous two decades, Rodney has left deep footprints on Nashville's Music Row. Back in 1980, the Oak Ridge Boys scored a No. 1 record with his "Leavin' Louisiana in the Broad Daylight." In 1982 Crowell hit publishing pay dirt when Bob Seger recorded "Shame on the Moon." Then in 1983 Crystal Gayle topped the country charts again with one of Crowell's finest compositions, "'Til I Gain Control Again." Crowell released a trio of post-Hot Band solo records from 1978 to 1981 on Warner Bros., then resumed his output in 1986 with a half dozen more records up through 1995. In 2000, Lee Ann Womack scored a country No. 1 with his "Ashes by Now."

In 1978 Crowell also produced Roseanne Cash's Right or Wrong *album. A year later the two were married and started a family. Rodney, with John and June Carter Cash as proud grandparents to his offspring, joined one of the elite families in Music City. The couple divorced in 1991.*

If an artist is only as good as his or her latest efforts, then based on Fate's Right Hand *and* The Houston Kid, *Rodney has moved way beyond his formidable talents as a singer-songwriter and producer, and reached the highest plateau as an evocative, fully realized recording artist and writer. Being philosophical without sounding preachy or pompous, he communicates to his listeners on a highly enlightened level, sharing his journeys and his mistakes. It's a calling from which many successful artists shy away. Like the late jazz saxophonist Dexter Gordon once said, "If you don't have heart in this business, then you don't belong in it." Crowell has regained control of his craft by climbing to the very top of his game.*

There comes a time when any man worth his salt arrives at a crucial stage in his career. He is who he is. The ego sheds its skin and the real man stands alone and exposed. Whatever he's accomplished or whatever lurks on the horizon is well and fine, but life experience isn't all that defines the quintessence of this man. It's about reaching a *personal* level of comfort. Dropping the trappings and pretensions. Some women characterize these kinds of men as being "comfortable in their own skin."

For Rodney Crowell, physical looks have not been a problem. Sitting behind a desk in his Nashville publicist's office the day after Johnny Cash's funeral, he is a handsome, slightly built gentleman in a Southern squire way, with gleaming eyes, striking angular features, and a cleft chin. When Crowell (born in 1950) neared the magical, golden year of 5-0 and began work on *The Houston Kid*, he was coming to terms with his *inner* aging self. He needed to prove himself beyond being a songwriter and a welterweight singing star. Questions arose. If he left this earth tomorrow, what mark would he leave and how would his children describe him after he was gone?

"I was at a place where I needed to stake my claim as an *artist*," explained Rodney. "I think it was a combination of my own feelings of discomfort and feeling pretentious. It's really easy to start putting on artifice when your music is on the radio. Then I started to feel myself walk into a room and become Rodney Crowell. We've all seen people do that. But I started dismantling it.

"After I got divorced and became a single parent, I realized that I didn't want somebody else raising my children. So I took a little time off to regroup.

The lord of the roots-rock manor. Whether it's rock 'n' roll or ballads written in Nashville structure, Rodney Crowell's music explores his subjects with a novelist's eye.

I started taking my kids to school, I was off the road, and all that pretense that had calcified around me soon fell away.

"I thought to myself, 'Man, I dodged a bullet.'

"Later, I decided to go back out. I had a kid in college and the other kids were with Roseanne. We had it all sorted out. I promised myself from that point on, everything I did was going to count. I wanted to spiritually articulate my place in music and make it real and palpable so my listeners could get into my world and see their own process going on. That's what I want to be remembered for, the work I did starting with *The Houston Kid*."

Looking over an entire body of work dating from 1978 to 2000 on the Warner Bros., Columbia, and MCA labels, Crowell is vigorously self-critical, yet proud of a portion of his past.

"I think I have a really fine body of work in terms of songs—'Song for the Life,' "Til I Gain Control Again,' 'Shame on the Moon,' 'After All This Time,' 'Crazy for Leaving,' 'Lovin' All Night,' 'Leaving Louisiana in the Broad Daylight,' and 'What Kind of Love.' If I could take all my earlier records, the first nine, and edit them down, I could probably make up two pretty good records.

"It took me a while to become a 'fully realized' recording artist. I don't think I truly arrived at that point until *The Houston Kid*."

The Houston Kid is a brilliant montage of 11 songs, sculpted from Crowell's blue-collar childhood. It's told mostly in the first person. Many of the tunes are actual snapshots from Rodney's upbringing in Houston.

The opening song, "Telephone Road," is a lyrical patchwork of colorful, single-line sensory images of sights, tastes, and smells: sheets of driving rain, cherry Cokes, roadside cheeseburgers, and mosquito trucks spraying clouds of DDT as shirtless kids unknowingly horse around in the noxious fog on the roadside.

"Memory is all about reassembling images and 'Telephone Road' is just reassembled images," said Crowell. "'Rain came down on endless sheets of thunder.' When I was a kid, my parents didn't go to restaurants. Dining out was a hamburger stand at the Princess Drive-In. Sawdust dance floors. Salty watermelons. We had watermelon stands along the road where they'd sell you a slice and you'd shake some salt on it."

The Houston Kid's warts-and-all storytelling tapestry weaves images of growing up during the Eisenhower '50s and Kennedy '60s. In between predawn family fishing trips and pastoral riverside strolls, Crowell recounts distressing episodes of abusive and violent husbands, and kids who went on to become convicts or HIV-positive junkies. Whenever Crowell needed to thicken the plot for a song, he simply looked to other childhood characters that lived down the street.

"*The Houston Kid* is my life, mainly about the environment I grew up in. When my own life experiences didn't serve up enough drama, I would access somebody else's.

"I never went to prison, but the kid three houses down did. We both grew up in domestically violent households. I had music, so I got out. The thugs gave me a pass. 'He's that guy in that band. He plays music. Let him go. Don't beat him up.'

"Music saved *my* ass, but how about the guy three houses down who didn't play music? He was sunk. The thugs would kick his ass, so he turned into a tough guy who wound up on death row."

The Houston Kid's catchiest tune is "I Walk the Line (Revisited)," Rodney's tribute to Johnny Cash's classic "I Walk the Line." The song is a snapshot of the first time Rodney actually heard the song. As a six-year-old boy, the experience transformed him.

"It was 1956 and I was going fishing in the predawn with my grandfather and my dad in a borrowed 1949 Ford," said Crowell. "Cane fishing poles were sticking out the windows. I had my chin on the backseat looking out the window at the pine-thicketed road in East Texas. We were going to a place called Canyon Creek where we fished.

"Suddenly 'I Walk the Line' came out of that big old 1949 chrome Ford dashboard radio. Show me a prototype for that song and I'll eat your hat, meaning there was no point of reference for what I'd just heard. I was taken out of the car and sent off somewhere. I remember later as a teenager thinking, how do I write about that? It took me until I was in my forties before I could actually sit down and recapture the experience on paper. I was abducted by a song. That's what happened."

As the verses of Rodney's song relay the story of a boy hearing "I Walk the Line" for the first time, the chorus, sung (not sampled) by Johnny Cash, is the identical first four lines of the tune. Looking back, Crowell admits it took a lot of gall inviting Johnny Cash back into the studio to mess with his signature tune.

"My melody was different than his, but the syllables fit perfectly. I called him and asked, 'Man, can you shake free? I've stumbled onto something here.' He probably thought he was coming in to sing his version."

Rodney's version soon gave way to Johnny's.

"Johnny had a hard time with it, but I kept singing my melody back to him. Finally he said, 'Stop. I've been singing this song for forty-some years. You got a lot of nerve changing my melody.' I thought, wow, I guess I do. But he took it as a challenge and nailed it in two takes with two performances that were totally different."

As a musician who just happened to also be Johnny Cash's son-in-law (for 13 years), Crowell had to strike a delicate balance within Nashville's imperial clan.

"I always had a great relationship with Johnny," admitted Crowell, choosing his words carefully. "From the very beginning I made a point of not kissing his ass as a son-in-law. I let him know that I was my own man and I didn't want or need anything from him. At the same time I let him know that I admired him deeply. He was a great guy and I loved him. There were a lot of ass-kissers around him, and he knew I wasn't one of them. He'd get mad at me when it was right to get mad.

"John and June Carter were as sweet as they could be. But in order to enter into the inner circle of Johnny and June, you had to burn through the people in the sycophantic outer layer who watched over everything. They had six daughters, so there were six hundred hound dogs trying to sniff their way in.

"The people whose lives revolved around John and June set up a gauntlet that you had to literally break through. When I first showed up, man, it was as if I were trying to break into Fort Knox. Those people later grew to love me, but at first, it wasn't worth it. Then I realized it wasn't John or June's fault, nor was it their kids'. They were royalty, elevated to the highest level, but they were just good people."

Who would have thought a young man from a poor East Texas family could have risen to such heights? As a boy, Crowell recalls first seeing Johnny Cash perform live, not long after the song on the radio zapped him.

"I was six years old, and my dad and mom took me to this place called Magnolia Gardens in Channel View, Texas. It was an outdoor venue. We were all there to see Johnny Cash, Jerry Lee Lewis, and Carl Perkins. Jerry Lee went on first. It was pouring down rain. There were tables on the sides with a dance floor out in the front amid a typical East Texas downpour with lots of thunder and lightning.

"That didn't stop the hoods or the tough guys from going out onto the dance floor in their ducktail haircuts, doing the dirty bop to Jerry Lee's set. That blew me away. Next came Carl Perkins. It was still raining. There were leaks in the roof over the stage. Hot microphones lay everywhere; surely somebody was about to die from electrocution. There was another deluge of rain during Carl's show as I watched from over by the side of the stage. My mom and dad were carrying on out on the dance floor."

Just as Johnny Cash was ready to come on, the clouds parted and the sun came out. Johnny walked onstage. "How high's the water, mama?," he sang out, as the water flowed off the dance floor.

"It was performance art at its finest. Johnny played the environment! Even as a kid, I was hit hard. I was dumbfounded. Years later I figured it out. He was performing for the moment."

Three years separated *The Houston Kid* and the next release, 2003's *Fate's Right Hand*. Supporting guests on those sessions included Flecktone banjoist Béla Fleck, dobro master Jerry Douglas, harmonica ace Charlie McCoy, and singer-songwriters Gillian Welch and Kim Richey.

"*Fate's Right Hand* is a spiritual look at where I am in my life right now. It didn't take long to write," Crowell noted. "I tried to exercise neutrality, to just let the songs tell *me* what they wanted to be. Normally songs just happen. I let the language come through so that I'm showing not telling. And that's what happened. I woke up one morning with 14 songs looking at me saying, 'We're here.'"

A cold-light-of-day self-portrait is depicted starkly on "The Man in Me." In the lyric, Crowell reveals himself as aloof, cold, and suspiciously on his guard, an alter ego who speaks in four-letter words. His teeth are crooked and a face stares back at him from the mirror, ugly and distorted.

"'The Man in Me' is dark, but I was once that guy. Truly. I couldn't write about him while I was still him. But having lived past it, my self-acceptance and self-compassion took hold. I wrote about that guy hoping someone passing through on his or her own personal journey might hear me articulate my self-hatred, so this song might help them get past their own self-hatred."

Fate's Right Hand's first single and video was a twangy, mid-tempo rocker titled "Earthbound," featuring banjo and mandolin embellishments by Béla Fleck and John Jorgenson. Only on a Rodney Crowell number could references to the Dalai Lama, Charlie Brown, Ringo Starr, Aretha Franklin, and Irish poet Seamus Heaney coexist so blissfully.

"We showed up for this shitty gig at some ugly looking club in San Antonio when I said to my friend [guitarist] Steuart Smith, 'Whoa, this is going to be brutal tonight. Let's go grab some food and share a fine bottle of wine.' We found this nice Italian restaurant and halfway through the second bottle of wine, Steuart looks over at me and says, 'You know, I could die tomorrow and that would be okay with me.'

"I looked at him. 'Pardon? Come again?'

"'No, really,' Steuart said, 'I love my wife; I adore my daughter. But I could check out tomorrow and it would be okay with me. I'm pretty sure I've seen and done all there is to see and do.'

"I flew out to California the next day and I kept thinking about what Steuart had said. He was earthbound. That word kept turning over in my head, so I turned it into a song. I hooked up with Steuart a little while later. He told me the Eagles had called him and hired him away for a shitload of money. I told him, 'Aren't you glad you stuck around?' It was an odd place for a song to come from."

In his mission to become a more earnest, meaningful songwriter, Crowell takes his fellow country artists to task for not speaking up on important issues like war and the environment. The death of Johnny Cash, according to Crowell, has left a gigantic void in American country music and its societal impact.

"I'm frustrated more younger artists aren't taking a stand in their work. While I have a small audience, there are some performers with millions of people hanging on to every word they say—and they're not saying dick. They probably feel it would be professional suicide for them to speak up. But God, if you already have enough money . . ." Crowell's voice trailed off.

Reflecting on the Dixie Chicks and the price they paid for their honesty in criticizing President Bush during the height of the Iraqi War, Crowell sighed, "It's a sore point with me."

One of *Fate's* most poignant songs, the song that gives the record its spiritual backbone, is a confessional ballad called "Time to Go Inward." In a particularly telling passage halfway through the song, Crowell equates the wisdom of Jesus and Buddha with Minnie Pearl.

"In the early '80s," Rodney explained, "when I first started rubbing elbows with the Nashville hierarchy, Minnie Pearl and I sat next to each other at an awards show. People were winning their awards and at the time I was snobbish and acting pretty snotty. She would smile and say to me, 'Look at her. Isn't she a darling? She's so sweet. She's precious.' I was into my standoffish, rebellious, Holden Caulfield thing while Minnie was this open person."

Her goodness had a lingering effect on Crowell. "I found myself drawn to her. I truly fell in love with her. How did she do it? I needed to find that quality within myself. I wanted to be more accepting just like Minnie, and stop being such a jealous individual.

"One day we ran into each other at the Kroger market, standing outside with our grocery carts, having a conversation. She paused and looked at me, all-knowing, 'You know, Rodney,' she said, 'there will come a time when you're going to need to go inside yourself to find something new to give to your audience. When that time comes, don't be afraid.'

"That was 1982. It took me 20 years to get to that point. That's the reason I used that line, 'Jesus and Buddha and Krishna and Minnie Pearl knew.' Minnie Pearl had a divine wisdom as powerful as anything from Jesus or Buddha in terms of compassion, love, self-acceptance, and love for other people. It *was* time to go inward and look for that better part of myself."

Life is Messy. That was the title of a CD Crowell cut in 1992, just after he and Roseanne Cash divorced. Rodney had been through thick and thin. It all started in 1975 when, after selling songs to singers like Jerry Reed, he moved to Los Angeles to work alongside his friend Emmylou Harris on a bold new music genre concept. Emmylou signed a record deal with Reprise and her label told her to assemble a "hot band" and tour. She did just that.

"When we first went to England as members of the Hot Band, some British music journalists came to interview us. I was this Houston kid who grew up under the influence of Roy Head, Bill Haley, and Big Joe Turner. They asked me, 'Do you think the Byrds and the Burritos paved the way for country-rock as we know it today?'"

Rodney laughed as he fingered a new copy of the double CD reissue of *Sweetheart of the Rodeo* sitting on the desk.

"I said, 'Hell no. Haven't you heard of Jerry Lee Lewis? Carl Perkins? Johnny Cash? Elvis Presley?' Smiley Lewis and Big Joe Turner turned those guys on as gospel, country, and rock 'n' roll was defining itself.

"That's where country-rock music comes from, Bill Haley and the Comets ripping off Big Joe Turner. Remember, Bill Haley and the Comets was a country band until they heard Big Joe Turner. Then they recorded 'Shake, Rattle & Roll' and 'Rock Around the Clock.'"

With his youthful looks, genuine country roots, and tenor vocal style, American roots rock enthusiasts often look at Rodney Crowell and speculate whether he could have become the heir apparent to Gram Parsons as a member of Emmylou's famous Hot Band. Crowell disagrees.

"Emmylou and I hooked up because we both loved the Louvin Brothers and the Everlys. The Louvin Brothers begat the Everly Brothers, who begat the Beatles, who begat Simon & Garfunkel, who begat Gram Parsons and Emmylou Harris. When Gram died, Emmylou stumbled onto me, so we carried on.

"Emmy and I both loved authentic country—Webb Pierce, Hank Snow, Hank Williams, Hank Locklin, Stonewall Jackson, Loretta Lynn, and all that stuff. We were hippies playing country music with a rock 'n' roll attitude.

"I'll never forget those days. One of my favorite things about it was going from playing Dodger Stadium with Elton John to a gig with James Taylor, then winding up on a brief tour with Conway Twitty. I remember Conway had this drummer they called Porkchop. I wore a George Jones Possum Hollow T-shirt with hair to my shoulders, smoking dope, drinking, acting crazy and having a blast. Porkchop walked up to me, 'You ain't country! You're just pretending.' I looked at him, 'Hell man, I'm not country? How come my mom and dad met in a high school gymnasium at a Roy Acuff concert in Buchanan, Tennessee, in 1942? If it wasn't for Roy Acuff, hell, I wouldn't even be here.' Porkchop walked away muttering. I was so proud of myself, but, damn, it was the truth."

Wherever the Hot Band played, the shadow of Gram Parsons seemed to follow.

"The first time we went to Long Island, there was a death threat against me. Some guy was outraged that I had the audacity to even think that I could take Gram's place. But I wasn't taking Gram Parsons's place. It was my job. I was gainfully employed as Emmy's songwriting partner.

"Gram Parsons was dead by the time I showed up. He'd burned it up long before I got there. Had he not, I probably would not have gotten the gig. So in that sense, the dots all connect.

"Emmy and I were both poets. We come from the same spiritual place. It felt good for Emmy to have me along as a co-conspirator. We were wide-eyed and innocent, just painting by the numbers."

Download This!

Rodney Crowell Walks the Line

Rodney Crowell the solo artist, producer, and songwriter has been covered by dozens of artists, ranging from This Mortal Coil and the Waterboys to Guy Clark and George Strait.

1. "Telephone Road"—Rodney Crowell (Vanguard).
   This is the opening gem off *The Houston Kid,* a groundbreaking effort that's highly recommended. The lines of poetic imagery are hard to beat.

2. "I Walk the Line (Revisited)"—Rodney Crowell (Vanguard).
   Another great tune from *The Houston Kid* CD. Who would have thought as a young kid that Crowell would become part of the royal Cash family?

3. "Seven Year Ache"—Roseanne Cash (Columbia).
   Crowell produced this tune from Roseanne's second album in 1981. A complicated tune about infidelity, it vaulted Roseanne's career as a singing star.

4. "Shake, Rattle & Roll"—Big Joe Turner (Atlantic).
   Turner came from Kansas City, home of Count Basie and a vivacious, bluesy jazz scene. Bill Haley & His Comets and Elvis Presley covered his Atlantic R&B hits for white audiences.

continued on the next page

Rodney Crowell Walks the Line *continued*

5. "If I Could Only Win Your Love"—Emmylou Harris (Reprise).
This 1975 vocal duet from Emmylou's second record with the Hot Band, *Elite Hotel*, is a Louvin Brothers standard. In 1976 Tammy Wynette covered the song wonderfully on the album *'Til I Can Make It on My Own*, which, sadly, is not available on CD.

6. "'Til I Gain Control Again"—Emmylou Harris/Rodney Crowell (Warner Bros.).
This tune is considered one of Crowell's signature compositions. It was also cut by Willie, Waylon, and Crystal Gayle. Crowell cut his own version in 1981 on his self-titled, third Warner Bros. record.

7. "I Hear You Knocking"—Smiley Lewis (Imperial/United Artists).
Before Fats Domino ruled the New Orleans R&B roost, Smiley influenced Cash, Jerry Lee, and the big Sun guns with hits like this, made famous by Fats Domino and later by Welsh rocker Dave Edmunds in 1972.

8. "Earthbound"—Rodney Crowell (DMZ/Epic).
Fate's Right Hand, arguably one of the finest releases of 2003, is a CD where Crowell ponders his own mortality and his public image.

9. "Ashes by Now"—Lee Ann Womack (MCA).
Womack's cover of one of Crowell's money tunes was recorded on her million-selling 2000 release, *I Hope You Dance*.

10. "Five Feet High and Rising"—Johnny Cash (Columbia).
"How high's the water, mama?," Crowell heard Cash bellow as a youth. It deals with a great flood in the Mississippi Delta region and was played on pop and country and western stations alike starting in 1959.

11. "Oh King Richard"—Rodney Crowell (Columbia).
Attention all you NASCAR moms and dads: this 1986 recording, with Booker T. Jones producing and playing organ, salutes the car racing legend Richard Petty. A-Moon-Pie-and-RC-Cola southern delight.

12. "After All This Time"—Rodney Crowell (Columbia/Legacy).
A moody and reflective ballad starts off with a train reference. Andy "Moon River" Williams cut a version in the 1990s.

chapter 16

Lucinda Williams

The Modern Day Hank

> *I haven't decided yet how I feel about reincarnation.*
> *But as my dad always used to remind me, I was born the*
> *same month and year Hank Williams died. January 1953.*
> —Lucinda Williams *to* Esquire Magazine, *April 2002*

A documentary filmmaker friend recently told us:

"Guys, it's no longer about rock 'n' roll. It's a hip-hop world now."

How true. Like it or not, rock 'n' roll has been relegated to the back burner of pop culture, no longer top-shelf explosive material. It is no longer the apple of the eye of the ragged youth, who now care far more about the release dates of PlayStation software than rock 'n' roll CDs. Kids' baggy, throwback athletic togs and futuristic footwear now take precedence over leather trousers and pointy mod boots. DJ culture and drum 'n' bass have eclipsed drum-bass-and-guitar music. Junkie-thin physiques slinging electric axes have given way to buff torsos and muscle-on-muscle. There hasn't been an honest-to-God rock 'n' roll icon since Kurt Cobain, and look what happened to him, his brains suicide-splattered all over the walls of the apartment above his garage.

Thank God for Lucinda Williams.

If it weren't for Lucinda Williams (and maybe the White Stripes), who knows where the fate and future of rock 'n' roll might hang. Not to put any undue pressure on her as an artist, but these days, Lucinda is truly a desert flower, an oasis with a small "o" in a parched wasteland, a rare American treasure—one of the few American musicians out there performing, producing, kicking it, and behaving like a true icon.

It's no coincidence that she's now a little bit north of 50. Just like a lot of us boomers, she's had to deal with the trauma of receiving that AARP application in the mail. But Lucinda needn't worry. So far, she's got the balls and

the back catalog to transcend the gravest fears of growing old and irrelevant.
Just as Keith Richards looked to Muddy Waters as an excuse to keep playing
blues-based rock 'n' roll (okay, perhaps Keith has evolved into a bad example),
so can American roots rockers take umbrage and inspiration in Lucinda's slim
but vital output of seven albums in 25 years. She's an artist with a history of
standing up for herself and taking her damned time even when she may not
have had the clout or leverage of financial success and stardom, only vision.
Of course it takes heaps of courage for anyone to stand up for one's beliefs in
the record business. By her own admission, Lucinda is an artist who can now
say with confidence that she's reached the point where she answers to nobody
on all levels—in business matters and in music-making.

The ultimate milestone came with the creative and financial success of
1998's Car Wheels on a Gravel Road. Released a full 20 years after her first
Folkways Records blues recording session, Car Wheels was six painful years
in the making and the by-product of numerous backfires, a couple false starts,
lost friendships, multiple producers, personal breakdowns, endless retakes,
and a couple ill-fated label deals. As a musical rule of thumb, records born
out of such turmoil are earmarked for disaster, destined for the dumper, or
worse, the cutout bin.

But Lucinda achieved the impossible. Not only did she stand up coura-
geously for her principles to the consternation of close friends, allies, and
advocates, but Car Wheels will cruise comfortably throughout modern mu-
sical history as a true masterpiece, putting her right up there with Dylan,
the Band, Petty, and the Dead. As English record producer Joe Boyd aptly
described it, Car Wheels is the Blonde on Blonde of its time. That's high
praise, especially coming from the same Joe Boyd who has worked with the
likes of Nick Drake, Hendrix, Fairport Convention, and Richard and Linda
Thompson.

Also in 1998, no less than Time magazine anointed Lucinda "America's
Best Songwriter." For once, mainstream Time had their watches set right.
Looking back, as difficult as those six years were, producing an album as
near-perfect as Car Wheels, it's difficult to imagine that Lucinda's musical
career would be half as luminescent without them. An artistic triumph, the
album she struggled to produce marks the difference between her current
status as a writer creating in the rarefied air of innovation versus living out
the rest of her career touring as a struggling, mid-level indie troubadour.

Recording a masterpiece is one miraculous feat. Following it up is another. Living in its shadow years down the line is yet another. We have a saying. If you love an artist, set them free. Sounds like a Sting song? It's not meant to. The greatest gift a fan can give a writer or performer they love and whose work they admire is the freedom (or enough rope) to reshuffle the deck and continue to experiment. Many an artist will attest that it's far scarier bouncing back from success than from failure.

Only an artist like Lucinda Williams could possibly follow up an effort like Car Wheels *with a more lyrically scaled down work like* Essence. *It's the rare artist who can make beautiful music drawing from a rich palette of intrinsically American music styles like ramblin', gamblin' folk, classic country, the dark side of the blues, raggedy rock 'n' roll, a taste of the Delta, the spicy spirit of John Coltrane, and the backwoods Southern literary roads of William Faulkner and Flannery O'Connor. Songs like "Passionate Kisses," "Sweet Old World," and "Lake Charles" didn't flow from the pen of a casual observer. They are works of someone who allowed their ideas to percolate, sometimes painfully, keeping them submerged, not allowing them to emerge a moment before their time.*

We couldn't have published this book in good conscience had we not checked in with Lucinda and gotten her take on the creative process of writing. And if a few of the questions seem selfish, geared more toward advice than information, well then, we plead guilty. As a result, we elected to stay as faithful to the original conversation as we could by presenting her words in "Q & A" form.

In 1979 and 1980 your first two records were released on the Smithsonian Folkways label. Even now, they serve as a useful primer for your current sound, an equal mixture of blues and country influences. But you probably didn't get a bunch of money up front.

You know how much I got? They gave me $250 for *Ramblin'*. It was when Moe Ash was running the label. I got to meet him before he died, this little old New York curmudgeon. His hearing was bad and he was this seasoned, crusty guy. Folkways had done all of those field recordings, so you could literally sit in a kitchen, make a tape of your songs, and they would put it out. For the second record, *Happy Woman Blues*, Moe gave me $500.

You got a 100% pay raise.

This was 1979 and I didn't have a manager or a lawyer or anything like that. I had been living in Houston. Then I had moved up to New York for about a year. I was going to do the whole Greenwich Village folk scene, but it was already dead by that time. There was a pretty healthy singer-songwriter scene going on. I played at Folk City and all these little off-the-wall coffeehouses, like the Flushing Local Coffeehouse. I'd take the train and run all over the place by myself. When I got my deal with Folkways, I didn't have any original material on the first album. But the second record was all original material so I had to get it published. I signed this real simple contract, which was real basic. A few years after, I was on the phone with a music writer friend of mine from Austin who said, "By the way, I got a call from one of your fans, who claimed he heard one of your songs in this film." "Oh really, what's the name of the film?" "*All American Girls In Heat #2.*" I said, "What? Are you sure?" He said, "The fan swears up and down he heard one of your songs off the Folkways records." Those were the only records I had out at the time. I didn't know

Lucinda Williams is America's most gifted contemporary songwriter. She interweaves rustic blues, country, folk, and roots rock like no other modern tunesmith.

whether to laugh or cry. By then I had a manager who worked for the Rosebud Agency to help me get a deal. He went out and rented the film, and sure enough, one of my songs from the Folkways record was in it. It was a song called "One Night Stand," a parody on country songs. There was my little innocent song on this hardcore porno film. I was devastated. What are people going to think? But when I tell people, nobody has ever known. Those films come out and disappear without a trace and there's nobody's name on the film to trace anything. I saw it and it was pretty hilarious.

Aren't you glad you cut those records?

Oh, yeah. They made up the extra thick vinyl LPs with the heavy cardboard album covers.

The Essence *album sounds like you cut out half of the words to the songs—a musical act of paring down. It signified taking a work and boiling it down to its very essence. Is it that obvious?*

What happened with *Essence* was that I was feeling some pressure. It was time to write new material and get ready to do the next record. Now, I'm not used to writing on demand. I'm not really good at it. I have to wait for the mood. I can go for years without finishing anything. One time I went through about five years and I started getting worried. But now I realize there's a pattern when I kinda get into that writer's block thing. I don't worry about it anymore. What happens is I end up with this big spurt of songs, and a bunch of music comes around later, all at the same time. That's what happened with the *World Without Tears* record. I was holed up in this little motel apartment in 2002 and wrote and wrote and wrote. But the *Essence* music was an exercise in getting out of the trap of feeling that every song had to be this narrative, an involved song like "Drunken Angel," "Lake Charles," or "Car Wheels on a Gravel Road." I worked on some of those songs off and on for years, so they're like little short stories. I didn't just sit down and spit them out.

But there is a songwriting process.

Normally what happens is I'll get a skeleton of a song, and continue working on it until I get it up to a level I think is lyrically acceptable. The lyrics are the hardest thing to perfect. When I started writing some of the songs on

Essence, they were loose and simple. Like "Steal Your Love" or "Are You Down?," I threw lyrics together. At first I thought, "This isn't okay. It doesn't come up to the standard of 'Car Wheels on a Gravel Road' or 'Lake Charles.'" At first I thought, "I can't get away with this." Then something switched inside me and I decided, "Why not? What the hell? Why can't I just do this whole other thing?" I'd seen Dylan do it. I watched him from a distance go through that transition. He's been one of my secret mentors. My dad is one, too. But as far as musicians go, I watched Dylan over the years. The music he's known for when I first discovered him is stuff like *Highway 61 Revisited* and *Blonde on Blonde*. They were those intense metaphorical works—deep heavy stuff, like poems. Then his writing started getting simpler. Even on *Time Out of Mind*.

Some people feel uneasiness when starting up a new project. Is it something that you learned to live with?

That's what I was saying about the creative pattern—after years of going through a dry period, then there's this big bunch of creativity. A lag, and then a spurt. Now I don't worry about it. Part of it is a confidence thing, too. After you've been doing it for a while, you grow more confident. You're more able to experiment and not be so worried that it has to be done in a certain way. Since *Car Wheels*, that set the standard. So I got a lot of negative feedback when *Essence* came out. Some of the songs were so simple, like "Lonely Girls."

The pared-down aspect of Essence *is what makes it such a brilliant record.*

A lot of people feel that way, but some say I'm repeating the same lines over and over. "Lonely girls. Heavy blankets." They didn't get it. They didn't get the Zen of it. I was experimenting and for the first time I allowed myself to come out of my singer-songwriter mode. I was trying to emerge from that overly serious writing thing. I allowed the music and the band to do its thing, rather than having all the emphasis on the lyrics, which was how it had been up until then, for the most part. On *Essence*, I felt for the first time as if I was branching out and doing a rock thing, not stylistically, but having a band and letting the music do its thing. The first time I experimented with that was on the song "Joy" [from *Car Wheels*]. I remember writing that and thinking it wasn't finished yet because it didn't have enough lyrics. I remember when I first taught that piece to the band. We jammed out on the song and it turned into this cool musical ride. I remember thinking, "What the hell, I'm just going to leave it like it is." It had only two verses and I repeated a lot of the same lines. But it worked. Really, when you think about it, that's what's going on with all the old blues stuff that has influenced me.

Is the blues the hardest style of music to play correctly, and the easiest music to play badly?

Not everybody can do it. I've been very careful about treading into that territory because I'm a little white girl. I've been in awe of all the great Delta blues artists. I've felt, out of respect, that they own that music. I can borrow it and do my thing with it, but I'm certainly not a blues singer nor do I ever profess to be one. It's in my roots; I've inherited part of the roots of blues in my music. I feel a little more confident in delivering a blues song. Actually, I've been getting feedback from people that I should do a blues record.

You should. When you're playing blues, how do you figure out what hasn't been done before and how do you handle the challenge of breaking new ground?

You can't think about it intellectually. That's the thing. There's a fine line there that can't be taught. You just have to know. It comes with time and age. For a long time, and I still go through this, there was anxiety, fear, and dread every time I had to go into the studio to make a record. I'd get into the studio and I would be a nervous wreck. I would think, "God, this is so permanent. What if I don't like it later on and I want to do things over and over again?" Those feelings go away with time because, really, I haven't made that many records compared to somebody like Steve Earle. When I was recording with Steve, he would get frustrated. At one point he said, "Lu! It's just a record. Lighten up!" That's how he approaches it. He's able to write really quickly. He's good at writing on demand. If he's asked to come up with a particular song for a movie, he can sit down and do it. Steve would already know that we had a vocal take or whatever it was. But the process I work with is a lot more deliberate. I like to take my time. Steve just goes in and does it. That's why we butted heads a little bit when we worked together in the studio. He has a different way of doing things, and I need to be coddled. "It's going to be okay." If I feel like I need to do something over, you just need to let me go in and do it, even though we know we already got it. Sometimes I have to do it again, so I know, too.

If you put all your records in a stack, do you wish there were more?
   I don't think about it that way.

You've worked fast and you've worked slowly. Which is better?
   I like to work slower. Maybe a combination of the two. It's a good idea to let things breathe and don't get too anal about things when you're in the studio—try to get it as live as possible. At the same time, I like to be able to go back in and fix things a little bit, here and there. *World Without Tears* was completely live. I didn't do any of the vocals over again. *Essence* was completely the opposite. We used Pro Tools quite a bit. I didn't have a regular band at the time, and I had hired outside musicians to come in, like [drummer] Jim Keltner and [bassist] Tony Garnier. It was done in a whole different way, but I love the production on that record.

How much is songwriting an acting process?
   Not much. I've always wanted to be able to write and create a story, which, again, Dylan and Steve are really good at. I've done it a couple of times. There's this song from *Sweet Old World* called "He Never Got Enough Love." That was taken from a newspaper article that I read about this guy who was on death row. I created this whole story around it. I wrote "Memphis Pearl," which is also on that record, after I saw this homeless lady digging through a trashcan one day. I created a story around that. But most of my songs are about actual people I've known and real experiences I've had. It's either stuff I've been through or am going through, or there's some connection with that person I'm writing about. It's pretty close to the bone, songs like "Lake Charles" and "Bus to Baton Rouge." There's a lot of stuff hidden in there.

When you listen to a sexual song like "Righteously" off World Without Tears *or "Right in Time" off* Car Wheels, *one realizes how tough it is to write about raw sensuality. You've approached sexuality on so many levels*

and different genres—blues songs, rock songs, and personal songs. How
difficult is it to go there?

I get off on it. I'm a rebel by nature. I like pushing people's buttons. You
see, I grew up around a bunch of poets anyway—Charles Bukowski, e.e.
cummings, and all that stuff. They don't censor themselves. It's all right out
there. That's probably where I got a lot of that. I like being on the edge, creatively and lyrically. Plus, at the time, I'm really not thinking about it that
way. I'm just doing it. It doesn't occur to me that I'm being [sensual]. I'm
not intellectualizing to that extent. It's another example of how you can go
back to the blues. Listen to Robert Johnson singing about "squeezing my
lemon until the juice runs down my leg." There are all kinds of graphic references when you go back to the blues. Jim Morrison influenced me like
that, too. I was really into the Doors, and he borrowed that same idea from
all those old blues songs, especially when you listen to his unedited stuff.
I like that attitude: "I'm an artist first. This is my art and I'm doing my art,
my thing. If somebody doesn't like it, they can leave." That's how I approach
it from an artistic perspective. A painter isn't going to stand there and censor himself while he's painting. I don't want to offend people, but I do it in
as subtle a way as possible.

Blues has this dark, spooky side.

But it's very joyful at the same time. This, again, has to do with good
art. It's not supposed to be sugarcoated. I come up against this quite a bit.
"Your stuff is so dark and heavy." People think that's a bad thing. Well, life
is dark and heavy. Deal with it. Deal with the pain and feel it. People don't
want to feel any pain. They want to go to Wal-Mart, live in their little house
on their manicured lawn, and go to their boring job everyday. I don't know.
Everybody has the blues; I don't care where they live.

Is there any escape from fear and anxiety in the creative process?

Like Jim Morrison said, you're not going to get out of this alive. I remember thinking when I was younger, "Is this it?" Then I remember somebody
older telling me, "Did you think you were going to get a free ride out of here?"
Bob Neuwirth said something like that to me. "What made you think you were
going to get a free ticket out of here?" You're an artist; there's a price to pay.

When I get into mood swings and everything else, I think, "Well, if I didn't have this, then I wouldn't have all these songs." Unfortunately, it's hard to have one without the other. You have to accept it and not beat yourself up about it.

How do you cope with it?

I think I'm doing pretty well, considering. I'm not sure what kind of demons you're carrying around, but I have quite a few. I battle with them all the time. But that's why I write to begin with. The creative process is a very cathartic process for me. That, in and of itself, means that I can't hold back. I have to dig way down in there and pull it out. That's what probably saved me from going completely insane. I would have become a juvenile delinquent. It doesn't matter if you live in the suburbs in Ohio, you can feel it. That's what it's all about for me. First and foremost, that's why I do it. It's a therapeutic process. That's what people are hearing. It's almost as if you were reading my journal. Then the next step of the creative process is to put it out there so that other people can share. You put it in this art form so that the listeners can get it. That's the craft part of it.

"Sweet Old World" was such a watershed song for you.

What sometimes happens with these songs is I'll have this seed of a song, maybe one line, that I'll carry around with me for years. I wanted to write a song about suicide for years and years. My first, earliest experience with that was this person who I didn't know very well. I remember going up to the Bread Loaf Writers' Conference at Middlebury College in Vermont with my dad in the summer. I was 17. It was a real pivotal time for me, two weeks of an intense environment around poets and short story writers. People would come to this big converted barn with a fireplace at night and sit around and drink and talk. I'd get my guitar out and sing songs. It was an amazing experience. I had met this guy there, a young poet. I guess I had fallen in love, but I don't really remember. He made some impact on me and we stayed in touch. He sent me poetry. Then one day I got a call out in California in 1972 from a friend of his saying he had taken his own life. I asked the person what had happened and she said, "He was just too sensitive for this world." I remember thinking, "Wow, what a fucking cop-out." It stayed with me. I tried to write a song about it, but I couldn't get it to come out right. But the seed was planted and over the years I picked at it and thought it through. Then in 1976 another friend, Frank Stanford's suicide, made a big impact on me. I wrote "Pineola" about that. Finally, when I was living in Texas in the early '80s, a friend of mine's father, whom I hadn't met, shot himself out of the blue. It was one of those shocking things. So now I had these three different vantage points, and I was ready to finish the song. I wrote "Sweet Old World" in 1990. I labored over that song for years. It took a lot of work. For me, when I'm writing something like that, it's for myself, too. When something like that happens, it forces you to look at your own mortality and examine your own life. What does it all mean? Again, that was my way of dealing with the process.

In terms of your career, you've really stuck to your guns, being yourself.

Yeah, I'm pretty stubborn, but don't give me too much credit because a lot of it comes out of fear of being controlled. I don't need to be that worried about stuff, but I'm just so afraid of losing control over my own creativity. Sometimes I go too far and worry too much, like when I'm in the studio recording and I get freaked out—paranoid or uptight. I worry too much about stuff. But the positive end of it is that nobody tells me what to do because they will incur my wrath. But I have gone overboard. I've worried about my music being too over-produced so I've kept a tight rein on things. That's been a growing process for me, too, trying to be more at ease and not worrying so much about things being too slick. I remember when I made that second Folkways record, *Happy Woman Blues*. I didn't have a drummer or a band. At the time I had just been playing acoustically. We went into Sugar Hill Studios in Houston and did the record on the fly. Then Mickey Moody brought in a drummer after we put down the songs acoustically with guitar, bass, and fiddle. He put down drum tracks on the songs and didn't even tell me. I went in the next day and he said, "Hey, listen to this. What do you think?" I was shocked. It was a huge deal adding drums to my little songs. I was pretty much a folkie. I was upset he did it without him discussing it with me first. That's what set everything in motion from there on out. That might have been what traumatized me to the point where I'm so hands-on today.

Are you at the point where you can do whatever the hell you want?

Yeah.

Can anybody get to that point?

Oh, yeah. Bob Dylan and Neil Young are that point. Prince is at that point. I'm definitely at that point. It was really hard in the beginning. I had to be a pain in the ass. I was accused of being a prima donna, an artist that was difficult to work with, stubborn, etc. Part of that comes from the male-female tension, a control issue that comes up quite a bit. But it's paid off at times being a royal pain in the butt.

You managed to be stubborn in your career when you didn't have all that much success as leverage.

I've walked off of major labels before. They know I don't care. That's the thing. You have to be willing to leave it all behind. You can't let them think they have anything over on you. I also can do it because I have something they want. That has to be established first. It wouldn't work for everybody, because somebody might walk away and everybody would just wave good-bye. For me it's worked at the risk of pissing people off. Now, the trade-off is that I'm in control. At the end of the day, I have my songs and my art. I have my fan base. I'm going to have that and I'm going to be able to go out and play and make a living. I'm self-sufficient. That came from doing it the old-fashioned way, going out and playing live. I played in bars and built up a fan base by myself without depending on songs on the radio or having a video. Those are marketing tools that allow you to reach more people. But by the time I started getting successful I had already reached a bunch of people on my own on the strength of my live performances and my little records I put out, like the [self-titled] record on Rough Trade. They were a great record company, totally independent. After that record took off [in 1988], that's when I was introduced to the world of major labels, which, frankly, has been a series of battles.

How do you look at the business today?

I would like to see the independent label industry get stronger because I think that's going to be the saving grace. Big companies and big business are falling apart, which I think is a good thing. In the wave of the future, I would like to see strictly indie labels. They're the only people trying to work in the creative realm, trying to put the artist first and do the right thing. I would be going full circle, because I started out on an independent label. They were the only ones who would give me a chance. Nobody else would sign me at the time. Somebody asked me if I was interested in forming my own imprint label so I could sign artists. I would love to because every so often I'll run across a great young act. But it's so frustrating when you try to turn labels on to them. They don't want to take a chance. Then I remember what it was like when I was trying to get a deal. The more original you are, the harder it is.

Another good reason to do a blues record.

Here's an example of major label thinking: we went to our label at one point and asked about the idea of doing a blues record. They said we could do a blues record, but it wasn't going to count as a record on my contract. It would be seen as an extra project. They basically said it wouldn't count.

After nearly two and a half decades, isn't it time for a live record?

Yeah, we're in the process. We recorded a bunch of stuff at the El Rey Theatre in Los Angeles. Then we recorded at the Fillmore Auditorium in San Francisco. Those were the only places we recorded because it was cost-prohibitive to do the whole tour. Originally that's what I wanted to do, and I was bummed out because I thought we could just stick a tape into the sound system. But you don't get as good a sound, and you don't have control later when you go into the studio and mix it. I wish we had been able to record more shows, but we couldn't afford to have a mobile unit out there every night. Initially when we listened to everything, the Fillmore stuff sounded the best, in terms of audio quality. The audience vibe was better there, too. It might turn out that we may use just all the tracks at the Fillmore. Then I can call it *Live at the Fillmore*—like the Allman Brothers or Miles Davis.

Do you ever get into the zone onstage, like a basketball player does on the paint when every shot goes in?

Yeah, I definitely have those nights. I know when it's happening and the music comes out better than I realize. Sometimes I don't think I'm having a good night, and then later if I listen back, it surprises me.

Download This!

The Essence of Lucinda

Lucinda Williams has released only seven albums in a 25-year period. Here are some highlights that would make up our *Greatest Hits* collection. (But first, get on with that live album, Lu.)

1. "Stop Breakin' Down"—Lucinda Williams (Smithsonian Folkways).
   The first album, *Ramblin',* from 1978, is all blues and country tunes. Recorded in the Deep South, none were written by Lucinda. She covers Robert Johnson with a blues-folk finesse.

2. "Jambalaya"—Lucinda Williams (Smithsonian Folkways).
   A Delta blues treatment of a Hank Williams tune with Lu strumming a fat, 12-string acoustic.

3. "I Lost It"—Lucinda Williams (Smithsonian Folkways).
   This original pedestrian version appeared on her second Folkways record, *Happy Woman Blues,* back in 1980, and then reappeared in full splendor on her *Wheels on a Gravel Road* masterpiece.

4. "Sweet Old World"—Lucinda Williams (Chameleon).
   A trademark Lucinda Williams song that literally took years to write, "Sweet" demonstrates her skill at communicating tactile sensations in verse form (i.e., the touch of fingertips or feeling the pounding of another person's heart in tight embrace). Alongside Roger Miller's "One Dyin' and a Buryin'," it's the second-best song written about suicide.

5. "Memphis Pearl"—Lucinda Williams (Chameleon).
   All acoustic and no drums, but lots of fiddle, slide dobro, and mandolin drape this tale of a Tennessee bag lady's everyday struggles.

6. "Pineola"—Lucinda Williams (Chameleon).
   Using her acute powers of observations, Lu traces the aftershocks of another suicide, from discovering the body to mourning at the burial.

7. "Passionate Kisses"—Lucinda Williams (Koch).
   When this tune became a solid country hit for Mary Chapin Carpenter and earned Lucinda a Grammy, Lucinda's self-titled 1988 Rough Trade album helped establish her as a viable Nashville songwriter.

8. "I Just Wanted to See You So Bad"—Lucinda Williams (Rough Trade/Koch).
Another song from her self-titled late '80s record, made under the auspices of multi-instrumentalist band member Gurf Morlix, who toured with and produced Williams for a long period of her career.

9. "The Night's Too Long"—Lucinda Williams (Rough Trade/Koch).
Patty Loveless picked up this song for country radio. Subsequently, Williams spent nine years living in Music City when she wasn't on the road playing in bars.

10. "Big Red Sun"—Lucinda Williams (Rough Trade/Koch).
Lucinda's uptempo, Tex-Mex tribute to Doug Sahm and his Sir Douglas Quintet. Distant Farfisa-style organ blends with a lucid slide dobro.

11. "Right in Time"—Lucinda Williams (Mercury).
Car Wheels on a Gravel Road was scrapped and redone over and over. It was delayed for years only to become a Grammy-winning, million-selling album. "Right in Time" is Lucinda's unabashed anthem to the art of "self-pleasuring."

12. "Car Wheels on a Gravel Road"—Lucinda Williams (Mercury).
The difference between the finished *Car Wheels* album and its original sessions overseen by Gurf Morlix are rather striking. The original vocals possessed little of Williams's quirky vocal personality. It was as if she was reading through the lyrics.

13. "Lake Charles"—Lucinda Williams (Mercury).
A good example of a song that Williams slaved over to make it one of her most crafted ballads. Lots of real-life observations and memories of her birthplace— another strong trait of Lucinda's songwriting.

14. "Concrete and Barbed Wire"—Lucinda Williams (Mercury).
Lucinda Williams and Steve Earle strum through this rootsy duet. Country changes with lots of accordion and slide guitar.

15. "Greenville"—Lucinda Williams (Mercury).
A brilliant duet with Emmylou Harris. The year 1998 was a vintage one for the lady from Lake Charles.

16. "Lonely Girls"—Lucinda Williams (Lost Highway).
This is an exercise in American songwriting worthy of college study, with its symmetrical phrasing and minimalist lyrical repose.

continued on the next page

The Essence of Lucinda *continued*

17. "I Envy the Wind"—Lucinda Williams (Lost Highway).
Another one of Williams's finest compositions, from *Essence*. *Essence* is
to *Car Wheels* what *Nashville Skyline* is to *Blonde on Blonde*. Economy of
description, but heavy on impressionism.

18. "Essence"—Lucinda Williams (Lost Highway).
The first picture inside the booklet of this 2001 release tells the whole story.
A coffee cup, Martin guitar, a pen, note pad with lyrics, empty cassette tape
case, and a Walkman player with headphones. Her vocal performance on the
title track is so convincing, the listener actually believes Lucinda Williams is a
strung out love junkie.

19. "Righteously"—Lucinda Williams (Lost Highway).
Lucinda Williams gets downright sexual again as she sings about experiencing
the glories of getting felt up. Forget that she lays the sensuality on thick, but the
provocative part is likening the experience to listening to John Coltrane. A love
supreme?

20. "Ventura"—Lucinda Williams (Lost Highway).
Another day-in-the-life tune as Lu writes about driving up the California coast
on U.S. 101, past Ventura and the surfers at Santa Barbara, and probably on
up north to Pismo Beach. Neil Young is turned up loud on the radio and there's
a languid steel guitar wrapped all over the arrangements. It's Lucinda Williams
at her artistic best, from the *World Without Tears* CD.

chapter 17

The Low Stock of the Current Music Industry

F ebruary 8, 1996. Nobody knew it at the time, but for many music fans, that was the day that modern music went into decline.

It wasn't an iconoclastic dark day—not like the murder of John Lennon or the suicide of Kurt Cobain, where folks can remember exactly where they were the minute they heard the news. No, it was the day President Bill Clinton signed into law the congressionally enacted Telecommunications Act of 1996.

Looking back, that day was the first rumbling of an avalanche of huge changes about to take place in radio and the music industry. For the record business in particular, it was the beginning of the end of a lucrative business cycle that started around 1966 and flourished for three decades. As the stock market rose to near death-defying heights during the bull market 1990s, who could possibly suspect that music's own "stock-price" would plummet in the face of corporate and government power plays?

By the year 2000, with the record industry already suffering double-digit sales drops, the 1996 Telecommunications Act's rules had shaken the music business to its core. Depending on which side of the idealistic fence you straddled (free trader or consumer advocate), the Telecom Act's laws governing how many stations one broadcast company could own would soon redefine both radio and the record business for better or worse.

The laws and statutes that comprised the Telecom Act were originally meant to be a long-overdue, modern overhaul of the telecommunications structure of the United States. Many government and business leaders approaching the new millennium believed that vital services such as radio broadcasting, cable, utilities, and communications could no longer be pigeonholed, isolated, and protected. Gone were the days when "the telephone company" provided phone service or "the utility company" dispensed natural gas and electricity, or "broadcasters" solely provided radio and TV entertainment.

The borderlines were blurred. Internet access could be purchased through a cable entity. Long distance phone service and satellite television could be ordered through a local Baby Bell. Someone's favorite music station could be piped in through a DSL line connected to a home computer. Lawmakers decided to "level the playing field" for telecommunication concerns in the US.

It was time to deregulate.

Although the 1996 Telecom Act regulated many facets of modern communication, including cable and network television, telephone and long distance rates, wireless services, and Internet access, no sector was more radically impacted or transformed than the radio broadcasting world.

Essentially it came down to this: the quantity of radio stations a broadcast chain could own in one local market increased from two stations (one AM and one FM) to *eight* across the AM or FM dial (in a region that carried 45 stations or more). The Telecom Act also allowed broadcast companies to own as many stations *nationwide* as they pleased. Essentially, a broadcast media company that had previously owned 30 stations across the country could now own hundreds or even thousands. When the Telecom bill was being written in 1995, nobody predicted such a scenario would happen. But within five years, that's exactly what occurred.

By 2001, a San Antonio company, Clear Channel Communications, through a rapid series of mergers, acquisitions, and accumulated holdings, controlled 1,200 mostly music-oriented radio stations across the United States. Cumulus Broadcasting Inc. and Citadel Broadcasting Corp. owned 266 and 213 medium- and small-market stations, respectively. Yet another major conglomerate, Infinity Broadcasting Corporation, accrued 180 stations in 40 of the largest population centers in 22 states. Infinity's holdings included six stations in New York City alone, five stations each in Philadelphia and Washington D.C., and seven stations in Chicago and Los Angeles. Radio had gone super-corporate. Infinity's parent company, General Electric, owned global media giant Viacom, whose holdings also included CBS Television, Simon

& Schuster, Paramount Pictures, and numerous cable channels including MTV and Showtime.

Eric Boehlert, a senior writer at www.salon.com, was working at *Billboard Magazine* at the time the deregulation process began.

"While I was at *Billboard* covering radio," Boehlert recalled, "I didn't speak to anyone who thought five years from [1996] there would be two radio companies running America—Clear Channel and Infinity."

Before 1996, radio, governed by the Federal Communications Commission (FCC), was plodding along financially. In 1992, radio was cast into such a deep recession that 60 percent of all American stations were not profitable. In response to a dour situation, the FCC permitted "duopoly" ownership, where a company could own two AM stations and two FM stations in a single market. That was supposed to help radio cut its operating expenses and bolster sales packages.

"In the early '90s," said Boehlert, "I was writing about what bad shape the radio business was in. Advertising revenues were down. They were getting beat up by the newspapers. For instance, an FM station in Boston couldn't even sell for ten or twenty million dollars. Back then the catchphrase was 'duopolies.' You were able to sell ads on more than one station in a market. It was [radio's] way out; they would be able to sell more time and cut costs. Then after the 1996 Telecommunications Act was passed, it became [like] duopolies [were] on rampant steroids."

While the 1996 Telecom Act was pushed through a Republican Congress under Newt Gingrich's and Bob Dole's leadership, and signed by Democratic President Clinton, the House and Senate strangely dominated the process, keeping the FCC far in the background. Before the legislation passed, there were no hearings and virtually no public debate. There was no debate on the floor of the House or the Senate. Radio deregulation statutes were buried deep inside a 300-page bill that nobody seemed to report on or know much about.

Mainstream press ignored (or completely misjudged) the impending impact the Telecom Act would have on radio, and then on music. Attention mostly revolved around three Trojan horse issues inside the act, none of which pertained directly to Congress repealing radio's ownership limitations. Issue one, the press reported, was that television manufacturers were required to equip all new TV sets with a "V-chip" to help parents block out violent or sexually explicit viewing from children. (Today, the V-chip is a tangential piece of technology at best.) The second issue was Internet censorship. Criminal penalties were discussed for anyone knowingly transmitting obscene materials over "an interactive computer service." (Realistically, it was a futile effort to legislate obscene content on the worldwide Web.) The third issue was the formation of a voluntary ratings system for cable and broadcast television programs. (While the ratings guide still exists, are most TV viewers even aware of the existence of television's rating system? One needn't ask that about the current ratings of the Motion Picture Association of America.)

The license renewal process for radio station owners was also made easier. Seven-year licenses were expanded to eight years, and the FCC was barred from considering alternate owners during renewal time. The only way the FCC could revoke a license or force a station to change hands was if the present owners were guilty of any serious FCC infractions.

"What was so bizarre about the [1996] Telecom Act," noted Boehlert, "was [that] it wasn't handled by the Federal Communications Commission. Prior to that, nothing had been done on the AM or FM dial without the FCC's fingerprints all over it or [after] years of FCC study. Congress came along and decided to handle it, and in eight months, passed the act. 'Radical' doesn't begin to describe what they did to the radio business."

By early 1996, a few broadcast players represented by shrewd Wall Street brokers and venture capitalists went on buying sprees across the country. One company, the feisty Jacor Communications, quickly bought up 450 radio stations. While a buying frenzy continued throughout the late '90s, media watchers snickered at the notion that any one company could possibly rack up 1,000 radio properties. Along with Jacor, early media goliaths included Chancellor Media, American Stations, AMFM Network, and Evergreen Media. Month after month, American music lovers watched as the buying and selling of the people's airwaves surged valuations of local stations on the buying block. By the year 2000, almost every city and town in America saw radio stations across the dial bought and sold for record prices. Soon there were only a few independently owned radio stations left operating in each region, and mostly at a huge financial disadvantage. Consumer advocates worried about the monopolization of the American people's commercial radio airwaves.

"[Originally] everyone thought someone would get to two or three hundred stations," said Boehlert, "while there probably might be five, six, or seven different companies with a hundred or more stations."

Today, however, few if any of the early participating broadcast companies even exist any more. American Stations divested their position. Then Clear Channel Communications gobbled up Evergreen, Jacor, Chancellor, and AMFM, until they controlled 1,200 radio stations in 247 of the top 250 largest radio markets in America.

"I remember," said Boehlert, "one of the major [broadcast] CEOs telling me that when the act finally passed after all the wrangling, he and his other officers were together in a hotel room. They high-fived each other and ordered champagne."

Clear Channel is now a dominant figure in the world of radio, music, and entertainment. Besides their radio empire, Clear Channel has also ventured into other major media ventures.

"It's not just that Clear Channel owns 1,200 stations," Boehlert pointed out. "You have to take a step back because now Clear Channel owns everything. They've replaced whoever ran the music business to become their own music business. They now own the largest radio syndicator, Premiere Radio Networks. They now have their own marketing consultants, research company, and trade magazine. They now have their own trade shows. They now have their own [nationwide] concert promotion company and billboard company. And I'm leaving stuff out. They've had such a stranglehold, that within five years, they went from this sleepy company to this outrageous and—critics would say—power-hungry company."

The next entity to bear the brunt of such sweeping "reforms" was the music industry, including record labels large and small as well as the artists who recorded for them. For decades, major record labels had perfected a system in which they could expose their artists' music on radio at will, signing whatever creative artists they chose, and doling out tour support to try and turn those acts into superstars. If extra strong-arm tactics were needed to make a record become a hit, labels hired a network of "independent promoters" to "convince" radio program directors "with nontraditional revenue" to add their records to a station's playlist. And that included *all* artists, from the baby acts to the world's most famous performers.

"The record industry in 1996 had operated as it had for the last 50 years," observed Boehlert, who wrote an April 2001 investigative piece for salon.com on Clear Channel, calling them Radio's Big Bully.

"By 2000, the music business became unrecognizable because one [radio] company became the proverbial 800-pound gorilla. If you couldn't get your record on Clear Channel stations, particularly if you were a mainstream R&B, rock, or pop act, then forget it.

"Back in the earlier days," Boehlert continued, "if [a label] didn't get on one broadcast chain, you might get shut out of 18 stations. So you took your hits and moved on to the other 324 markets left. Now, if you have a pop record and you're having trouble with Clear Channel, then why bother?

"Nobody had seen anything like that. The only thing that came close was the network of independent promoters who could decide if a record was or was not getting on the air. But that was a whole different game, and the record companies really understood how that game worked."

The other unforeseen outcome of the 1996 Telecom Act was the end of competition between rival radio stations. Throughout the 1950s, '60s, '70s, and '80s, "radio wars" thrived in many small to major markets. Competition was fierce and well executed. If a label had an airplay-friendly rock record, the label promotion department held multiple options in most markets. They could play one set of radio call letters against another. If a label couldn't get their record on one station, they'd try another. They could circle a major market station with smaller but influential secondary markets and "force them" on a record. Today, with big chains like Clear Channel and Infinity controlling up to eight stations in many different top markets, call letters that once ruthlessly competed against each other for all-important Arbitron rating points now find themselves working under the same corporate umbrella. What were once bitter radio competitors are now strange bedfellows sharing audience research and other synergies. To the horror of die-hard music fans weary of homogenous-sounding radio, one brash Clear Channel executive bragged that the consistency of their radio stations' sound was comparable to the consistency of Wal-Mart stores across the country.

"Station managers and program directors want high ratings," said Boehlert, "but there's no major incentive to break [introduce] artists and to come up with that secret weapon record that some music director might have found, that his or her rivals didn't have, that would take three weeks for the competition to get on the air. By then you owned the band, and when they [performed live in] your market, they were yours. Consolidation has eliminated such competition. Now artists don't have that leverage anymore."

As a result, the number of new artists being broken each year by commercial radio has dwindled. Consequently, the number of new artists being signed onto major labels has dropped, while many established acts have also been unceremoniously purged from their longtime label homes.

"While the labels now are in the marketing and distribution business, they don't have tentacles into broadcasting or the concert business," Boehlert commented. "It's bad, and I think it's another chapter in the collapse of the music business as we know it. Anyone who was in the business ten years ago really wouldn't recognize the music business today."

Artists who specialize in American roots rock (as opposed to teen-oriented, mass appeal pop) seem to have less and less reason to record for a major label. More and more major labels have dropped what they call their "niche artists" because they have less of a chance of making "home run" bestseller status in the multi-millions. As the major label groups such as Warner, EMI, Universal, BMG, and Sony become global conglomerates, they in turn become beholden to the bottom-line concerns of their stockholders and boards of directors, and less to the signing of quality, adult-oriented roots acts.

In the intervening time, over on the radio side, when the conglomerates first began their "consolidation" process, radio professionals were promised there would be more job opportunities and room for promotion within the new, larger broadcast groups. DJs, programmers, managers, promotion directors, salespeople, and other radio professionals were all supposed to benefit by being part of a wider network of stations spread geographically across the country. Unfortunately, instead of expanding opportunities, layoffs and cutbacks became the order of the day. As group station holdings in each region became "clusters," general managers, sales managers, and program directors from the top to the bottom were laid off or forced to oversee multiple corporate properties. Local air talents were let go in favor of nationally syndicated or taped shows owned by the same broadcast conglomerates.

Over on the record label front, jobs were also eliminated at a fast pace. Legendary and reputable imprints both large and small, such as Island, Motown, A&M, MCA, DreamWorks, Elektra, and Reprise, were gutted, absorbed, consolidated, or eliminated by their corporate parents. Signings slowed down as each major label group was either in financial play or about to be downsized. Artist and repertoire (A&R) staffs were now extremely hesitant to sign artists as briskly as they had in previous decades. Like every industry in America between 1999 and 2004, radio and the music industry suffered round after round of layoffs. The music business slipped from being a 40 billion dollar concern in 2000 to 28 billion in 2004. To many, the aftershocks of the 1996 Telecom Act seemed way beyond repair. An American tradition of radio and music had been destroyed.

"Radio consolidation can never go back to where it was before the Telecom Act," said Boehlert. "Washington won't re-regulate. There is no precedent for that. I don't see a day where Clear Channel doesn't own 1,200 stations. Someone is going to own 1,000 stations. The radio business as we once knew it is over. The 10,000 people drummed out of radio because of consolidation and layoffs probably will not return."

After all the buying and selling and firing, the question remains: was it worth it?

Radio, according to Boehlert, "pretty much lives on beer and soft drink ads. I think advertising is better. Today it is now easier for advertisers to buy national radio spots. Media buyers have an easier time than in 1990 picking up the phone and making major buys on behalf of a client. Today you can make a few phone calls and buy coast-to-coast advertising. That has improved for radio. The massive layoffs have created another windfall for station owners, but in terms of local broadcasting, it's gutted the radio business."

It's clear that record label and radio consolidation has caused a creative rift in the music business. Gone are the days when prolific bands and singer-songwriters wrote and recorded one album per year for a major label. Industry watchers bemoan the downfall of patient artist development (i.e., nurturing artists through three or even four releases). Today, most artists—new, emerging, or veteran—are expected to progress artistically and financially by releasing a full CD only every three or four years.

"The net effect is the collapse of one of the great American entrepreneurial industries," Bochlert explained. "The music industry was one of the great eccentric and wonderful industries. It was created in America, perfected in a bizarre way in America, and it was run by a wild bunch of characters that made a lot of artists' dreams come true. It also spit a lot of artists out in the process. Today, the business model is outdated, which is sad and too bad for artists and music fans."

The record label community, spearheaded by its trade organization, the Record Industry Association of America (RIAA), is fond of blaming steep annual sales declines on computer users who download music files illegally or burn extra copies of pre-recorded CDs for their friends. Yet for every label industry insider who points the guilty finger at technology, there are many who feel the decline in music sales is symptomatic of other problems. Many blame the quality of the music being nurtured and recorded under the current system. Also, the retail cost of a CD has jumped to an all-time high, close to $20 for an established act in the US. This comes at a time when music fans are lulled into the assumption that most CDs contain, at best, one or two good tracks. This spurs music hobbyists to download only the hits or their favorite tracks rather than spend twenty bucks on a CD.

Secondly, while music DVDs have doubled in sales, the public now views the 20-year-old compact disc technology as "old school"—not a good time for CDs to sport bloated price tags, shrunken artwork, and tired presentation. Activity in the "big box stores" like Best Buy or Wal-Mart shows much more consumer enthusiasm in their DVD and video/computer game sections than in their CD departments.

Customers might buy new and undiscovered music more often if they were pointed towards titles in clever and innovative ways instead of the standard media. One way to spike up CD sales would be to devise in-store and online sites where the average person could plug in or type in his or her favorite genres, artists, and sounds, and receive viable suggestions as to who they should buy next. If a customer were fond of, say, Allison Moorer or Badly Drawn Boy, or Pearl Jam or Bob Dylan, what other new and fresh recommendations could be made in the store or on the Internet? The music industry should get behind some kind of "electronic friend" recommendation technology. Finding new music could be fun and interesting again in the cyber age.

In today's volatile music climate, when radio and the record labels catch cold, the music retail outlets catch pneumonia. Sadly, music is being purchased less and less at local record stores, and more and more at large, electronics-oriented chain stores, where CDs are often dangled as loss leaders to attract sales on higher ticket items like televisions and audiovisual gear. The monolithic chains Best Buy, Target, Wal-Mart, and Circuit City are accounting for over fifty percent of total American prerecorded music sales.

"Many independent retail [record] stores are out of business," said Boehlert. "Even the [record] chains are suffering. Whereas over the past 30 years, the best place to have had a CD store was in college towns, now that's the worst place in America to own one. Retailers have been devastated, partly through consolidation, partly because of downloading and the burning of CDs, partly because of arrogance and ignorance on the part of the labels."

Unfortunately the biggest losers are the artists. They are the ones who put the most on the line, their art and their livelihoods.

"I don't know how artists even contemplate making a career [of music] if they haven't already established themselves. If they can play 90 to 120 live dates per year and make a living, that's great. But if they haven't already established themselves, I can't imagine how they make it. It's such a crapshoot and a lottery to begin with. How do artists get into the retail stores? How do they get on radio?"

One lifeline for American roots rock artists is to continue to reach out to audiences through noncommercial radio (and the few remaining commercial stations that program progressive roots rock music). This is very much a viable alternative. Artists can survive or even thrive on such a following. (While these older listeners, aged 35 to 54, are a loyal demographic, they're also a tougher sell to get to buy music, even online.)

Roots rock artists can consistently put out the highest amount of quality, timeless music without much need for commercial airplay support. Plus, American roots rock artists selling 50,000 to 100,000 copies on smaller, more homegrown independent labels can consider themselves successful.

As the music industry looks desperately into the future, one of the more intriguing up and coming technologies that might boost American roots rock looks to be satellite radio. XM Radio and Sirius Radio are seriously turning the heads of music fans who are currently fed up with boring mainstream radio stations. Many financial analysts, industry watchers, and stockholders who may have been skeptical in the past are now growing optimistic.

"I was a critic and a skeptic of satellite radio for years," admitted Boehlert. "I just didn't see the economics of people paying a few hundred dollars to get it up and running and then pay a monthly bill. Although people do it for television, my argument was that the relationship people have with their radio is different. Americans literally cannot exist without their TVs and don't think twice paying fifty bucks a month for cable TV. But listening to the radio is such a passive activity. While you turn it on in your car, how many people over the age of 21 listen to the radio at home?

"Another reason I'm being proven wrong about satellite radio is that people will always be passionate about their music," Boehlert noted. "Listeners today seem less willing to listen to 13 minutes of commercials. People want new music. You can make the argument that they're not getting that on commercial FM radio. It's the ultimate indictment of commercial radio that people are now willing to pay a hundred and twenty bucks for radio that they can't find anywhere else. Personally, everybody I know who subscribes to satellite radio really loves it. I haven't heard from anybody that feels it's a waste of money."

The early popularity of satellite radio among music fans may send a message to corporate terrestrial radio programmers who care more about increasing station ad revenues through tight playlists, more repetition, and less variety rather than playing unproven, niche-oriented music. But can satellite radio, programmers argue, break new artists like "local" radio does? Satellite radio needs to figure out the fine line between offering its customers 100 channels of choice and becoming mainstream enough to grow its subscription base on a long and bumpy road toward profitability.

Since 1996, creative people in both the broadcasting and music industries have endured extremely difficult times. They are sometimes forced to watch from the sidelines while other entertainment sectors like movies, sports, and electronic games continue to prosper—dazzling, challenging, and innovating their audiences. Unfortunately, commercial radio and the music industry need a nudge from time to time to stay interesting. For nearly a decade, a dark shadow has been cast over its ranks, and it's going to take a few more years for commercial radio to recover and relearn how to be clever, adventurous, and inventive again.

Barely a decade ago, working in radio or the music business was a dream job. Now it's a bygone era. User-friendly, legal downloading sites and iPod technology are a push in the right direction. But again, some observers feel that the business may be overpricing itself by charging even 99¢ per downloaded song. While Apple's iPod technology has reported brisk sales, it's the hardware sales, not the revenues generated from software tunes, that is raking in the profits.

Music's free fall is a "stock-price" issue all right, though not in a traditional Wall Street way of thinking. Music's current "stock" value among its fans, especially among younger consumers, has plummeted—thanks to uninteresting corporate radio groups and label conglomerates frightened of technology. These were industries that were once considered recession-proof. Nowadays, who knows?

One thing is certain. As long as music's "stock-price" remains low even among its core customers, the music industry will continue to live in difficult and turbulent times until it re-commands the respect it once enjoyed as an innovator before February 8, 1996—the day modern music went into decline.

chapter 18

The *Sing My Way Home* Top 100 Modern American Roots Rock Classics Countdown

Here are 100 influential discs that we feel make an excellent and impressive "instant collection" of the finest American roots rock ever recorded. There's a lot of territory covered here, including folk, rock 'n' roll, singer-songwriter, and bluegrass, all mixed in with a little American country and cowboy. This is primarily a modern list, so noticeably absent are Hank Williams and Woody Guthrie. Also deleted are American classic rockers, English bands, and blues artists. We threw in only a few "best-of" collections. To make matters easy and to break up the list, we arranged the albums in categories and in countdown order. Note this is not meant to be an all-inclusive, be-all and end-all list, but rather, an honest overview of the various styles that make up the world of American roots rock music.

The First Round

100. *Roots*—**The Everly Brothers** (Warner Bros.).
This overlooked 1968 classic included two Merle Haggard standards, "Sing My Way Back Home" and "Mama Tried."

99. *I Am Shelby Lynne*—**Shelby Lynne** (Island).
It's her only good record, but highly worthwhile.

98. *A Few Small Repairs*—**Shawn Colvin** (Columbia).
Shawn's music addresses a wide range of emotions and various stages of relationship turmoil.

97. *Old Five and Dimers Like Me*—Billy Joe Shaver (Monument/Koch).
The wide use of his songs made him the Thomas Paine of the 1970s outlaw country movement.

96. *The House Carpenter's Daughter*—Natalie Merchant (Myth America).
Merchant dabbles deftly in Appalachian ballads, American hymns, and early Fairport Convention.

95. *Spinning Around the Sun*—Jimmie Dale Gilmore (Elektra).
Jimmie Dale uses major label production (and dollars) to bolster his organic sound.

94. *The Charity of Night*—Bruce Cockburn (Rykodisc).
Cockburn is the pride of Canada. Each song here is wrapped in global or cerebral intrigue.

93. *Revival Time*—Gillian Welch (Acony).
Gillian is another important figure, alongside Uncle Tupelo, Whiskeytown, Wilco, the Jayhawks, and Son Volt, in the modern roots rock continuum that blossomed in the 1990s.

92. *See How We Are*—X (Elektra).
Roots rock perspective from a different angle, using rockabilly, punk, and hard rock. John Doe's vocal on Dave Alvin's "4th of July" truly sizzles.

91. *Guitars, Cadillacs, Etc., Etc.*—Dwight Yoakam (Reprise).
Yoakam's twang and roadhouse production puts Bakersfield back on the country map.

90. *Jackrabbit Slim* —Steve Forbert (Sony).
A fine modern folkie album. Entertaining song plots represent Forbert's best material.

89. *Heart Food*—Judee Sill (Asylum/Handmade).

Sill is an obscure Asylum artist from the label's early days who died as a result of heroin usage. Rhino's Handmade label has reissued both of her recordings: 1971's *Judee Sill* and 1973's *Heart Food*.

88. *Hang On to a Dream: Verve Years*—**Tim Hardin** (PolyGram).
    An indispensable visionary who fused folk, rock, and jazz in the early '60s Greenwich Village scene.

87. *Again*—**Buffalo Springfield** (Atlantic).
    A 1967 love beads, psychedelic guidepost to modern American roots rock.

86. *Hollywood Town Hall*—**The Jayhawks** (Universal).
    Are you a Jayhawk or a Bushwhacker? Nice harmonies and strumming from Gary Louris and Mark Olson on this 1992 modern roots rock effort.

85. *Paradise Lunch*—**Ry Cooder** (Warner Bros.).
    Years before *Buena Vista Social Club* gained him wide recognition, Cooder was an invaluable Warner Bros. artist during the label's golden years.

84. *Texas Cookin'*—**Guy Clark** (RCA).
    Guy Clark is a premiere Texas songwriter. This album includes his versions of "Desperadoes Waiting for a Train" and "L.A. Freeway."

83. *Wheels of Fortune*—**The Flatlanders** (New West).
    This 2004 effort is the best of the Joe Ely, Jimmie Dale Gilmore, and Butch Hancock reunion projects.

82. *Austin Skyline*—**Jimmy LaFave** (Bohemia Beat).
    An Austin talent by way of Oklahoma, Jimmy is, in our opinion, the supreme interpreter of Bob Dylan songs. Second only to Bob himself.

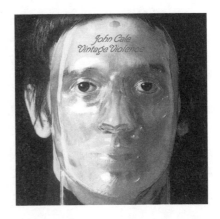

81. *Vintage Violence* —**John Cale** (Columbia).

John Cale is sacked from the Velvet Underground in 1968 and writes and cuts 11 country-flavored pop tunes in a few days' time. A work of genius.

80. *New Riders of the Purple Sage*
—**New Riders of the Purple Sage** (Sony).
Marmaduke and the New Riders were the early sages of country-rock, with the help of Jerry Garcia on pedal steel.

79. *Lost in Space*—**Aimee Mann** (Superego).
One of the most forward-thinking American artists today. Formerly an MTV video darling with the group 'Til Tuesday, the quality of Mann's records soared when she emancipated herself from the major-label system.

78. *Roger Miller—Golden Hits*—**Roger Miller** (PolyGram).
Miller was such a hot hit maker that this 11-track greatest hits package was only his fourth record.

The Second Round

77. *Sailin' Shoes*—**Little Feat** (Warner Bros.).
Even though leader Lowell George died back in 1979, his ability to combine rock, country, blues, and R&B into his own inimitable blend should not be overlooked today.

76. *The Light of the Moon*—**Los Lobos** (Slash/Warner Bros.).
East L.A., Latino roots aggregation band blends every possible Mexican and Spanish influence into their music.

75. *Crosby, Stills & Nash*—**Crosby, Stills & Nash** (Atlantic).
One of the early syntheses of rock, country, folk, and pop, with a supergroup concept that supported the major labels for decades.

74. *The Last of the True Believers*—**Nanci Griffith** (Rounder).
Originally released on a folk/bluegrass subsidiary label called Philo, this 1986 release marks the genesis of her expanded output on MCA and Elektra. Now she's back on Rounder.

73. *Hums of the Lovin' Spoonful*—Lovin' Spoonful (Buddha/BMG).
In our opinion, this was the first modern American roots rock experiment.

72. *Odelay*—Beck (Geffen).
Is Beck a modern day Gram Parsons? Both have a futuristic reach to their music.

71. *Pretty Much Your Standard Ranch Stash*—Michael Nesmith (RCA).
Many of Nesmith's early RCA records have been reissued in the UK. Here's the one well worth picking up.

70. *620 West Surf*—Michael McDermott (Giant/Warner Bros.).
This 1990 debut record is one of the best from this fine Chicago songwriter. Horror novelist Stephen King is a big fan.

69. *Blacklisted*—Neko Case & Her Boyfriends (Bloodshot).
Every record gets better and better for this headstrong disciple of Patsy Cline. Will the modern major label system embrace her?

68. *The Natch'l Blues*
—Taj Mahal (Columbia).
This is one of the finest
blues-rock records of all time.
Taj reinvents traditional songs
like "Corinna."

67. *Robbie Robertson*
—Robbie Robertson (Geffen).
Atmospheric, filmic, and super-
natural, but in a good way. Dan
Lanois's production is outermost on the edge.

66. *Flaming Red*—Patty Griffin (A&M).
This Boston/Cambridge folksinger followed up her acoustic ADAT debut with a denser, rocking sound. This 1998 release is her best.

65. *Honky Tonk Masquerade*—Joe Ely (MCA).
This 1978 release hoisted Joe into the roots rock experience and contains great Butch Hancock and Jimmie Dale Gilmore tunes.

64. *Silk Purse*—Linda Ronstadt (Capitol).
Elliot Mazer provided a rock-style production to this pioneering country-rock-pop crossover project.

63. *Bring the Family*—John Hiatt (A&M).
Recorded live on a soundstage in 1987 with Hiatt's ideal backup band—Nick Lowe on bass, Jim Keltner on drums, and Ry Cooder on guitar. Let's go to Memphis in the meantime.

62. *Sail Away*—Randy Newman (Warner Bros.).
A 1972 classic that has its moments of light and shade, sadness and satire.

61. *Strangers Almanac*—Whiskeytown (Outpost).
With Ryan Adams at age 22, this 1997 record is compelling in that it's equal parts Gram P. and Uncle T. Early strains of Adams's reckless, creative studio style.

60. *Come Away with Me*—Norah Jones (Blue Note).
Ms. Jones distills so many modern roots influences that she awakened upper-demo record buyers to support her with millions in sales. Meanwhile, the major labels are still scratching their heads.

59. *Exit 0*—Steve Earle (MCA).
An alchemy of Nashville country and Southern rock with a four-four "Texas Radio and the Big Beat" beat.

58. *Picnic*—Robert Earl Keen (Arista).
Robert Earl can't be ignored as another important West Texas songwriter. Has the sense of humor of a frat boy.

57. *Don McLean*—Don McLean (UA/BGO-import).
The musical equivalent to someone pulling the emergency stop mechanism on a speeding railroad train.

56. *Lonesome Jubilee*—John Mellencamp (Mercury).
This is one of Mellencamp's most roots-oriented works, featuring plenty of fiddles, accordions, and acoustic instruments.

55. *Nick of Time*—Bonnie Raitt (Capitol).
Great songs and a clean Don Was production sparked this 1989 worldwide bestseller.

54. *Too-Long in the Wasteland*—James McMurtry (Columbia).
John Mellencamp produced this debut 1989 record. Son of famous novelist Larry, James McMurtry has a deep, resonate voice. Plenty of Mellencampy slice-of-life scenarios in his songs.

53. *Baez Sings Dylan*—Joan Baez (Vanguard).
Love is just a four-letter word. Incredible Dylan interpretations and lots of roots influences to boot. Fine collection.

52. *Red Headed Stranger*—Willie Nelson (Columbia).
Released at the dawn of the outlaw country insurrection, this 1975 storyteller record made a huge, unlikely commercial impact.

51. *The American*—Martin Sexton (Atlantic).
Another major label gem worth seeking out. Lots of all-American influences, including yodeling and cowboy and desert lore.

The Regionals

50. *Songs of Love and Hate*—Leonard Cohen (Columbia).
Whole volumes could be, and have been, written about the enchantment of Mr. Cohen's music and persona.

49. *A.M.*—Wilco (Sire/Warner Bros.).
Wilco's 1995 debut rose from the ashes of the demise of Uncle Tupelo.

48. *American Pie*—Don McLean (Capitol).
The album with the song that fired up a million jukeboxes around the world.

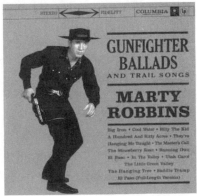

47. *Gunfighter Ballads and Trail Songs*—Marty Robbins (Legacy/Sony).
How many great songwriters of today listened to this record over and over with their fathers, uncles, or older male mentors?

46. *El Corazón*—**Steve Earle** (E-Squared/Warner Bros.).
This 1997 effort best typifies the multi-roots posture Earle is currently taking with generous elements of country, bluegrass, folk,
rock, and more.

45. *Pontiac*—**Lyle Lovett**
(Curb/MCA).
Lyle has made a bunch of great
records but this second record,
from 1987, has its own magic.
It's dreamy, clever, rootsy, and
the songs are enlivened by Lyle's
dry sense of humor.

44. *Proof through the Night*—
T-Bone Burnett (Warner Bros.).
This is the most obscure record of the list in that it is only available
in used or import vinyl. Packed with hard-hitting social and moral
commentary.

43. *Blue*—**Joni Mitchell** (Reprise).
Perhaps the most personal, transparent set of songs recorded.

42. *American III: Solitary Man*—**Johnny Cash**
(American Recordings).
Here the man in black reaches out to contemporary rock audi-
ences, just like he did throughout his 50-year career. We miss him.

41. *Full Moon Fever*—**Tom Petty** (MCA).
This is Petty's first solo album without the Heartbreakers, so it's
more personal. Produced by Jeff Lynne.

40. *Moondance*—**Van Morrison** (Warner Bros.).
Even though some of the songs are used on national TV commercial spots, this is Van Morrison at his most organic.

39. *John Prine—Great Days: The John Prine Anthology* (Rhino).
One can make the argument that John Prine is the finest roots
music songwriter alive today, and damn few would disagree.

38. *Working Man's Dead*—**Grateful Dead** (Warner Bros.).
The Dead's roots rock opus, Part One.

37. *Acadie*—**Daniel Lanois** (Opal/Warner Bros.).
Lanois captures the magical texture of blending sounds from Cajun Louisiana and French Canadian Montreal. This debut is a record to ponder your life choices over.

36. *The Pretender*—**Jackson Browne** (Asylum).
Between 1972 and 1980, Browne was the ultimate sensitive Southern California balladeer. Each release was a major music occasion.

35. *John Wesley Harding*—**Bob Dylan** (Columbia).
Essentially, this is Dylan following up *Blonde on Blonde* with a bunch of rock-solid songs backed by a power trio of bass, drums, and acoustic guitar. "I'll Be Your Baby Tonight" signaled Dylan's fascination with country.

34. *American Beauty*—**Grateful Dead** (Warner Bros.).
The Dead's roots rock opus, Part Two.

33. *Trace*—**Son Volt** (Warner Bros.).
Jay Farrar's spin-off, *Trace* is the best of the three Son Volt efforts from 1995 to 1998.

32. *Mermaid Avenue*—
Billy Bragg & Wilco (Elektra).
Woody Guthrie's music is raised
to another contemporary level
with this hands-across-the-
ocean collaboration.

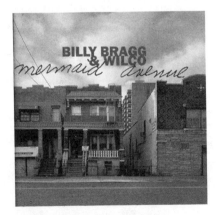

31. *Exile on Main Street*—**Rolling Stones** (Rolling Stones/Virgin).
Some may argue with merit that
this record doesn't belong here,
but it is when and where the Stones learned the nuances of country roots, with Gram Parsons standing off in the wings.

The Semifinalists

30. *Tumbleweed Connection*—Elton John (MCA).
   Here we "break format" again by including this all-British work,
   but the frontier imagery and roots influences are all-American.

29. *Fate's Right Hand*—Rodney Crowell (DMZ/Sony).
   Real emotions, authentic introspection, and cold-light-of-day senti-
   ments color this modern Nashville treat.

28. *Viva Terlingua*—Jerry Jeff Walker (MCA).
   This is simply one of the best Texas roots rock records, and holds
   up proudly to this day.

27. *If I Could Only Fly*—Merle Haggard (Anti/Epitaph).
   Here's a modern Haggard record that stands up to the best and
   most rigorous of Merle's vintage material on Capitol.

26. *Heaven Help the Child*—Mickey Newbury (Elektra).
   Brilliant music filled with chilling angst and elaborate splendor.
   There's no other artist like Mickey.

25. *Sweetheart of the Rodeo*—The Byrds (Columbia).
   A cross-generational work that resonates heavily to this day.
   Although the individual performances probably could have been
   better, the spirit of the work is eternal.

24. *Motel Shot*—Delaney &
   Bonnie and Friends (Atco).
   Another monumental roots rock
   experiment that changed music.
   Gospel, country, rock, folk, and
   blues are all accounted for in
   heavy doses, with Gram Parsons
   on hand as unofficial altar boy.
   Sadly out of print in the Western
   world.

23. *GP/Grievous Angel*—Gram Parson (Reprise).
   Okay, so we cheated by grouping these two releases together, even
   though they're available that way on CD.

22. *Small Change*—Tom Waits (Asylum).
    Since 1973, when he started writing about skid row bums and grimy Greyhound bus depots, Waits has remained one of the most treasured American roots rock writers.

21. *Copperhead Road*—Steve Earle (UNI).
    Earle leaves mainstream country on a dusty, deserted roadside and drives off.

20. *The Houston Kid*—Rodney Crowell (Sugar Hill).
    A magnificent total-concept record of boyhood memories, filled with detailed Americana imagery. Literary images abound.

19. *Elite Hotel*—Emmylou Harris (Warner Bros.).
    The post-Parsons oeuvre that launched another country and rock dynamic. She'll do it again decades later with *Wrecking Ball*.

18. *Kristofferson*—Kris Kristofferson (Legacy/Sony).
    The songs are as powerful as the performances on Kris's debut 1970 solo record. Like Mickey Newbury, they broke the mold after Kris.

17. *89/93*—Uncle Tupelo (Sony).
    A healthy compilation of modern roots sounds from the band that begat Wilco and Son Volt.

16. *Guitar Town*—Steve Earle (MCA).
    Now that's "country-rock."

The Next Big Ten

15. *Burrito Deluxe*—Flying Burrito Brothers (A&M).
    Gram Parsons's final effort at capturing the Cosmic American Music zeitgeist.

14. *At San Quentin*—Johnny Cash (Legacy/Sony).
    Music from a man who understood the minds of men locked up behind stone walls. "San Quentin may you rot and burn in hell," he snarls defiantly.

13. *Gold*—Ryan Adams (Lost Highway).
Half of Ryan's fans, indie and proud of it, say this effort is far too polished; the other half, an older and more refined group, say it's his best work.

12. *At Folsom*—Johnny Cash (Legacy/Sony).
The current reissued CD contains the full concert in its original order without those annoying censor beeps.

11. *Blood on the Tracks*—Bob Dylan (Columbia).
In 1975 Dylan returned with a healthy dose of his previous, defiant "Another Side of . . ." side. Earlier studio versions unearthed from box sets are just as amazing.

10. *Harvest*—Neil Young (Reprise).
There's no denying the importance and the popularity of Neil's 1972 blend of rock, pop, and country.

9. *Music from Big Pink*—The Band (Capitol).
The Band's 1968 studio debut persuaded the top musicians in rock to adopt a more roots-conscious point of view.

8. *Gilded Palace of Sin*—Flying Burrito Brothers (A&M).
The legendary stoned-out classic that many credited having started the entire modern American roots rock revolution.

7. *Honky Tonk Heroes*—Waylon Jennings (Buddha/BMG).
When Waylon Jennings recorded an entire album of Billy Joe Shaver tunes, he was messing with the Nashville powers-that-be and making history. *Honky Tonk Heroes* is the *Sgt. Pepper* of country.

6. *Wrecking Ball*—Emmylou Harris (Elektra).
When Emmylou Harris collaborated with producer Daniel Lanois on *Wrecking Ball*, her music was as difficult to categorize as music

by masters like Hank, Kris, Willie, or Mickey. It's quite complex to invent a brand-new roots rock sound, but Emmylou did just that.

The High Five

5. *Blonde on Blonde*—Bob Dylan (Columbia).
The virtual Dylan Desert Island Disc. Every song is perfect, including "Rainy Day Women #12 & 35," which initially pissed the record company off when Dylan forced them to release it as the first single.

4. *The Silver Tongued Devil and I*—Kris Kristofferson (Monument).
In the movie *Taxi Driver*, Travis Bickle buys an album to impress Betsy. So director Martin Scorsese has him walk into a record store and grab a copy of *Silver Tongued Devil*. No better endorsement than that.

3. *Essence*—Lucinda Williams (Lost Highway).
Essence is actually our favorite Lucinda Williams album. Lu is an artist who embodies everything we love about American roots-rock music, including a reverence for Hank, country, folk, blues, rock 'n' roll, edge, and exceptional songwriting. As the title infers, the songs on *Essence* are stripped down to their bare, well, essences.

2. *Nashville Skyline* —Bob Dylan (Columbia).
Simply put, Dylan composed a 27-minute roots rock masterpiece. He totally transformed

his singing voice and radically altered his songwriting style to be as concise and direct as Hank Williams. Contemporary music was never the same.

1. *Car Wheels on a Gravel Road*—Lucinda Williams (Mercury).
   Joe Boyd, the famed English producer of Fairport Convention and Nick Drake, succinctly described *Car Wheels* as "the *Blonde on Blonde* of the 1990s." We heartily agree.

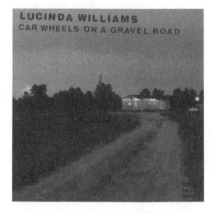

acknowledgments

All the artists and experts we interviewed, plus Richard Johnston, Fritz Clapp, Amy Miller, Julie Herrod-Lumsden, Steven Rybicki, Deborah Zimmerman, Gladys Zimmerman, Kevin Becketti, Nina Lesowitz, Jon Grimson, Kimiko Tokita, Matthew Greeson, David Bendett, Sonny Barger, Matt Kelsey, John Vernile, Kay Clary, Lynne Kirkwood, Marty DeAnda, Robert Rowland, Luke Lewis, Kate Henderson, Sarah McMullen, Mindy Giles, Dennis Newhall, Paul Bradshaw, Bob Johnston, Scott Crawford, Jeff Cook, and the Americana Music Association.

A special shout-out to Rob Bleetstein (an unsung musical hero) and to the guys in H-Unit.

—the Zimmermen

Keith and Kent Zimmerman spent several years in the music industry as chart editors and journalists before devoting their full attention to writing books. Their first literary collaboration was *Rotten: No Irish, No Blacks, No Dogs*, John Lydon's acclaimed memoir of the Sex Pistols and the London punk scene. *Rotten* was nominated for a Ralph J. Gleason Award in 1994. In 2000 the Zimmerman brothers scored their first *New York Times* bestseller with *Hell's Angel: The Life and Times of Ralph "Sonny" Barger and the Hell's Angels Motorcycle Club*. Subsequent books written with Sonny Barger include the short-story collection *Ridin' High, Livin' Free*, the *Freedom* handbook (due in 2005), and two fiction thrillers, *Dead in 5 Heartbeats* and *Six Chambers, One Bullet* (due in 2006). Their sixth book, *Soul on Bikes*, is a true tale of an all-black/all-male/all-Harley motorcycle club called the East Bay Dragons. Know as the Zimmermen, the twin-brother writing team is currently at work on books dealing with sports, television, music, and American pop culture.